NIGHT THOUGHTS

Night Thoughts
The Spectator Bedside Book

Edited by Patrick Marnham

CHATTO & WINDUS · THE HOGARTH PRESS

LONDON

Published in 1983 by
Chatto & Windus · The Hogarth Press
40 William IV Street
London WC2N 4DF

Night Thoughts.
  1. Anthologies
  I. Marnham, Patrick
  082   PN6014

ISBN 0 7011 2735 X

Printed in Great Britain by
Redwood Burn Ltd
Trowbridge, Wiltshire

Contents

Cartoons by Austin and Heath

Introduction

Wondering how best to introduce a selection from the *Spectator*, I remembered the circumstances in which I first came to write for it. In those days, the early seventies, the *Spectator* was not a fashionable paper and the young journalist trying to establish himself preferred to send his work to the *New Statesman*. But there was a problem about the latter; it had Views. Contributors were not encouraged to write what they thought if that happened to be out of line with the paper's views on a particular subject. In my case this led to the rejection of a piece about the corruption of Jomo Kenyatta's government, and its eventual publication in the *Spectator*. And there was a more celebrated occasion when the *New Statesman* defended the Newcastle Politician T. Dan Smith, later to be jailed for corruption, against attacks on him in the press simply on the grounds that he was a *Labour* politician. All papers make ludicrous mistakes, but at least any made by the *Spectator* in the recent past have not been caused by a blinkered concentration on some party political line. And the contributors, as well as the readers, have benefited from the absence of such restraints.

If the freedom from political direction has been one important reason for the *Spectator*'s excellence there has been a further freedom as well. It is a cliché to say that good journalism depends on the absence of proprietorial (or political) interference. In the case of the *Spectator* it has also depended on the absence of editorial interference. This is not the same as saying that the paper has lacked an editor. It has been transformed by Alexander Chancellor since he took over as editor in 1975. But his method has generally been to choose those who contribute and then to let them get on with it.

The life this has given to the contributors' work is increasingly valuable. There is a deadly phrase in Fleet Street, familiar to many freelance journalists, 'Wonderful piece old man, thanks very much. *We'll just run it through a typewriter.*' When he hears those words the freelance contributor knows that he might as well lose all further interest in the piece. The pay will be handsome, the by-line probably rather bigger, but the words, his words, will have been lost. A 'rewrite' specialist is about to take his work and bend it into some preordained shape deemed more suitable for the paper's style. Faced with this problem many journalists have, happily, succumbed to the temptation to submit a routine report to a wealthier publication and reserve their best work for the *Spectator*.

At the *Spectator* the underlying editorial principle seems to have been that if an article is not right it will be returned, but it will not usually be edited unless for length. In the age of the sub-editor, the advantage has been clear in every issue. People who are invited in this way to write what they think, tend to write and think better: if they fail to do so it is painfully obvious where the fault lies. And there is a further advantage, in that the range of opinion to be found in the paper is greatly increased and harder to predict. The reader too is invited to think for himself. Surely few other papers could accommodate articles as varied as those written with the elegance of Harold Acton, the authority of Patrick Devlin and the characteristic inspiration of Richard West, so effortlessly?

In the period of four years (1979–82) covered by this selection the *Spectator* has published over 5000 signed articles and a total of about six million words. The task of selecting roughly one and a half per cent from this total has meant that many of my favourite pieces have had to be omitted. My only principle, apart from trying to make this book as interesting as possible, has been to make it as varied as possible. But leafing at random through the final selection I was interested to see the number of new names. Roy Kerridge, Andrew Brown, Tim Garton Ash, Xan Smiley, Eric Christiansen and Gavin Stamp all first made their journalistic reputations in this period and in this paper, and Nicholas von Hoffman was first introduced to an English readership. At the same time the paper has been able to attract writers with the experience of Enoch Powell, William Deedes, J. S. Collis, C. H. Sisson, Michael Wharton and John Hackett. To any reader who does not yet read the paper, and who would like to know where to begin, I would recommend the autobiographical fragments contributed by Peter Paterson and Anthony Blond, Ferdinand Mount's summary of the trial of Jeremy Thorpe, Auberon Waugh's memoir of his Uncle Alec, Richard West's reflections on the painful subject of infibulation and anything by Jeffrey Bernard; deciding which of his weekly contributions to exclude took up more of my time than any other part of the task.

I would like to record my thanks to Charles Seaton of the *Spectator* whose learning has been an invaluable resource, shamelessly plundered on so many occasions by those who write for the paper. I must also record the debt which everyone who enjoys good writing owes to Henry Keswick and Algy Cluff, who have successively kept the *Spectator* going since 1975.

PATRICK MARNHAM
Doughty Street,
March 1983

1 The State of the Nation

Orphanage life
Peter Paterson

Of Christmas Day at home before I reached the age of four, I have no recollection whatever. Nor can I recall the festival in 1936 when I was at the infants' department of the orphanage in a small seaside town on the Kent coast, except for one memory: we were taken to visit the local toy shop shortly before Christmas, where we were allowed to pick a present, and this we were presented with from a Christmas tree on the day itself.

Christmas Day at the main orphanage in South London – at any rate on the 'boys' side', for we never encountered the girls at all – was quite different from any other day, particularly for those unfortunate boys who habitually wet their beds. It was the one day of the year when they were not obliged to rise before the morning bell sounded, make their way to the bathroom and rinse out their sheets. Failure to wake earlier than the rest of us meant running a gauntlet of punching, kicking and towel-flicking tormentors, egged on, it must be said in extenuation, by the house matrons.

Other rules and restrictions were also relaxed on Christmas Day. We were not required to parade before each meal for an inspection to ensure that our boots and fingernails passed the scrutiny of the ex-sergeant major who carried out the odd maintenance jobs around the place, and who then marched us four abreast along the drive to the dining hall, insisting that we stamped our right feet at every fourth step – a drill, I learned many years later, which had once been a ceremonial march practised by the Rifle Brigade. Failure to pass muster on these inspections meant missing the meal, and then spending the time between the end of school and lights out marching round and round the playground 'marking the fourth', or spending hours brushing our cropped heads with a hard bristle brush, or

cleaning our two pairs of boots without the benefit of the usual Day and Martin's spit-on blacking.

Nor were we obliged on Christmas Day to eat all meals in silence, as was the rule for the rest of the year, with the exception of Sunday tea, when the supervisory staff withdrew, leaving the dining hall to the bullies and gang leaders to exact their tribute from the smaller boys – forcing us to surrender the thick slice of currant cake which was doled out once a week at this meal.

Christmas Day, by contrast, was bliss. Certainly by contrast with Christmas Eve, known to generations of boys in the orphanage as Devil's Eve, when the staff, keyed up, no doubt, by the unalloyed joy due to be unleashed the following day, were invariably in a filthy temper. With a singular lack of imagination, the terraced houses where we hung our paper chains, were numbered rather than named. Each boy also had a number: hence, in the twice daily roll call and prayers in House No. 8, I shouted 'Twenty-Six!' to show that I had not absconded.

At one end of the terrace of houses, with staff accommodation on the ground floor, dormitories above, and with classrooms on the top floor, stood the play hall, for use in rainy weather, fronted by the playground. At the other was the dining hall, while in between was a large and enticing field which was strictly out of bounds, except on the annual Founder's Day, when we performed a pageant for visitors.

Visitors were also in evidence on Christmas Day, for members of the board of governors liked to put in an appearance, no doubt taking pleasure from their charitable efforts. Each of us woke to find a stocking at the end of his bed, containing the traditional mixture of small toys, sweets, nuts and an apple and orange. Presents sent to us by relations or friends outside were handed out before we assembled for our Christmas dinner – the midday meal was never known as lunch.

After turkey and Christmas pudding, the chairman of the governors, a bald man with a huge nose and a diamond pin in his cravat, placed a bright new shilling from a large cash bag beside each boy's plate. It was a bequest from an 'old scholar', but one who must have been somewhat shaky about the rules of the institution, for no sooner was the money on the table than the house matron, following on behind, scooped it up. No boy was allowed to possess cash, although the odd would-be escaper (there was no point in having money except for this purpose) did amass a small hoard by hiding illicit coins in the knot of his tie. In fact, 'running away' entailed a huge risk, for on being returned the malefactor faced a public flogging, with sixteen strokes of the cane as standard punishment.

To be fair, the Christmas shilling did not disappear into the pockets of the staff, but was returned to us at the rate of a penny a week to spend at the school tuck shop (opened on Saturday mornings only), always assuming that one could pass the special house inspection after breakfast on that day. This entailed a microscopic search for dust on any of the surfaces in the dormitories, plus the production of two pairs of gleaming boots and one's underpants, which after a week's wear were still required to be spotless.

After Christmas dinner most of the staff disappeared for their own meal, leaving the most junior master in charge of the two hundred or so boys. Adjourning to the play hall, we were paired off and spent the afternoon working off our turkey and pudding in a series of wrestling matches, until it was time for tea. In the evening came the carol

service, followed by a silent film show invariably featuring, I recall, the adventures of an Alsatian dog, a precursor of Lassie, known as Rin Tin Tin, and a cartoon featuring a character called Felix the Cat. And so to bed.

These pre-war Christmas traditions were kept up by the orphanage when it managed to reassemble its scattered inmates from the first, disorganised, wartime evacuations and re-establish itself in a bankrupt private school in Surrey. Portraits of the Victorian founder – not unlike Karl Marx wearing wire spectacles – glowered down from the walls as they had done in the old premises, and the ritual of giving away the shilling with one hand and taking it away with the other continued, along with the wrestling matches.

It was a world which, thankfully, came to an end for me in 1945, when I reached the leaving age of fourteen, and which finally disappeared in its old form with the operation of the Butler Education Act – one reason why I always had a soft spot for Rab. From then on the orphanage was no longer recognised as an educational establishment, and the children had to be sent out to ordinary day schools, thus making it impossible to continue the frequent canings and other humiliating punishments which can scarcely have changed since the place was founded at the turn of the century.

Yet looking back, my most enduring memories are not of the harshness of the regime, but of the warm companionship and vast resourcefulness of my fellow wrestlers, several of whom ran away, guided only by a map of England torn from a pocket diary, making for some half-remembered place where they had once lived, despite the inevitability that they would be returned. And, particularly, of the boy whose wit devised the funniest joke I have ever heard, assuring me, one miserable Saturday morning, that he had seen our matron's knickers on the washing line – and they had been far from clean. I cried with laughter.

18 December 1982

Dancing
Alexander Chancellor

Although at my prep school I repeatedly won the slow waltz competition in partnership with my cousin Simon Elliot, I have never since had a dancing lesson. This is painfully apparent on the rare occasions on which I take to the floor. My brother, on the other hand, has had innumerable dancing lessons. My brother is twelve years older than I am. He is an antiquarian bookseller and the author of distinguished biographies of Darwin, Wagner, Audubon and, now, of Edward I: not a man you would necessarily expect to be so concerned about the standard of his dancing. But concerned he is, not only to shine in the ballroom but to be familiar with all the latest steps which unfortunately tend to drop out of fashion almost before he has learnt them. His first instructor was the celebrated Miss Vacani, who taught him the quickstep. Miss Vacani was also the Queen's dancing teacher. Before her Coronation, Princess Elizabeth once danced with my brother. 'We might both be wondering, ma'am,' he said to her, as he shuffled her around the floor, 'why each of us dances so well. We have the same teacher!' 'She's a great character, isn't she,' replied the Princess enigmatically. But that was long ago. More recently my brother decided he should learn to dance 'disco', which apparently requires more than a wonderful sense of rhythm, lack of inhibition, and immunity to embarrassment. It is a step which can be taught. Accordingly he looked through the Yellow Pages and found the telephone number of a branch of the Arthur Murray School of Dancing in Kensington, the neighbourhood in which he lives. A welcoming voice on the telephone told him that for £45 he could have five hours of private tuition and three group lessons in both 'disco' and 'Latin' dancing. Along he went, and after some preliminary gyrations with a young lady from Texas whose voice, however, had a curious hint of cockney in it, he was ushered into the office of a flashy fellow with a moustache to be told that he hadn't 'a cat's hope in hell' of learning to dance properly unless he enrolled for a much longer course. He stuck to his guns, however, and insisted on the £45 course, which, he was then told, was not really a £45 course at all, but a £135 course with an astounding beginner's discount of £90. Halfway through his next lesson, the lady from Texas said he must be tired and sat him down for a pep talk. 'I am your psychiatrist, I am the architect of your dancing future,' she said. 'Here is a form for you. Fill it in and bring it back. It will enable us to help you in the future.' He didn't like all this emphasis on the future. Nor did he like the form, which sought, by means of a number of questions, to discover why he wanted to learn to dance. Did he wish to get on better with girls? Did he think it would help him in business? He later threw the form away in a fury, but returned for his next lesson. The instructress was outraged at his failure to fill in the form. He implored her to stop pressurising him. She was ruining his lessons, he said. 'I could see you were cynical when you came in here,' she replied. His fellow students included a little Indian girl whose guardian had already paid £4,500 for her lessons, and an environmental officer from Watford who had paid £2,500 so far, coming up three nights a week and regretting it not at all ('I used to be a wallflower. Now I can talk to girls'). My brother completed his course, refusing to the end to reveal why he wanted to dance and why he was not interested in a 'dancing future'. The manager's farewell was less than friendly: 'We like to help people on a long-term basis. If you want a few quick lessons, go somewhere else.'

24 May 1980

The Bhagwan
Roy Kerridge

Bhagwan Shree Rajneesh, leader of the Orange People, is no ordinary Indian guru. The things that other priests either forbid or forgive, he insists on. Sannyasins, or followers, are expected to drink, smoke, swear and indulge in casual sex.

Some friends of mine had 'taken sannyasin', no doubt surprised to learn that their normal behaviour was in reality a Holy Meditation, and they had been issued with Indian names, every boy a Swami and every girl a Ma. Few, if any, Indians join the cult, which takes it nickname from the orange clothes once worn, sold at the Bhagwan Boutiques. The uniform is now maroon red, and perhaps one day sannyasins will be known as Purple People. I was urged to spend a weekend at Medina, formerly Herringswell Manor, the cult's stately home in Suffolk. Bhagwan now lives on a ranch in Oregon, but he is supposed to be at Medina in spirit, where he sits invisibly in a sacred easy chair.

It was a fine spring evening when I set out for Medina, and I swung jauntily along beneath an avenue of beech trees, my pyjamas in a plastic carrier bag and a song on my lips. Soon an eerie mock-Tudor water tower loomed before me like a turret on a fort. A stud farm for racehorses adjoined Medina, convincing me more than ever that this was really a case for Jeffrey Bernard. Dusk fell before I reached the late Victorian manor house, built for the racehorse magnate whose heirs no doubt huddled beneath the water tower.

In the hall hung a notice reading 'Leave Shoes and Minds Here'. I took a firm grip on my mind and proceeded. Marred only by large photographs of the bearded Bhagwan everywhere, the interior was a model of opulence and good taste, with leather-bound chairs, oak panelling and potted ferns in hanging baskets. Before long I was signed up for a course in Self Experience and shown to my room, where a mattress and blankets lay on the floor. 'There's a disco tonight in the Omar Khayyam pub next to the Great Hall,' I was told, so I went along to see.

Squeezing into the packed room, where the bar did a roaring trade, I saw the red-clad sannyasins leaping wildly about, while others cuddled in corners. I looked round for Bernard Levin, said to be a convert to this cult, but could not find him. A record player boomed out a song called 'There Ain't Nothing Like a Gang Bang'. Altogether it was a scene of debauchery only equalled by every other disco I have seen on any Friday night in any town anywhere in Britain. Whatever happened to the waltz?

One or two of the young men looked arrogant and sensual, but most of them were mild and may have been scholarly before they had left their minds behind. There was no intellectual life in Medina as far as I could see. Everyone took for granted that they must do everything Bhagwan wanted, as if he were Jehovah to their Chosen People.

Preparing for bed, I found that there was a communal bath and shower room, where naked couples larked around splashing each other. A spiv I know in Brighton runs a mixed sauna, and I now realise that if he called it a Meditation Retreat he could treble the entrance fees.

'I've got these red marks – it's the acupuncture,' a bearded young man told me. A blonde girl without a stitch on walked past us, but he never batted an eyelid. 'When they tear the pins out, it tends to hurt a bit.'

Next morning I and nine others sat on cushions while our self-experience teacher instructed us in Dynamic Meditation. We were a mixed bunch, mostly in our thirties, and included a freckle-faced housewife from Lowestoft, a fat bald man with a curly black beard and a childish face, who later confessed to being 'infatuated with all women', and a tragic yet defiant-looking girl whose short spiky hair somehow accentuated her Edwardian drawing-room features. Everyone except myself had been there before, and some worked there.

Our teacher also had an Indian name, but I shall call him Dave. He looked like a Dave somehow, wiry, tough and bearded, the sort of person you see tinkering with a motorbike while rock music blares from a transistor. From the beginning I regarded him as an enemy. His lecture on the Dynamic Meditation, which turned out to consist of snorting, screaming, barking, standing in silence and finally dancing, was peppered with four-letter words. Spoken deliberately, they sounded very odd, and I later found that a Bhagwan tape of therapeutic effing-and-blinding was being offered for sale in the Medina shop.

After the snorting, 'breathing outwards with the whole body, but not inwards,' came the screaming. We were issued with blindfolds, but I insisted on keeping my spectacles on underneath, claiming that they were an integral part of my Self. This was uncomfortable, but as the blindfold was kept askew, only Dave and I could see what was going on. He told us to do whatever we felt like. Everyone at once rolled around on the floor screaming and savagely fighting the scattered cushions. Picking up a cushion, I hurled it at Dave's head and scored a bull's-eye. Turning in surprise, he copped another cushion right between the eyes. The Edwardian girl was having a severe fit of hysterics, having taken on two cushions at once, but another well-aimed cushion soon snapped her out of it. Dave ran over to me. 'You're supposed to do whatever you like in relation to yourself, not to others,' he hissed.

After this Meditation came an Awareness Walk. Forming into couples, we were sent out into the beautiful grounds, with orders to speak non-stop for half an hour apiece on whatever we were aware of at the moment. I was paired with the sad-eyed Edwardian girl, who had a sensitive nature, and was chiefly aware of buds and unfolding leaves on the trees in the woods. Every sentence was supposed to begin with 'I am aware of . . .' but she kept forgetting and exclaiming 'Oh look, these buds are dark on one side and pale on the other!'

A botanist was lost when, in her own words, she 'fell in love with Bhagwan'. If society had not crumbled, and we were Edwardians, she would have enjoyed pressing leaves and painting in water colours. When it was my turn, I became Aware of a dear little house in the undergrowth, made from discarded cinema screens by the Medina children, and we ended up sitting cosily inside while I entertained my companion with shadow pictures on the screen walls. This was an art I had learned years before from the *Children's Encyclopaedia*. Good old Arthur Mee never lets you down, and the Encyclopaedia is still a guide for any circumstance.

After this idyll came a vegetarian lunch, and then we confronted Dave once more. This time we were formed into couples again, and from his aggressive four-letter chat, with references to 'your lover', it appeared that converts were being enticed to take further and more expensive courses by the promise of sensual delights.

I had to dance with the freckled Lowestoft housewife, whose absent husband was 'not interested in religion', and probably imagined her to be praying and fasting. Then we were blindfolded, spun around and told to find one another. Many of the Bhagwan's 'meditations' were pretentious versions of childhood games, and after Blind Man's Bluff came Cosmic Pass the Parcel, Therapeutic 'Simon Says' and Neo-Reichian Musical Chairs.

'You have a Psychic Bond with your partner, and can find him or her blindfolded across a crowded room,' Dave announced. 'You will probably be friends for life, or else enemies. Embrace when you find one another, and remember, when you are together once more, you are at Home.' I waited impatiently while my blindfolded partner embraced someone else, not very flattered to note that she later identified me by sniffing. Dave told us all to remove the blindfolds and sit on the floor facing our Psychic Partner. Each had to ask the other, 'Who are you?'

'My name's Roy, a bloke, aged forty, brought up near Wembley,' I told the freckled one, who asked the question first.

'What do I do now? He keeps giving me the wrong answer,' she asked Dave anxiously.

'Just keep on asking,' he advised, but I could do no better. Then it was her turn, and I saw, with admiration, how the job ought to be done.

'I am Truth, I am Space, I am Mystery,' she began in her East Anglian accent. 'I am Me. I am You. I am Silence. I . . . I am getting a little confused actually. I'm always confused for two months after I leave here, and then I feel wonderful and come back again.'

'Don't you think it just takes two months for the effects to wear off?' I inquired, but she didn't think so. The dancing and leaping about gave her considerable pain, and I wished she would go back to her husband. I tried to imagine their home life together.

He: Could I have some toast, dear?

She: I am Time, I am the Universe! Gerrit yourself, you gurt idle oaf. I am All-Knowingness . . .'

Muttering 'That's a lot of squit!' and other Lowestoftian expressions, he slams his way out of the house and enrols for a course of Self Realisation with the glamorous Ma Prem Anandibear (formerly Doreen). So the fabric of the home is being destroyed.

No more was said of the Psychic Bond after this, and we were all partnered with others later on, for more soul-searching questions. Most of the girls seemed to want a varied sex life and a steady partner at the same time. Bhagwan's substitute for marriage was called a 'relationship' and seemed insecure and impermanent. Many of the girls had haunted, spinsterish expressions. I felt very sorry for them, but could no more rescue them from Medina than I could from Fairyland. In old legends, Fairyland seems delightful at first but once you have eaten the food you can never leave, trapped in a false world of 'fairy glamour'. What seems to be a prince is really a hideous goblin, just as what seems to be the beloved Bhagwan at night turns out, in the morning, to be a stranger from Harlow New Town.

After their meditations, sannyasins sat talking of times when they had actually seen Bhagwan drive by in his white Rolls-Royce. A party of starry-eyed day visitors was shown around by an Orange guide, in stately home fashion and I was able to slip a girl a note reading, 'Beware – Never Come Back.'

'Take a risk and have a treat,' Dave urged us at the end of the first day, 'For example, if you want to ask Ma Deva Geeta to go to bed with you, then just ask her! Take a risk and have a treat!' Ma Deva Geeta, sitting crosslegged on a cushion, looked down modestly.

My chosen risk was to break into the children's house, where I found the well-cared-for infants bouncing on their bunk beds in pyjamas. As a treat, I hope for all concerned, I told them bedtime stories. Unwittingly I won the gratitude of their parents, who seemed worried about leaving them in a commune of their own all day. Young housemothers cared for them, and their school seemed the equal of anything I had seen in the outside world.

Next day we had Sufi Whirling, which turned out to be spinning round and round until you fell to the floor unconscious or retching. My Psychic Partner of the previous day ricked something and was taken to the doctor sobbing in agony. Observing all through my 'blindfold', I took two spins and sat on a cushion, my fingers in my ears to drown the deafening, reverberating sound of Music of the Spheres apparently played on heaps of scrap metal.

'The Beginning drives you crazy,' Bhagwan intoned sepulchrally from a tape recorder. To conclude our course, a Sufi Dance was held, which would have surprised any ancient Persian philosophers present. A Bhagwan band played square dance tunes and we had to sing a ditty beginning 'I'm Just a Cosmic Cowboy'.

That night, sipping vodka in front of a log fire, I made small talk with a Swami and his Ma, a sannyasin couple who had been together for some years. Their sons had learned to read from hippie comics. While the man talked of his heyday in the late Sixties, his Swedish girl friend looked at me curiously. 'I should like you to go to bed with Swami and me tonight!' she commanded. This rather stunned me, but Swami nodded in agreement. What would Jeffrey Bernard have done? Before I could decide, the girl suddenly had a row with Swami, and rushed out of the room.

So ended my course in Self Experience. As the Bhagwan himself remarks: 'How can you seek yourself? You are already that.'

8 May 1982

Fox-hunting
Raymond Carr

The campaign against fox-hunting may provide future historians with yet another example of the Jacobin effect. A sect of fanatics, replete with the self-righteous moral superiority and ruthlessness that comes from a conviction that their cause is just and that history is on their side, through organisation and persistence can force their will on the course of events as the Jacobins did in the French Revolution. Immune to boredom and the discomfort of hard benches, they stuck it out, sitting up late to push through committee resolutions when their opponents, susceptible to human weakness, had gone off for a drink or to bed. I am not suggesting that Mr Richard Course is the Robespierre of the League against Cruel Sports ready to send fox-hunters *en masse* to the guillotine; but as its Executive Director he is a fine exponent of Jacobin techniques. His 10,000 crusaders and fanatics may succeed in banning fox-hunting in this country.

What is the passion that excites and inflames the members of the League against Cruel Sports and the activist wing, the Hunt

Saboteurs? All would answer, like Bentham, that animals are sentient beings with rights and that the law should not 'refuse its protection' against wanton cruelty inflicted on any sentient being. But no one who has studied the social and political history of fox-hunting and its adversaries can doubt that much of the passion of the antis is fuelled by class prejudice. Fox-hunters are under fire, not so much for what they are supposed to do, but for what they are supposed to be. To the great nineteenth-century radical Cobden fox-hunting was a 'feudal sport'; a recent president of the JCR of that great nursery of MFHs, Christ Church, described it as a 'bourgeois' sport – bourgeois being a more 'fashionable' synonym for evil than 'feudal'. That heroic lady, Jilly Cooper, after a day spent with the Hunt Saboteurs spraying hounds with aerosol and blowing hunting horns concluded it would be honest to call them the 'Anti-Blue-Blood Sports Brigade'.

To defend themselves against the accusation that they are a collection of snobs in fancy clothes fox-hunters have trotted out an argument that goes back to the eighteenth century: that foxhunting is 'democratic', that dukes and chimney-sweeps are equal in the sight of a stiff fence, that Welsh miners have a pack of foxhounds, etc. Beating about for ammunition to meet an absurd charge that the affluent should be prevented from amusing themselves in public is an absurd occupation. Like all sports, fox-hunting is only open to those who can afford it. It's true that, in spite of the braying of upper-class voices at smart meets, those who can afford it are no longer confined to the nobility and squirearchy. But even hordes of car followers do not make hunting democratic.

What is a humane way to control a population of vermin – beautiful vermin, but vermin nevertheless? To put it brutally, what is a good way of killing foxes since foxes *must* be killed? Here I think the balance of the argument lies with the fox-hunters. I wouldn't argue that foxes enjoy being chased by hounds, but at the end of the chase they are either killed instantly – usually their backs are broken by hounds – or they get away. The alternatives to hunting suggested by the antis are shooting or gassing. Having had to shoot foxes I can't say much for the efficacy of the first method, and no one, I imagine, conceives of gassing in a hole to be a pleasant form of death. The antis must answer this question fairly and squarely, and they don't.

All our relations with the animal world are riddled with paradox. The rational hunter becomes a conservationist, preserving the animals he hunts. Portugal's democratic revolution gave every citizen the right to shoot: the result was the slaughter of 3000 wild partridges on one estate, leaving three or four brace behind. Without foxes having been preserved by a hegemonic landowning class for hunting purposes they would have vanished from some parts of England – indeed even respectable masters imported bag foxes from Germany and Russia in the early nineteenth century. To a fox-hunter death except by hounds is a terrible social mid-nineteenth-century sole-cism. That great autocratic MFH, Thomas Assheton Smith, was once observed to pale over the newspaper at breakfast: 'The ladies present, supposing some great European calamity had occurred, hastily asked him what was the matter, when he replied, looking over his spectacles: "By jove, a dog fox has been burnt to death in a barn." '

Preservation of foxes is, by antis, regarded as shameful. How terrible to preserve animals in order to kill them. But then, how obscene to breed animals in order to eat them. Sensible fox-hunters should accept the objections of vegetarians. Self-denial on grounds of moral consistency deserves reward.

Fox-hunters should stop inventing arguments about the 'de-mocracy' of the hunting field, etc. They should acknowledge that they go hunting because they enjoy it – to those who have once tasted its excitements there is nothing in the world that can replace it – and that they are, as Christopher Sykes argued, infected with a kind of madness. A time-worn apologia is that hunting stops these madmen doing anything worse, freed by their exertions, as one mediaeval enthusiast wrote, from 'imaginations of fleshly lust'. Tired out after a hard day in the saddle you go to bed, presumably alone. An equally time-worn accusation is the old puritan charge that hunting debases those who practise it; but, as *The Times* has argued, to stop hunting because it is bad for those who hunt is 'to invade the sphere of the individual conscience'.

Nor should fox-hunters be browbeaten by puritans and progres-sives who dismiss them as brute beasts, unreconstructed High Tories or worse. How can one listen to the nonsense spouted in the

Berkshire Council debate about abolishing fox-hunting on council land: 'Hunting shows the sort of thinking that leads to concentration camps.' Supreme silliness is reached, as one might expect, among radical philosophers in the US: foxes' tails are phallic symbols and to hunt is to engage in a 'masturbation fantasy'.

The antis – particularly the League against Cruel Sports – are well funded and well organised to achieve their aim: to legislate fox-hunting out of existence. Hence a contribution of £80,000 to Labour's campaign funds on condition that the party pressed for the abolition of hunting. Labour lost in 1979 and fox-hunters breathed a sigh of relief. But they counted without Mr Course, who reminded Labour local councillors of his investment. Five local councils have expressed their determination to stop fox-hunting on council-owned land. Existing tenants cannot be forced to ban fox-hunting; new tenants, presumably, will have to accept leases which forbid it, just as nineteenth-century landlords put clauses in their leases forcing tenants to allow hunting – and were roundly abused by radicals as tyrants. What a turn-up for the books!

Labour has been fixed by cash as well as conviction – the TGWU has declared fox-hunting 'distasteful to the British way of life'. The Liberals and the SDP, as heirs to the radical tradition of Cobden in British politics, will be just as bad if not worse. The whole tactical weakness of the blood sports lobby is precisely here: a pressure group of 10,000 antis can kill the enjoyment of millions by playing on the fear of being caught out opposing what is presented as a progressive, humanitarian crusade. To oppose blood sports is electorally safe provided coarse fishing – a proletarian sport with TV coverage – is left untouched. Fish, perhaps, are not sentient beings.

Fox-hunters of Britain, unite. Your case is sound. Go into battle, your banners emblazoned with the words of Trotsky: 'Hunting acts on the mind as a poultice does on a sore.'

31 July 1982

BUPA
Alexander Chancellor

We were all exactly the same, like some alien race from another planet. We wore regulation blue dressing gowns with black stripes. We were cocooned in American-type luxury, far removed from the seediness of the Pentonville Road outside. I suspected that I might have been the only person there who had come of his own free will. We were at the BUPA medical centre having our health 'screened'. The others, I felt, had probably been sent by their companies. I was there on my own account in the hope of reassurance that, in middle age, with many thousands of cigarettes and alcoholic refreshments behind me, I might still be in a satisfactory state of health. I have still to hear the results of the innumerable tests to which I was subjected. But I already feel better for having undergone them. Unquestionably the most intriguing part of the session was the conversation I had with a computer. I was put in a cubicle and confronted with a talkative television screen, beside which were buttons saying 'Yes', 'No', 'Don't know' and 'Help'. 'Help' was obviously the most tempting button to press, but all it did was to summon a nurse to give advice if one felt unable to answer any question that appeared on the screen. There were some very difficult questions on the lines of : 'Are you happy in your work?', 'Do you feel up to your job?', 'Do you feel you are given enough responsibility?', 'Do you ever feel you are completely worthless?', and so on. To most of them one was not allowed to answer 'Don't know'. On the screen appeared a firm refusal to accept such a dithery reply. So I tried to give answers that would present me to the computer in the most endearing light. Some of the questions, it has to be said, were extremely personal. That is why, at the end of the interrogation, when the computer asked if I had enjoyed it all, I answered 'No'; and when it asked if I would rather have been asked the same questions by a doctor rather than by itself, I also answered 'No'. I hope that the computer contains some subtle mechanism for distinguishing between truth and falsehood. I also hope that it has been able to work out the sort of condition that I am in. But I rather doubt it.

20 December 1980

King's Cross prostitutes
Gavin Stamp

If my relations are horrified, my friends are amused that I live just off Argyle Square in King's Cross, currently London's most celebrated red light district. I have always liked the seedy older parts of inner cities and the prostitutes don't offend me, so I am quite content; but the humour of the low life has worn rather thin in the last week with the occupation by the so-called English Collective of Prostitutes of Holy Cross, Cromer Street, the local parish church where I was married. Local people are upset and outraged by the presence in their church of a bevy of masked, chain-smoking harridans.

The Collective, imitating French prostitutes who occupied the Madeleine in Paris, are demanding to see a series of public figures and announce that 'this action is our official complaint against police illegality and racism'. 'Illegality' refers to police 'harassment' of prostitutes on the street in Argyle Square but as, rightly or wrongly, the Street Offences Act of 1959 is still the law of the land, such actions are scarcely illegal. 'Racism' is, of course, a useful complaint and, as it happens, half of the prostitutes and most of the pimps are black. What is going on in King's Cross certainly ought to receive more attention from the various authorities but I do question whether the forcible occupation of an Anglican church is the best way to achieve this and, furthermore, whether the Collective has any right to represent the prostitutes in the area. None of the newspapers or television reporters who have taken such a prurient interest in the case – attracted, perhaps, by memories of 'Vicars and Tarts' parties – has asked who those occupying the church really are, for the girls trying to earn a living in the Square are scarcely likely to be able to afford to take so much time off. Some of them, indeed, have told the vicar that they are disgusted by what is going on in his church whose masked occupants are, needless to say, not prostitutes at all but middle-class radical feminists attached to the Women's Centre in Tonbridge Street under whose umbrella nestle such supporting groups as Women Against Rape and Black Women For Wages For Housework etc, and whose overlapping membership is all too familiar to the editor of the *Spectator* because they once occupied his office, as readers may recall. Furthermore, I note that the English Collective of Prostitutes receives an annual subsidy of £8,000 from the GLC, partly owing to the advocacy of the former vicar of Holy Cross, the Revd Peter Wheatley who chose, tactlessly and impudently, to give his support to the illegal occupation which is upsetting his successor's work.

Several newspapers, including the *News of the World* and the *Sun* have chosen maliciously to misrepresent the attitude of the present vicar. For what was the Revd Trevor Richardson to do when a force of masked women entered his church during an evening Mass and then declined to leave? To ask the police to evict them would have been to play into the Collective's hands, for nothing would please them more than the publicity that such violent action in a Christian church would provoke. Although well aware of the disgust felt by his parishioners, Father Richardson has quite rightly been concerned about the real prostitutes, recognising that they also have souls and that Our Lord befriended prostitutes and sinners and condemned the hypocrisy of the Pharisees. On the other hand, He also demanded repentance, which it does not suit the Collective to recall.

To distance the parish from those occupying its church, last Sunday's service was held in the hall of the nearby Tonbridge Boys' Club. Even so, the proceedings were histrionically interrupted by a member of the Collective who asked that members of the congregation should come over to the church to pray with those in there. After the service, a few people tried to do just this, including a seventy-six-year-old retired priest; they were turned away at the door: 'We don't pray with you. You're not Christians.' Enough said. It was, of course, naive to expect any rational or charitable behaviour from the Collective, consisting, as it does, of arrogant shrill feminists trained in the heady days of student sit-ins and consumed by hatred of men. None of them live locally. For all its vicarious concern with the plight of the community of prostitutes, the Collective seems little interested in the real King's Cross community which is, as it was in the 1880s when Holy Cross, a simple, dignified Anglo-Catholic mission church was built, largely working class and very poor. One elderly lady in the congregation, near to tears at the desecration of her church, complained with truth that the girls in Argyle Square earned more in a day than she did in a year. The real residents of King's Cross want not less police harassment but much more of it.

Argyle Square was part of the Battle Bridge Estate built by the junction of the Gray's Inn Road and the 'New Road', now the Euston Road, in the 1820s and 1830s. My house stands on the site of a famous giant dust heap, removed in 1826; Argyle Square is on the site of a failed pleasure ground. The speculation which built these typical Late Georgian, third-rate terraces was never successful; already by the 1840s the area was known for vagrancy and drunkenness. The opening of King's Cross station in 1851 did not help. It had been preceded by Euston station, further west, in 1837, and St Pancras station joined it in 1868. The presence of three main-line termini had the usual effect on the area, although in the nineteenth century the worst vice was to be found in Waterloo station. Today there is none near Waterloo, a little around Victoria and Paddington, and a great deal in King's Cross. Although prostitution has a long history here, in the last five years it has become much more extensive and blatant, the result both of unemployment and the activities of the Yorkshire Ripper. It is popularly believed that many of the girls are day-time commuters on 'Have It Away Day' tickets; certainly many come from Newcastle and the north.

The Street Offences Act, which the Collective wants repealed, took prostitution off the streets for very good reasons: it is a nuisance. Business begins at about midday and after dark the noise of shouting, screaming, of car-doors banging is intolerable. Nor is it pleasant to find in the morning that doorsteps and pavements are littered with used condoms and Kentucky Fried Chicken packets. Many female tenants of council flats are sick of being propositioned, and afraid of letting their children walk in the streets or play in the garden in

Argyle Square. As always, prostitution has brought corruption and violence.

The local MP, Frank Dobson (Lab), has taken an intelligent interest in the problem but, as a good believer in the role of the State, proposes legalised brothels as the solution. This the English Collective of Prostitutes opposes, and I rather agree with them. It is a repellent infringement of individual freedom to force girls to work in the sort of revolting sex warehouses to be found in Hamburg or Amsterdam. Local residents also do not much want to live near legalised brothels; they want strong action against prostitution, but the problem will not go away: it will just go elsewhere and I do not relish the idea of the police having more power.

Anna Neale of the English Collective of Prostitutes insists that 'giving the police *carte blanche* to "clean up the streets" means they can do whatever they please, which can and does include: demanding free sex, demanding money, assaulting or beating up women who refuse to be arrested, colluding with pimps to extract more money from the women.' Indeed. What I know of the local police only confirms that view. During the day, they roar around the Square in their cars making a lot of noise; at night they are seldom to be seen. They like arresting prostitutes during the day; the local pimps seem to engage their attention less. One night, at 4.30 a.m., my wife reported to the police that a pimp was beating up a girl outside our house; they seemed only interested in my wife's occupation and possible connection with the incident and took over a quarter of an hour to arrive – too late, of course. My neighbour, who is Italian, was told by an Inspector that he had no business complaining about the prostitution as he was foreign – even though he is a taxpayer and ratepayer. And when some enterprising cameramen filmed some members of the force conducting unorthodox interviews with suspected prostitutes in the backs of cars, the video film was seized by the police.

Offensive as its manifestations may be, I see no reason why prostitution as such should be illegal and to prohibit kerb-crawling and the availing of a prostitute's services – as has been seriously proposed – seems to me an alarming infringement of individual freedom. In fact, no new laws are required, for there are perfectly good laws on the statute book to protect the interests of the ordinary citizen and make King's Cross return to normal. They merely need to be enforced with fairness and with consistency: laws against soliciting in the street, laws about committing nuisances and breaches of the peace, laws about keeping disorderly houses and living off immoral earnings. But prostitutes do deserve our sympathy and understanding, and the £8,000 given to the Collective (let alone the other subsidies to the various overlapping manifestations of the Women's Centre) would seem to be better spent on ways of trying to give some of the girls another occupation. There is a wonderful irony in a militant left-wing feminist organisation choosing to identify with prostitutes, for prostitution, in theory, is surely a perfect expression of individualism and capitalism. Unfortunately, there are flaws – or is it Original Sin? – for the poor prostitute is always manipulated by others, whether by pimps or, now, by the clever activists of the English Collective of Prostitutes. Despite the bigotry and hypocrisy often present in the Christian communion, the doors of the church are often the only ones open without strings attached. It would be more appropriate if my parish church had been dedicated to St Mary Magdalene – but she, it should be said, came off the game. Nor, as far as we know, did she ask Our Lord to campaign against 'police illegality and racism'.

27 November 1982

Churchill's lying-in
John Stewart Collis

It was the last week of January 1965. Churchill's funeral took place on Saturday 30 January. The Lying in State lasted throughout the previous fortnight. The queue, starting from the gates of the House of Commons, curled round over Westminster Bridge, then along Lambeth Palace Road, thence over Lambeth Bridge to Millbank leading to Westminster Hall in which the catafalque was placed. I understood that it meant about four hours in the queue before reaching the Hall. It flowed on throughout every day and every night.

It occurred to me that this was one of those historic occasions in which it would be good to participate. I was living in Ewell in Surrey at the time, and I thought that if I drove up on the Tuesday of the second week in the middle of the night, arriving at about 3 a.m., the queue would surely be short, and I wouldn't have to join it for more than an hour before reaching the catafalque. So I went up and parked my car in the vicinity of Parliament Square – for no policeman was making the slightest objection as to where one put a car on this occasion.

I hastened to walk across the Square and was pleased to find no queue in sight. Then in high spirits I walked quickly over Westminster Bridge, and turned to the right into Lambeth Palace Road – to be confronted almost at once by an enormously wide queue, a long distance from the bridge. My heart sank. It is an eccentricity of mine to do things on impulse without taking simple precautions. It was a cold night, and I was wearing only a light overcoat and thin socks, and absolutely the wrong kind of shoes. By the time I had reached Lambeth Bridge, I had become alarmed by my predicament, but hoped that I would make it.

I looked round at this great queue of people, so long and wide. Many were young and must have been children during the war, perhaps not yet born at its outset. Many others were middle-aged – they had heard that voice coming to them over the wireless, whether to groups or into lonely rooms. Twenty years had passed since the final triumph of this man. But neither the young nor the middle-aged were thinking of those last years, but of what he had been, of what he was in their imagination. He was the man who had overcome Hitler. He had promised nothing. He did not rant. He never smiled. There was melancholy in his cadence, and there was understanding of simple people when he spoke of 'that bad man over there'. Now his body was soon to disappear from the surface of the earth.

I spoke to nobody, and I heard no memorable remark. It had become very cold. I welcomed this. It was far more appropriate for the sombre scene than a warm summer night would have been. But on account of my faulty clothing I became anxious. Something must be done. After we had at last crossed Lambeth Bridge, the queue took an enormous loop around a Green before joining Millbank. In the middle of this Green a marquee had been erected to serve the purposes of a lavatory. I had a hat on and it occurred to me that if I stepped out of my place in the queue, entered the tent, and then emerged hatless from it, I could join the far end of the loop without attracting any notice. And indeed I did accomplish this quite easily.

This reprehensible tactic cut out at least an hour of my queue-crawling, yet it was not until 6.30 a.m. that I was able to mount the steps of Westminster Hall and go inside. What a change! I came into wonderful warm air and a cathedral peace. A long staircase led down to the floor of the great hall in which the catafalque stood. Our queue, the river of people come to pay homage to Churchill, flowed slowly down this long staircase. We were not chivvied by any policemen, there was no 'keep moving please', all was discreet courtesy. In fact I paused on my way down and stood still to watch something. There were four sentinels stationed at the catafalque, one at each corner. They were relieved at regular intervals by fresh guards. It was my good fortune while descending the stairs to see a relief party in action.

From a door on the left side of the catafalque, and higher up, four sentinels appeared. The other four standing by the coffin had their rifles in the 'at ease' position, their legs apart, their heads bowed. They were motionless as any statue. Gradually the four men from above, in obedience to no verbal command, with incomparable grace of movement, each soundlessly approached the separate sentinels, and stood behind them. Then quietly the statues came to life; their limbs assumed slow motion; their bowed heads were raised: silently they came to attention and sloped arms, and each with the same rhythm left the catafalque by the way the others came – who now slowly ordered arms, stood at ease, bowed their heads, until at last their figures too were frozen.

After passing the catafalque I stopped before the exit to look back at the steady stream of people descending the stairs. That stream had flowed during all the previous week, night and day, and would continue day and night until the ending of this second week.

As I left the Hall I stumbled and fell to the ground. Two policemen quietly restored me to the perpendicular. This indignity did not bother me at all. I had seen something I would not forget. After seventeen years I put it in words now as if, for me, it had been yesterday. There was a message too, could I but read it, as to the meaning of Homage and of Leadership.

30 January 1982

Lord Denning
Patrick Devlin

Justice, Lord Denning and the Constitution
P. Robinson and P. Watchman, eds. (Gower)

Lord Denning is a highly exceptional or unaccountable fact or occurrence. This is the definition which, after covering the more esoteric settings for the word, the OED gives to a phenomenon. He has been for thirty-three years, as compared with the twenty of the next in order, one of the small number, now about thirty, of the appellate judges (those in the House of Lords and the Court of Appeal, the senior judges as they are sometimes called) who settle the development by judicial process of English law.

From the beginning he has been noted for nonconformity. But it is only since he became an octogenarian that the full extent of his phenomenality has been revealed. Taking the licence which the British invariably accord to octogenarians, especially nonconformist ones, he has displayed himself on television as a superb communicator with the public and one also who is ready to satisfy their anxiety to know how the great live. It would not be a good thing if all judges did likewise, but fortunately few have both the talent and the inclination. As an exception, Lord Denning has done a real service to the administration of justice by giving the public a sight of one of its great administrators.

Lord Denning has also written books in a popular style but exhibiting all his lucidity and learning. Famous trials can make saleable stuff. But if anyone had asked me before the event whether it would be possible to get two volumes of the adventures of an appellate judge on to the best-seller lists, I should have ridiculed the idea. It could not have been done, however, simply by the impartial extraction of passages from the law reports. There had to be a dramatic and unifying theme. The theme is the struggle by the Court of Appeal to modernise the law and the efforts of the House of Lords, especially in recent times, to thwart it. Both those books are in effect Lord Denning's appeal to his readers from the reverses he has encountered in the Lords.

There is some improbability in a theme which puts all the progressive sheep into the Court of Appeal and all the obstinate old goats into the House of Lords: most of the existing goats were once shepherded by Lord Denning. There was bound to be a reaction. This has now appeared in a number of essays put together by a group of academics, mostly young, I imagine, and with a strong element of the Scots who as lawyers are often said to be stricter than the English. Each essay is in form and substance an article for a law review.

The title of the book headlines the theme, which is that Lord Denning's addiction to the sort of justice he personally favours is unconstitutional. Since the British have no written constitution it is never easy to decide exactly what we mean when we say that something is unconstitutional. Sometimes it means simply that some body, exercising power, has failed to observe the degree of restraint that is customary. It is in this sense that it can be applied to the judiciary.

The judiciary has the sole power of applying the law and application sometimes requires implementation and extension. In this manner judges make law. True, they are only subordinate legislators and anything they say can be changed by Parliament. But the unwieldiness of Parliament ensures that often judicial legislation will last a long time, affecting meanwhile the rights and liberties of many people. So the judicial power, which is undemocratic, must be exercised with restraint. The customary restraint is obedience to precedent.

The doctrine of precedent requires every new decision to be attached to an old decision. Thus the judicial animal, be it sheep or goat, is hobbled; it may not advance by leaps and bounds. Innovation must be left to Parliament, not only because the judges cannot speak for the community but also because the forensic process, which is designed for the production of a decision in a particular case, is not apt for the formulation of general law.

Looked at in this way the doctrine can be seen as restricting. Looked at from another angle it is revealed as the essential condition of judicial lawmaking. A single judgment decides a case but contributes to the law only to the extent that it is followed by other judges. To keep their power the judges must move as a fleet in line. For the Court of Appeal judicial discipline is simple. The Court sits in divisions: each division must follow the signals of the House of Lords and also those of every other division that have not been cancelled by the House. If this discipline is not maintained the fleet will scatter and lose power.

The reason why judge-made law is still powerful is because Lord Denning is the only judge, past or present, who disobeys the rules. It is his lack of discipline rather than their lack of audacity that is the prime cause of his quarrels with the Lords.

This is the indictment that emerges from the book, though not with singular clarity since it is framed by different hands. Some document the indiscipline; others inspect without approval the actual results of the audacity. One author searches unsuccessfully for 'a coherent pattern of legal thought'. Does Lord Denning accept the doctrine of precedent and acknowledge its obligations? If so, what are his departures from it but the abuse of power for which he rebukes others, notably the trade unions? If not, what is his guiding light?

I think that he is lit by a diffuse passion for justice. Not the usual passion which can tempt a judge to strain the law in a particular case. He does not, for example, succour a single deserted wife 'in the exceptional circumstances of the case': he takes up the cause of all deserted wives. He does not decide regardless of law, but the law which he applies is not the law as it is but the law as he feels that it ought to be. He is impatient with what some call formalism – others call it the principle that the end does not justify the means – which retards the development of law. He has indeed a luminous mind and has often been the first to carry the torch into the dark places of the law. That is good. But it is bad that he should be the Lord Lucifer who will not serve.

This is the mainstream of the book. Thereafter the water flows out in a delta of diverse topics. The Constitution as the third element in the title is replaced by Morality, Negligence, the Rent Acts, Administrative Law and so on. Each heading is the subject of a critical essay in which Denning's social ideas and his ways of giving effect to them are examined. Of these I thought the one on trade union law by Kenneth Miller to be the best.

It is a pity that the mainstream split. If there had been a single author, he might have proceeded from a study of Lord Denning's unconstitutional activities to a study of those in which, acting within the magisterium, he has improved the law. Here his achievements are very considerable. His own books distract attention from them. There he seems concerned only to establish that his social ideas were always right. It is true that a reformer's reputation will be diminished if he spends himself on what posterity condemns. But the fact that his ideas (which are usually shared by many others) eventually turn out to be right will not make him famous, except perhaps as a preacher. For any practical reformer, whether he be political, social or legal, success is to be measured by the extent to which he can himself effect change within the constraints that limit him.

The value of Lord Denning's work in this respect has yet to be assessed. This is interesting reading for the present and necessary reading for the future biographer. It will be the task of the biographer, a task which also is untouched by the book, to explain Lord Denning's phenomenal popularity. I think it is, leaving aside his warmth and friendliness, because to a large number of people he appears as the protector of the ancient liberties which Parliament seems to have forgotten about.

16 May 1981

Lord Devlin, a former Lord of Appeal in Ordinary, was a senior judge for sixteen years.

Anatomy of Britain
Peregrine Worsthorne

The Changing Anatomy of Britain Anthony Sampson (Hodder and Stoughton)

'If you *do* succeed at first, try it on, try it on and try it on again' would make a good motto for Anthony Sampson who has just re-published his best-seller *Anatomy of Britain* for the fourth time. Although much of the detail has been brought up to date – not always accurately – the central theme remains unchanged, as if the author had learnt nothing and forgotten nothing (like the Bourbons) since the book first appeared in 1962. This is a bit odd under the circumstances, since Sampson's central theme has always been the reluctance of the British ruling classes to open their minds to new ideas, or to recognise that things ain't quite what they used to be. To nobody could this criticism apply more aptly than to Mr Sampson himself who seems quite amazingly set in his 1960 ways, a veritable museum piece from that long vanished era. As an exercise in nostalgia, the book is quite perfect, repeating all the familiar clichés, all the old tunes, so to speak. If one wants to be reminded of the fashionable nonsense that then passed for higher wisdom, who better than Mr Sampson, who concocted much of it, to unlock the gate of memory. For any less essentially frivolous purpose, however, the book is most unsatisfactory.

Its intellectual complacency is quite staggering. Back in 1962 Mr Sampson purported to demonstrate that Britain was still governed by a lot of *ancien régime* institutions populated by fuddy-duddy aristocrats unwilling or unable to recognise contemporary reality. If the country was to have any hope of escaping the fate of other empires in decline, like Spain and Portugal, it must get rid of the class system, embrace the white heat of the technological revolution, recruit new blood into the élites, go into Europe, produce more engineers; in a word *modernise*. Mr Heath, then as now, was his hero. Meritocracy, not aristocracy, was the answer.

Twenty years later Mr Sampson is saying exactly the same things, still purporting to put all the blame for everything on the old order, the public schools, Oxbridge, the class system, and so on. Not for one instance does it occur to this anatomist that his original analysis may have been inadequate, superficial, blinded by prejudice; or that the particular body politic under dissection may possess features which he overlooked. Surely a genuine scientist, returning to his task twenty years later, might have made some effort to use the scalpel rather more subtly, to probe a little more deeply, possibly even this time to try to examine certain organs – the heart, for example – previously ignored. Such good resolutions, however, are quite alien to Mr Sampson, since he is not really an anatomist at all.

What purports to be an anatomical attempt at dissection, with a view to laying bare the bones of the British body politic, is in truth merely a tailor's pitch to sell a new set of clothes, SDP clothes, as it happens, which the author thinks might fit better.

This is not to suggest that Mr Sampson is consciously selling his book under false pretences. Like all the most successful salesmen, he has come to believe his own patter, about the implausibility of which he appears totally oblivious; totally oblivious, for example, to the absurdity of continuing to attribute Britain's ills to a refusal to change or to the influences of traditional values rooted in the past. During the last twenty years Britain has experienced sweeping changes, fallen under the control of 'new men' whose meritocratic skills are exactly those recommended by Mr Sampson himself. The truth is that his prescriptions have been tried and found wanting. Modernisation has been all the rage, and if the public schools and Oxbridge are still on top this is not because they have failed to adapt, or hidden behind privilege but because they have adapted perhaps too successfully, proved too competitive: made themselves, that is, even more indispensable to the new order than ever they were to the old. Vast sums have been spent on building new universities, introducing a new system of comprehensive education – exactly as recommended by Mr Sampson – but the likes of Mr Sampson refuse to patronise them for their own children because they are simply not good enough.

To go on blaming the 'old order', or 'reactionary' institutions for the current mess, if mess it be, is to fly in the face of all reason and common sense. Surely it is time for any open-minded observer, any true anatomist, to start locating the cause of the trouble, not in the reactionary old establishment, whose influence has been on the decline, but in the new progressive establishment, who have been having it all their own way. It is not the Cavendishes and the Cecils who should take the blame, but the Wilsons, Heaths, Jenkinses, Jays, and Anthony Sampsons. After all, which was the most successful administration of modern times in terms of economic growth? Not Wilson's or Heath's – those Sampson-approved models of modernity – but Macmillan's, filled with fuddy-duddy aristocrats. And surely even Mr Sampson cannot have failed to notice that the effect of modernising and democratising the Tory Party – so strongly urged in 1962 – has not been to make it more 'progressive' but very much more 'reactionary'. Thus Mr Sampson now finds himself adversely comparing Mrs Thatcher, a modern meritocrat if ever there was one, with Lord Carrington and Sir Ian Gilmour, products of the very *ancien régime* which in 1962 he was so anxious to get rid of.

As for industrial relations, can it really be supposed that Mr Sampson's new meritocrats – like Sir Peter Parker, for example – have proved all that more successful at man management than their privileged predecessors? Surely there is enough evidence in this field, as in so many others, that all that class obsession of the 1960s – the idea that Britain was being held back by an out of date hereditary aristocracy – was and is a bit puerile. If anything, it is precisely the old institutions – those which have refused to kow-tow to progressive fashion and have bravely disregarded Mr Sampson's advice – that seem to be doing the best job, the most *efficient* job. Take, for example, the armed forces in general and the Brigade of Guards in particular, or the monarchy and the House of Lords, or Eton and Christ Church, or the City and the Inns of Court, all these bastions of privilege which are supposed to be out of touch with contemporary realities, might it not be that they have demonstrated a surer feeling about the real Britain than anything dreamt of in Mr Sampson's philosophy? Yet when Mr Sampson writes about these institutions he adopts an ironical, quizzical, supercilious approach, as if unable to take them seriously, except as symptoms of the British disease. Their survival is deplored. In fact, however, the most remarkable and fascinating aspect of Britain during the last twenty years has been the way these ancient institutions seem to have outlived the egalitarian *zeitgeist*. In a profound sense, it is *their* values which are now returning into fashion, to the point where it is not them but Mr Sampson who begins to look like the proverbial dodo or dinosaur. Far from handicapping Britain, could it just be that the ancient institutions have been responsible for slowing down her decline: not so much brakes preventing progress, as their critics allege, as brakes preventing retrogression. Without their resilience, and refusal to fade away, the fate of Spain and Portugal might have overtaken these islands even faster than it has. For the truth about Britain since the war is that its people have gone on enjoying a standard of living incomparably higher than they had any reason to expect, far higher, indeed, than they deserved. In many ways the record is astonishingly impressive, for which those in charge deserve some credit. And if Mr Sampson is right in insisting that it is the old institutions which have remained dominant in spite of all the modernisation, then the proper conclusion might well be exactly the opposite of the one reached in this book: namely that the old institutions are sources of health rather than sickness, pride rather than shame; buttresses to be preserved rather than burdens to be jettisoned.

That of course, is the one conclusion Mr Sampson dare not reach because it would make a nonsense of his whole approach. For no anatomist can be expected to admit that what he took to be a corpse under dissection is in fact very much alive, particularly when the anatomist in question has made such a successful career out of pronouncing it dead, not once but four times. Thus the only way that

'The older generation are so irresponsible.'

Mr Sampson can escape his dilemma is to argue that such sources of life as do remain – Oxbridge, the public schools, the Brigade of Guards, the monarchy and all the other feudal relics – ought to be dead, so as to make way for healthy new tissue like . . . the Social Democratic Party. What a farce when an anatomist is so blinded by prejudice that his scalpel reveals vitality in a new organ that is already beginning to wither after a few months of existence, while dissecting all the old organs, which have survived for centuries, as coarsely and unsubtly as a butcher might carve up some flea-bitten hobby horse from the knacker's yard.

2 October 1982

Journalists as tin gods
Paul Johnson

Journalists in the United States have always, in my opinion, received too much deference. They have a constitutional status. Government and business make their jobs easy. Politicians fawn over them. Mr Peregrine Worsthorne, who thinks Britain behind in this field, is never tired of pointing out that when John Kennedy learnt he had been elected President, his first call was on the columnist Joe Alsop. And that was even before the apotheosis of the journalist brought about by Watergate, in which the Woodward and Bernstein team of the *Washington Post* were credited with the destruction of the Nixon presidency. Prizes rained down; fortunes were made; the saga was jacked up into a preposterous film. Universities reported a rush of young men and women into a profession now regarded as uniquely glamorous and rich in gravy. Newspaper proprietors, editors, columnists and even lesser fry began to behave with insufferable arrogance. When, last year, the head of the CIA talked about asking US journalists to give him a hand occasionally, you should have heard the feeling of outraged dignity set up by the newspaper establishment and the snorts of dowager-like disgust at the very idea of journalists – that hieratic caste of unsullied seraphs– associating with grubby fellows like intelligence agents. When I tentatively suggested that there might conceivably be another point of view, I could not get the *Washington Post* to print it.

As it turned out, the era of journalistic triumphalism has been mercifully short, and it is appropriate that the *Washington Post*, having enjoyed the *hubris*, should have been the first to be engulfed by *nemesis*. The case of Janet Cooke, who faked the story about the child-addict, is bad from every point of view. It is a condemnation of the thoroughly disreputable system of 'affirmative action', as it is called, in which a particular group is favoured solely because of its skin. Black women are doubly privileged, especially in Washington, and if they have a good education the world is their oyster. The *Washington Post*'s editor, Ben Bradlee, conceded: 'The fact that Janet Cooke is black and her immediate editor was black made me trust them more, not less'. That is a very damaging admission. More serious, however, is that the reporter was not asked to name her (non-existent) sources for what was a sensational story. An editor has an unqualified right to oblige a reporter to identify his informants, and in a case like this, where the public health authorities and possibly the police should have been involved, he has a positive duty to do so. Stories based on anonymous sources should be sparingly used, in my opinion, and never made the basis for journalistic awards. A reporter unable or unwilling to satisfy the editor about his sources should be sacked.

The case of Michael Daly, the *New York Daily News* columnist who has been publishing pro-IRA propaganda, is in some ways even worse. His exposure reflects great credit on the *Economist* and on the *Daily Mail*, which rightly decided to give the scandal big treatment. Of course the *News* is not much of a paper and is going downhill. Its sales have fallen from 1,911,000 in 1977 to 1,491,000 at the latest count, while Murdoch's *New York Post* has climbed from 503,000 to 732,000. All the same, Daly's behaviour, on his own admission, is staggering. He is quoted in the *News* as saying that his column, which was more or less a piece of Irish imagination, was no different from any of the others he had written over the past two years, and that what he had the effrontery to term 'reconstruction' was his normal mode of procedure. The *Washington Post* has at least made ample amends for behaviour it admits is indefensible. The *News* has been much more grudging. Daly has simply been allowed to resign, and the editor, Michael O'Neill, says he has 'only the warmest feelings' for Daly, though his deceptions may well have led idiot Irish-Americans to contribute to IRA funds and so have cost British and Irish lives.

A de-mythologising of the US press is now under way, thank God. A *Newsweek* poll reports that sixty-one per cent of Americans believe 'very little' or 'only some' of what they read in newspapers. Some thirty-three per cent apparently think reporters make stories up 'often'. With the change of mood, it wouldn't surprise me if some of the big triumphs of the past begin to unravel. Who, now, believes in the existence of 'Deep Throat'? There is, indeed, an excellent case for an investigation of the behaviour of the press throughout the Watergate spasm, the methods used to get certain stories, or 'stories', the prejudice created against Nixon administration officials before and during their trials, the actual conduct of these trials, and the extraordinary sentences imposed. From the vantage point of 1981, the entire episode is beginning to look like a shameful witchhunt.

However that may be, the end of divine right journalism is to be welcomed on both sides of the Atlantic. It is wrong that journalists should claim special privileges, as do (with some justification) priests and doctors. There is no such thing as a 'professional secret' in journalism; indeed, it is not a profession but a trade. A journalist in court should be treated like any other witness. The notion that his sole job is to report the news, and that he has no obligation to assist the police, the army or any other legal authority in the discharge of their duties to society, is not only wrong but immoral. In a democracy a reporter may well be in duty bound to help the security or intelligence services in certain special cases. He is no different from everybody else and has all the normal responsibilities of a patriotic citizen.

British journalists have never been treated as little tin gods, but I regret the increasingly lavish use of by-lines and the star system in our quality papers. There has been a good deal of nomenclaturial inflation, too, with 'political editor' and similar nonsense. This is a temptation, indeed a positive incitement, to self-important journalists to introduce their views into their reports. Nothing is more fatal to a serious paper than 'viewy' news-columns. In the United States, where good newspapers once enforced an absolute distinction between news and views, there has undoubtedly been a decline in standards, with the *New York Times* and the *Washington Post* setting a poor example. One hopes that the present disgrace of the medium will lead editors to reimpose objectivity.

23 May 1981

A British Jew
Anthony Blond

'Sir, why do people dislike the Jews?'
'Because, Blond, they killed Christ.'

Forty years on such an exchange would be unlikely in any schoolroom in the world, but my Eton housemaster was not being particularly unkind or prejudiced. He was simply delivering the current matter-of-fact Christian view of the crucifixion. Now, attitudes towards Jews have changed. Auschwitz, the successes of the Israeli army, and the formal forgiveness of the Pope had not yet happened in that lovely summer of 1940.

Eton, though the largest school in England, had only eight Jewish pupils at that time. We were the Rossiter twins, Montagu, Goldblatt, Haskell, Vos, Blond *ma* and, later, Blond *mi*. Goldblatt, Haskell and Vos were all scholars. (I almost forgot – he would not forgive the omission – Harold Sebag-Montefiore who became the polo correspondent of *The Times*, who flogged from horseback the plaque of a co-religionist Karl Marx and is a pillar of the grandest synagogue in London.) The Rossiters were tyros at Eton football. The Hon. Montagu was excused games on account of some debility, but was nevertheless a popular figure. Goldblatt had a sweet smile, became the Captain of the School and was the son of the Liberal MP who founded the Trade Practices Committee which balled out Jewish black marketeers during the war. Haskell, never perhaps lovely but always loved, was the son of the ballet critic Arnold Haskell. Nobody liked Vos. He had to barricade himself in the lavatory on VE Day to escape the attentions of an infuriated mob. He had a genius for making himself disliked and this was the only incident I recall of a Jew being harassed. It was really out of anti-Vosism, so that when I was asked that same summer about anti-semitism at Eton by Marcus Sieff, now the second life peer of that ilk, I could truthfully answer: 'Anti-what?'

How did I come to be at Eton? Not because my family were part of that assimilated *haute juiverie* like the Pintos, the Mocattas, the Sebag-Montefiores. I was not one of these, though my mother's family is of ancient Italian stock. My grandfather, Bernard Blond, arrived in Hull in the 1880s, mistaking it possibly for New York. This was not uncommon; many Jews were illiterate and often taken for rides by ticket touts. And, according to my uncle, my grandfather was nice but not very bright. His name was Blond, a Russian sobriquet for a fair person (we have his passport). He settled in the ghetto in Hull, now destroyed and replaced by the Lister comprehensive school. He then moved to Manchester and caught the eye of Rachel Laski (so called from the Kingdom of Lask in Poland), aunt of the now famous Harold and, more to the point, sister of Nathan and Noah, of Laski and Laski, India merchants and rich. They sailed regularly to Bombay to sell the Indians saris. Nathan, my great-uncle, was a magistrate and the chief Jew of Manchester. He made a practice of never sentencing co-religionists. He nourished Chaim Weizmann, whose eloquence was such that both Balfour and Churchill came to Manchester to hear him speak in Yiddish. The latter was clever enough to stay with Nathan at Smedley House in Cheetham and dandled Harold on his knee. Bernard Blond and Rachel produced my father, who produced me. My father was three years in the trenches, ending up as a major in the Horse Guards and covered with glory. He insisted that if he had sons they should go to Eton. So my social preferment derived from military prowess.

How did the Jews get to England? There were Jews here in Saxon times, and they possibly came even before there were Christians –

with the Phoenicians on their tin-collecting expeditions to Cornwall. But the first wave of settlers came with William of Normandy who, like an earlier invader, Julius Caesar, favoured the Jews. They could not own land but were encouraged to lend money and became mortgagors, possibly the world's least popular profession. So when a small boy called Hugh was found upside down in a ditch near Lincoln, his body drained of blood, the Jews were blamed for the murder. This was the origin of the blood libel, revived by Hitler. To this day some Jewish families drink white wine on Passover to avoid misunderstanding. In 1290 their royal protector turned on them and they were expelled; for three and a half centuries England was officially *judenrein*.

They were let in again by a different kind of Protector, Cromwell, possibly influenced by his gunpowder merchant, a Maltese Jew. In 1659 was started the first Jewish society, the Inspectors of He'Eschaim of which I was once honoured to be a member – who gave out prayer books to the poor Jews of Cochin. A few years later a Quaker architect built, at no charge, for the tiny congregation of Spanish and Portuguese Jews, a synagogue in Bevis Marks just within the gates of the City of London. The ancestors of all those Pintos, Mocattas, Nabarros and Waley Cohens were more likely to have been pedlars and tinkers, so the marriage registry shows, than bankers and bullion brokers. But by the end of the eighteenth century the congregation had prospered sufficiently to include a typical free-thinking, financially independent Whig gentleman with a house in Gray's Inn, a place in the country and a boy at Winchester, Isaac d'Israeli who, more out of pique than conviction, had Benjamin baptised as a Christian.

The next and greatest influx of Jews to Great Britain was from Poland and Russia in the 1880s. Refugees from pogroms, these Jews were Ashkenazim (lit: Hebrew Germans) – a different breed from the Sephardim. Some of their names, dished out to them by snotty officials, were unattractive – Grob, Lipschitz, Goldberg, Stein and Fink. They were not welcomed by their established and well-nourished co-religionists. At first English society was not aware of the New Jews. There's no point in keeping a man out of a golf club if he's never seen a golf ball. But by the Twenties and Thirties when they appeared in their Jaguars ('Jews' Bentleys') in Maidenhead at the weekends, overran Bournemouth, infiltrated the Carlton at Cannes and the Captain's table on the *Queen Mary*, they *were* noticed. The Jews prospered in their traditional trades. The cheapest piece of capital equipment is a sewing machine – hence the rag trade and the fifty shilling suit. Some retail trades in England were transformed by Jewish expertise – timber (Times Furnishing), jewellery ('a Bravington Ring and the Girl is Caught') and usury in the form of hire purchase. By the mid-Thirties the Burtons, the Wolfsons and the Marks were millionaires demanding, if not a place in society, at least a flat in Grosvenor Square. They were not, according to commentators like Chesterton, Belloc and Eliot, very nice. They were so unlike dear (queer) Siegfried Sassoon or that elegant Major Goldsmith, the Liberal MP for Cavenham, Jews one was happy to number among one's best friends. In the Thirties English society was anti-semitic at all levels. At the first meeting of the Mere Golf Club, Cheshire, one of the committee said in a ripe Lancashire accent: 'Now let's get one thing straight – we're not 'aving any common Jewish buggers in 'ere.'

Worse, it was precisely this *nouveau* lot who noisily proposed distinctly unpatriotic plans for the British Mandated territory of Palestine. For fifty years, from the Balfour Declaration of 1917 to the Six Day War of 1967, Zionism was an irritant for the British establishment and an embarrassment to *haute juiverie* on both sides of the Atlantic. In 1948 when Begin's group (the Irgun) hanged two British sergeants in Palestine and the poet Abraham Stern's gang shot nice, Beethoven-loving Superintendent Conquest, Jewish grandees like Lord Bearsted in London and the Sulzbergers in New York were not Zionists. The *Daily Express* angrily splashed the stories. Synagogues in London were set on fire. It may be unkind to attribute the distaste for Zionism of assimilated Jews in England and America to fear of social degradation by association. Their motives may have been mixed and possibly contained sincere British patriotism. In those days, to that sort of English Jew, the state of Israel was a social threat. They could not have been more wrong.

Anti-semitism ceased to be socially acceptable during the Six Day War of 1967. This sounds orotund, but please consider it; for more than a thousand years Jews have been crumpled by a string of unattractive adjectives and anecdotes. Roman Jews were disliked by Cicero, Suetonius and Horace for their greasiness, their diet of tunny fish tails, etc., and this odour has clung to them throughout history, and can be detected, for instance, in the novels of John Buchan. Suddenly the Jews' social problems – in the West – evaporated. The Six Day War was compulsive viewing on television. The world gasped as it saw the six-foot sons of immigrants who had crawled into Haifa harbour in leaky little boats only twenty years before, wallop the armies of three nations – Egypt, Syria and Jordan – allowing two days for each.

International Jewry which had seeded the world with genius (and for what?) was at last 'kosher', thanks to the bayonets of Israeli soldiers. For the first time since the destruction of the Temple, Jews walked tall. Zionism was now respectable. Lord Bearsted sent two large cheques to Michael Sacher, the chief fund-raiser, in one day. The British Government placed no restriction on the amount of money sent to Tel Aviv. The clubs and bars of the Home Counties had a new joke about Jews, the Israeli joke high on arrogance and cockiness – not a Jewish joke at all. The Oxford English Dictionary was forced to abandon, through a court of law, its definition of the verb 'to jew'.

The social position of Jews in society is now impressive, whatever their origins. They are over-represented in both Houses of Parliament, as captains of industry in the public and private sectors, at the top of every profession from architecture (Sir Denys Lasdun) to zoology (Lord Zuckerman) and are high up in the Catholic and Anglican Churches (the Bishop of Birmingham was bar-mitzvahed in my synagogue). Much has changed. Of course anti-semitism occurs in odd flurries. Some years ago six girls were expelled from Heathfield for Jew-baiting. Richard Ingrams continues to snipe away in *Private Eye*, but he has always been rather an old-fashioned young man. And Harold Wilson did 'know all the wrong Jews', and honour too many of them – *ipsissima verba* of a Jewish peer who added, 'I could have told him'. But anti-semitism has lost its venom and effect. Consider the case of Leslie Hore-Belisha who was destroyed by the military because of his Jewishness. He attended the Jewish house at

Clifton – what ever happened to that? – was a wit of the Oxford Union, knew all the right people, but they got him. He was, 'more Jewed Against than Jewing', as Christopher Hollis wrote, and he preferred monks to members of his own religion, but they got him. The same fate could never happen to Sir Keith Joseph, for instance. The social prestige of relatively new Jews like Goodman, Lords Weidenfeld, Lever and Selim Zilkha would have been unthinkable in pre-war England when it was not done to shop at Marks and Spencer, now the most respected institution in the land, with, I am told, the best pork pies.

But why not? Many Jews, like another minority, the Parsees, have higher than average intelligence, civic sense, and – ask anybody in the spastic and spina bifida business – compassion. They are good citizens, pay taxes, go dutifully to war and, except in the area of business fraud, don't bump up the crime rate. Is it not right and proper that Jews should have a higher than average share of the world's goods, and of decision-making? Except in those countries dominated by Karl Marx, the most famous anti-semite of all, they do.

The door of my house in Chester Row sports a mezzuzah (a little silver badge of Jewishness). At a *Spectator* party my wife remarked to Enoch Powell that she often saw him walking past the house. 'Ah,' remarked the observant statesman, 'You must live near the Jew'. 'No', she replied, '*with* the Jew'.

English society today is 'with the Jew', and this article, which may not please the professional seekers out of anti-semitism, or those who have no objection to Jews as such but just-wish-they'd-shut-up-about-it, is in celebration of an outbreak of pro-semitism, which may or may not be permanent. One wonders: God has dealt his People some tricky hands. It was a rabbi who drew up the contract of marriage between Ferdinand of Aragon and Isabella of Castile which led to the Inquisition. The Jews who most identified with their country were the Jews of Germany.

24 April 1982

2   The Churches

The Pope in England
C. H. Sisson

One could almost find it in one's heart to leave the Archbishop of Canterbury alone with his sorrows, as he awaits the Pope's visit. This little ecumenical occasion cannot be quite what he imagined. It may perhaps have the healthy result of bringing out differences which the authorities of the Church of England have been trying to smudge ever since they were given their head in 1974. However that may be, a church of so many alternatives should not be altogether surprised if some people are unable to see that a multiplicity of differences points infallibly to unanimity. Not all have been sanctified in the coffee-bars of Synod. But, however it may be with these high theological matters, there are more sordid considerations.

That the Pope should pay a pastoral visit to his followers in England is clearly something he may do if he wishes. One might think that he risks confusing himself as well as other people by his taste for travel, and that he might be better employed at home in the Vatican, but that is for him to judge. That he should, while he is here, exchange some civilities with the Archbishop of Canterbury, even with the Governor of the Church of England, is reasonable enough. That the visit should be made the occasion for meeting leaders of other denominations, in order, in his flying visit, to get a slightly less misleading picture of ecclesiastical dispositions in these islands, is also no bad thing.

It is surely rather puzzling, however, that the Archbishop should lay on simultaneous visits by heads of the Anglican communion overseas, as if he should wish to say, not exactly, 'My church is bigger than yours' – which he cannot say – but that he is not just the Archbishop of Canterbury but a bit of a traveller himself, with friends he can visit in other countries, and so cuts quite a figure in the world-wide Church of his aspirations.

Hasn't it all got rather out of hand? A disintegrated church at home is not healed by fixing its gaze on distant shores and the residual politics of post-imperial times. And the Pope surely, for all his talents, will have his work cut out to get even a plausible tourist's picture of this country during his short stay. He has been to Africa, he has been to South America, to the United States, to Ireland; he is always keen to pop home to see how things are going on in Poland. No doubt he has other jaunts in mind. Surely on this occasion he had better concentrate on the United Kingdom? It is a puzzling enough place for those of us who live here, and the airborne businessman, in less exalted lines of business, does not always take in all that he needs to be able to listen critically to the propositions of his branch managers.

If the Pope knocks over the furniture when he is here we shall have to pretend, out of courtesy to a distinguished foreign visitor, that he has not done so, or that it doesn't matter. We could even forgive our own archbishop if, in the heady atmosphere of a clerical get-together, he injudiciously laid on too large and too miscellaneous a party. It is a big occasion and it is not likely to happen again, in his time. But the truth is that this confusion between local and international affairs has become part and parcel of the office of Archbishop of Canterbury, as at present conceived. It is not too much to say that, as things are, the executive head of the Church of England is so preoccupied with his more far-flung collaborators that the Queen's realm of the United Kingdom is small beer to him. This natural preoccupation with the widest dimensions of Anglicanism is understandable enough, for what is more flattering than to be a World Figure? But it is a drawback for the Church of England, the historic entity to which the see of Canterbury has been related since the days of Augustine.

All the most notable developments in the Church of England, in recent years, have been coloured, one might think excessively, by these international preoccupations. Of course there *are* international preoccupations, and someone has to attend to them, but even a good Foreign Secretary is not a substitute for a Prime Minister. The local sheep look up and are frankly puzzled. We like to hear about foreign parts but we have our own parts. They have been left to wither. That is not how the Archbishop and those who aid and abet him would put the matter. But in fact, we have seen our Prayer Book thrown away, our superb version of the Bible demoted to a position of no importance, and a new sectarianism, which looks only to its own members, sweep over the parishes. Of course it is all in the name of holiness, like every other iniquity carried out in the name of the Church over the centuries – including the centuries before the sixteenth.

Let us pay no attention to holiness – or none to claims to it. It is, really, not the Anglican way. But now, one might say in all churches, not only in our own, the folly of sanctimonious claims knows no bounds. The degradation of current conceptions may be compendiously studied on the BBC's Sunday programme (at 8.15 a.m. every week on Radio 4). In this ramshackle collection of what passes for religious news, not a week passes but some more or less ill-informed person is put up to say, with no authority whatever, that 'the church' thinks this or that about some fashionable event of the day. Politicians may be worried but, bless my soul, Christians know the answers! It is no sillier than some other programmes but it takes all the prizes for pretentiousness – unless, of course, one treats theological pretensions with complete contempt. One might suppose this to be the object of the organisers of the programme, but in fact one hardly believes them capable of such duplicity.

What is the local shepherd doing? Encouraging all this, as far as one can make out. It is, in fact, a natural outcome of the deliquescence of the Church of England, of which the abandonment of the Prayer Book has been more than a symptom. Bandaging their eyes and holding out their flabby hands as far as they would go, the leaders of the Church of England have exhorted its poor browbeaten members to avert their eyes from their duty in the commonwealth of the United Kingdom and to join in whatever wild-goose chases are proposed for the improvement of other people. It is not that some of these causes are not as deserving of support as political causes are likely to be, but that the miscellaneous spokesmen who claim our adherence to them because we are supposed to be Christians have no special competence to judge of these matters. The largest element of competence required is generally to be well-informed, which in a world buzzing more than ever with half-baked rumours it is extremely hard to be. Another element is that members of the Church of England have a duty of loyalty no less than other people; if our leaders think otherwise, they have changed the character of our church without authority and without telling us.

It has long seemed to me that, with the loosening of constitutional ties which has followed the dissolution of the Empire and entry into the Common Market, England stands at a disadvantage as compared with other components of the United Kingdom – with Scotland, Wales, even Ulster, though that is a more dubious case. I prefer England to the late Empire, and I should like it to survive. But whereas the other components expect to be reckoned with separately, England has to make do not only with the institutions but the personality of the United Kingdom. We are supposed to like to be smothered. With the Church of England it is even worse. We are blotted out under the Anglican robes of the Archbishop. Why not promote him to the role of Pope (new style) in the Anglican International, and give us an archbishop who could keep his mind on England?

Admittedly this proposition has become more difficult now, with the publication of the report of the Anglo-Roman Commission. A 'universal primacy' sits better with a notion of national churches, holding all Christians in a particular territory, than with a gaggle of churches of opinion each scattered across the world and making for more or less disruption. But that would mean a universal diminution of the authority of Rome, and the assertion of the primacy of Canterbury over Westminster.

10 April 1982

'We still believe that the old methods are best, Mrs Simmonds'

Muggeridge submits
Auberon Waugh

On Sunday, in the church of St Teresa, Taunton, we sang a hymn whose words, written out in the hymnbook, went like this:

'Kum-ba-ya, O Lord, Kumbaya
'Kum-ba-ya, O Lord, Kumbaya
'Kum-ba-ya, O Lord, Kumbaya
O Lord, Kumbaya.'

They were words I had first heard sung by Judith Durham and The Seekers twenty years ago, but it did not occur to me to wonder what they meant. The song is said to be a Negro spiritual, and presumably the Negroes who sang it in the southern states of America retained some folk-memory of a meaning it might once have had in some West African language or tribal dialect. But if this was so, the meaning has long since been lost, and there was no indication in the hymnbook that any particular meaning should be attributed. To the congregation, mostly composed of Irish Tauntonians, the words were quite simply double Dutch.

There is a coherent argument to be advanced for preferring double Dutch over any other language for the purpose of expressing the ineffable, but such an argument sits oddly on the lips of those who have just destroyed the Church's ancient liturgy in mediaeval Latin on the grounds that they had just noticed how nobody spoke mediaeval Latin any more. So far as I know, the hymn 'Kum-ba-ya' is the only one yet to be written in an incomprehensible language, but it might well be the precursor to a whole liturgy in double Dutch. The preference for double Dutch (or possibly uncomprehended nineteenth-century Gambian) over the beautiful, hallowed phrases of Church Latin would be in keeping with the deep hatred which the modern Church shows towards the last 1500 years of its own history, the violent repudiation of its own accumulated wisdom.

As things are, I suppose we can invest the words 'Kum-ba-ya, O

Lord' with any meaning we choose. I chose to sing them as a little anthem of welcome and congratulations to Malcolm and Kitty Muggeridge, who had been received into what remains of the Catholic Church the day before. Malcolm spoke of 'a sense of homecoming, of picking up the threads of a lost life, of responding to a bell that has long been ringing, of finding a place at a table that has long been left vacant', but there was a suggestion, I thought, in the press coverage of the event (it scored front-page photographs in all three quality Sundays) that the bell had been ringing suspiciously long, that the Muggeridges, both approaching 80 years old, had cut their Augustinian 'but not yet' *(sed noli modo)* rather fine.

Never mind. I am happy they have got away with it. 'They both exuded happiness, as though it was bursting from their hearts,' said the priest who received them, Father Paul Bidone. He it was who introduced a coachload of mentally handicapped children to fill the moments of silent prayer in the service with what were variously described as 'inarticulate cries and murmurings', or 'occasional cries and clapping'.

I observe that the place at table which was waiting for him after the ceremony was at the house of Lord Longford, who was his sponsor or godfather. Since Lord Longford (or Mr Pakenham as he then was) also sponsored my own reception into the Catholic Church forty-three years earlier, this might be a good occasion to compare notes.

There was no chorus of mentally handicapped children to welcome my reception into the Church with whistles, hoots or shrieks. Nor was any such chorus available in St Teresa's church on Sunday. Perhaps they are produced only on solemn pontifical occasions, as the *castrati* used to be in earlier times. I just had an older sister, a female cousin and a collection of aunts. Nor, I fancy, did I exude happiness as though it was bursting from my heart after the ceremony. In those days, one was expected to bellow like a Turk. But the chief difference, as I maintain, is in the sort of Church to which our common godfather introduced us. One could agree that just as my Mr Pakenham has developed and expanded from being a sickly private soldier in the Ox and Bucks to becoming first a baron, then an earl, a member of the Privy Council and Knight of the Garter, so the Catholic Church has grown richer and better in the intervening period. But whereas anyone can see that Lord Longford is one and the same person, it is much harder to spot any resemblance between the two Catholic Churches. I wonder which one Mr Muggeridge thinks he is joining.

In former times, I should explain, the priest muttered away in Latin at one end of the church and the congregation followed or not as they chose, often getting on with their private meditations or devotions instead. Nowadays, everything has to be done together, like some spiritual PT class. To rub in the idea that religious devotions are a communal effort, and that man's relationship with God is now a communal, not a personal, one, people are required to shake hands and recite the Creed in its earliest form of 'We believe' rather than 'I believe'.

I find the new emphasis personally distasteful and historically inappropriate: there might have been a case under the special conditions of the early Church for stressing human fellowship in religion, but not since Thomas Aquinas; most particularly today there is every need to emphasise the opposite, that man's relationship with God is essentially and uniquely a personal one, so is his accountability. To pretend otherwise is to degrade human nature still further just when it needs to rescue itself from the pressures of collectivism.

Whatever Mr Muggeridge may say to the contrary, I suspect that he is a modern (i.e. early) Christian rather than a traditional (or evolved) one. He writes of his joy in the Christian fellowship exactly as if religious belief were some sort of high-minded football supporters' club. More revealingly, he writes of his particular admiration for St Augustine of Hippo (354-430), the second greatest intellect of the Catholic Church, who was nothing if not a Christian communist.

St Thomas Aquinas (1225-74), who was the greatest Catholic intellect in the Church's history, absorbed everything of value Augustine had to contribute into the evolving philosophy of the Church. But present conditions are exactly the opposite of what they were in Augustine's time. Then, with the collapse of the great Roman Empire, the danger was social disintegration: nowadays the danger is social despotism.

In other words, I fear that the Church's new recruit has not really worked out his position inside it. But the fact that he welcomed the chorus of mentally handicapped children proves not only how his heart is in the right place, but also how his beautiful intellect is still working. There are many explanations for his pleasure, all admirable.

At its simplest and most traditional, there was the reminder that simpletons (*pace* Ms Anne Stanesby, of Springfield Hospital's Advice and Legal Representation Project) have always been thought to occupy a special place among God's children as holy innocents. Less traditionally, there is the pleasant thought of Channel Four edging its way into a TV personality's holy moments. Then there is the agreeable commentary these young people provided on the Church's present preference for simplicity in all things.

Finally, where lesser men would have been appalled to see a solemn event reduced to something approaching black farce, there is the reminder, enshrined in the gargoyle decoration of so many cathedrals, that Jesus was an inveterate joker, and that one explanation for everything must always be kept in reserve, that it was all a practical joke. So long as Mugg retains that perception, he can never be lost. All that remains, I suppose, is to wish him a hearty Kum-ba-ya.

4 December 1982

Mervyn Stockwood
A. N. Wilson

Chanctonbury Ring: An Autobiography Mervyn Stockwood (Hodder and Stoughton/Sheldon Press)

Christian autobiography ought to be a contradiction in terms. People who subscribe to an ideal of self-forgetting should surely be repelled by the exercise of sustained self-contemplation. Yet, they have been at it for centuries: ever since that supreme egotist St Paul gave us those fragments of unappealing self-portraiture in the Epistle to the Galatians. Some of the great books of the world have been the result of Christian self-obsession – St Augustine's *Confessions* and Newman's *Apologia*. Others have been intent on telling their life-story in the spirit of Dogberry, pining to be written down an ass.

Which is Mervyn Stockwood: a Saint Augustine or a Dogberry? While he was Bishop of Southwark, it was hard for an outsider who knew nothing of his brilliance as a pastor and an administrator (fully described here) to take him quite seriously. His public performances and utterances were so persistently foolish, and over such a long period of time, that it seemed he must have had a clownish compulsion to draw attention to himself. He loved to be seen as the advocate and defender of things specifically condemned by Scripture and the wider wisdom of Catholic tradition. Spiritualism, socialism and sodomy all found their champion in him. So did the ordination of women to the priesthood.

He is not, of course, the first bishop to espouse unchristian causes. In the pages of his book he reminds us of Archbishop Fisher, who was a Freemason, a body that substitute the term *Architect* for the Holy Trinity and who deny the divinity of Christ. In our own day, we may doubt, while Archbishop Paul Marcinkus skulks in the Vatican, whether it worries him that Christians are forbidden to give money upon usury. In palmier days, that cleverest of prelates Hensley Henson neglected Gospel warnings of hell fire to those who said, 'Thou fool'. And most bishops in history, certainly most Anglican bishops, have been able to reconcile their consciences to vengeful wars and to capital punishment. By the standards of most bishops, in fact, Mervyn Stockwood has been impressively orthodox.

When I opened his memoirs, however, those dangerous scriptural words, *Raca, Thou fool* came irresistibly to mind. It was impossible to feel otherwise when skimming through the photographic illustrations. Here we see the bish, hooting with mirth at his own jokes at a Foyle's literary luncheon. By his side, Dame Barbara Cartland, resplendent in ostrich feathers, reveals a merry set of dentures. Here again is the pontiff driving a dodgem-car at a party given by David Frost in Alexandra Palace; his car-sick passenger is Lord Longford. Here again: 'the author with the Bluebell girls'. Lounge-suited he stands with fists firmly clenched, while the beauties glitter at his side, bare thighs and cleavages a-dangle with diamante.

Next, I skimmed through the index: two pages apiece to exorcism, incense and homosexuality. That showed a proper sense of priorities. The only time I ever heard the bishop preach he was reading a spooky homily about seances, the Other Side, and the Astral Plane. It was ages ago. Thinking of it called back to memory the murkier acquaintances of my theological past. Those were the days where any ordinand sacked from a more strait-laced diocese for illiteracy, shoplifting or semi-criminal sexual lapses could turn their steps towards Southwark, confident of receiving the laying-on of Merv's apostolically-consecrated hands.

Since then, he has retired, comparatively young, and gone to live in Bath. When a supreme exhibitionist leaves the stage early, one naturally fears the worst. But this book explains his departure from Southwark very clearly and movingly. The opening chapters are as innocently conceited as one would expect: a curacy in Bristol in the 1930s (Stafford Cripps's constituency) made the Young Conservative Mervyn into a Red. He had just enough sense not to become a Stalinist. The chapters covering his Bristol years, and his time as vicar of Great St Mary's in Cambridge are a catalogue of unashamed boasting about his own independence of mind, his personal charm, and his ability to attract thousands of people to come to his church. After he becomes Bishop of Southwark, the success story continues. From the moment he excited Geoffrey Fisher's disapproval for refusing to wear gaiters at his investiture to his swansong in the *Morning Star* attacking Donald Coggan, he established his role as court jester to the *bourgeoisie*, the tame *enfant terrible*, whose comments about Race, Russia or Sex really shocked no one.

It was an easy role to play. What emerges (unsurprisingly and attractively) in this most readable book is how boring and depressing Stockwood found his public persona. He left Southwark plunged into the most hideous depression against which he had been struggling for five years. He had not lost his faith. Indeed, he is obviously a prayerful and spiritual figure. But he was bored stiff with being a bishop and bored stiff, one suspects, by the demands of having to be controversial. Now he lives in retirement in Bath, with

Midge his cat. He has mellowed, though, after a lifetime of following trends, we do not expect an old dog to learn a completely new set of tricks. At the time of going to press, the Social Democrats were evidently in the ascendant; for, after lamenting the fact that he was not made a Life Peer, Stockwood writes: 'At the next election I shall vote for the man who approximates to a Christian socialist in his endeavours, a man like Stafford Cripps or Clem Attlee whose approach is based on the teachings of Jesus of Nazareth'. No comment.

By the time you reach this stage in the book, it is impossible not to have become rather fond of old Merv. The glimpses of his nervous loneliness, his cold sweats and his sleepless nights are disarming. And there is something conversely cheering about the invigorating walks he always takes on Chanctonbury Ring (hence the title) when cares attack and life seems black. It was there, in 1981, that the cloud of his depression lifted, just as he was cured of a slipped disc by Our Lady of Washington five years before. His cat, Midge, asks him at the end of the book ' "If you had your time over again, would you reverse your collar?" I think a long time. "Well, Midge, the point you see is this: *yes* – if I could be convinced that the Church of England would leave me free to be a minister in the living Body of Christ; but *no*, if it meant being an undertaker for a decomposing ecclesiastical corpse." '

Assisted by a translation, one suspects that many *Spectator* readers

3   Power

Jeremy Thorpe's acquittal
Ferdinand Mount

Mr Jeremy Thorpe stands in the privacy of his own balcony, a free man. It is a riproaring finale – but a finale to what? Greek tragedy was never like this. Once again, you would have to riffle through Trollope to find such a mixture of high places and low life, such a meeting of the grand and the grubby. And this stunning reversal of fortune in the final chapter has more in common with the twists of a high Victorian novel than with the remorseless spinning of the Fates.

Even Trollope, though, for all his interest in ecclesiastical life, might have drawn the line at laying on a Thanksgiving Service in the North Devon village of Bratton Fleming for his hero. The rector describes this new *Te Deum* as 'a thanksgiving for the way God has answered our prayers for Jeremy and Marion in their ordeal.' Oh God, oh Bratton Fleming!

As to the conduct of the actual trial, only the most temperate and delicate comments are permissible; there is nothing much to be added to the points Alan Watkins made so well in the *Observer*. But it is worth harking back to the Minehead committal proceedings for a minute. Those who have criticised the reporting or indeed the existence of committal hearings usually argue that for the jury to hear the evidence twice may harm the interests of the defendant. But in both the cases where the dramatic nature of the evidence provoked this argument – the Thorpe case and the case of Dr Bodkin Adams – the jury *acquitted* the defendants. You could just as well argue that Mr George Deakin's decision to call for the magistrates' proceedings to be reported *helped* both himself and his co-defendants. The best argument against the existence of committal proceedings remains that they cost a lot of money and serve no good purpose; but if they are to stay, they should be reported, as Sir David Napley for one thinks.

would rather be 'undertakers' and weep at what Mervyn and his like have done to the 'decomposing ecclesiastical corpse' in the last twenty years. He does not ask himself why the corpse twitches when the surgeons hack away at its ancient liturgies and ordinals. Only in horror movies do corpses cry out. In real life, protest from such a quarter would suggest that the patient is still alive. But, although one ought to be angry with the foolish old men who are responsible for the decay of religion in the last few decades, I found myself illogically disarmed by this book and fully warmed to his frank belief that the modern church is thunderingly boring.

18 September 1982

Christmas*

Christmas is based on a fact; not on the literal accuracy of every word in the Gospels, but on the fact of the Incarnation. If it is not true that the Word was made flesh in the person of Christ, then the story of Christmas may, like all good stories, offer moral and psychological truths, but that is all. It will be no more than a legend, and the edifice of doctrine and worship which the Church has built upon it will be as false as the original fact. But it is also true that the Incarnation cannot be proved by ordinary historical or scientific methods: its fact only becomes apparent through faith. If the Church is to make anything of its duty to preach the Gospel at Christmas, it has to explain the fact in strictly religious terms.

Today's Church does not readily supply such an explanation. Some of its bishops do not even believe it themselves. Many more regard the exposition of religious truth as an affront to the good nature and patience of the few that care to listen to them, and are content to conduct their carol services, and make a few remarks about the lack of love in the world and the humble circumstances of Christ's birth. If they are sentimental, they will go on about how Christmas is a time for the children; if they are austere, they will complain about the enjoyment of carnal pleasures at such a time; if they are political, they will point out that while we eat our turkey, a third of the world is making do with rice.

If this is the Church's handling of Christmas, the 'commercial Christmas' regularly railed against each year is the last thing that Christmas need worry about. The cribs on show in big stores may well be the nearest representation of Christian truth that many children ever see, the atmosphere of festivity and consumption the only ghost many adults know of a great feast of the Church. Indeed, in the semi-secular, commercial Christmas, two vital principles are observed – that the occasion is for a family, however broken, and that the purpose of all the spending and effort is mainly to give. These are Christian principles which are reinforced by their widespread annual observance.

All that the commercial Christmas suffers from is its vagueness. It acknowledges that the birth of Christ was a Big Moment for mankind, from which we should learn and which we should commemorate, but on why, what and how, it is confused. If there is no institution ready to remedy the vagueness, the strength of belief will inevitably degenerate. The hungry sheep look up and, receiving little attention from their pastors, settle for Christmas pudding.

What makes the failure of the Church in this respect so odd, is the quality of the truth bequeathed to it. It would take a man of remarkable eloquence and clarity to bring the doctrine of the Trinity home to an ignorant audience, but in Christmas the Christian religion finds its most accessible moment, the moment when God, that most inaccessible of concepts, became a man.

Becoming man means becoming something that every man may understand, and therefore something which any clergyman should be able to explain. Where a generalised concept might mean nothing, a specific fact is intelligible. It is possible (though not especially pleasant) to visit Bethlehem today and experience the bleakness of the Judean hills in winter, or simply to point to a map to show where the events took place. The story of a particular time, place and person can be told.

The more often, fully and beautifully the Church relates the events of Christmas, the more inevitably will their 'relevance' appear to those who listen; and the more the listeners learn, the more they will wish to know what else happened, where the story b[e] whether it has ended. Souped up, watered down, over-ge[ ] Christmas is reduced to the ordinary things which, by its ev[ ] made extraordinary. The precise story of how the Word [ ] flesh is the most truthful that words can tell, and becomes le[ ] each alteration.

Nor does the Church have to speak with condescension[ ] simple events, as if they were a show put on to convince the[ ] They contain more than any intellect can ever grasp. It i[s] unbearably difficult, if delightful, to imagine the Redeeme[r] world being born in a stable, He 'whose glorious, yet contract[e] wrapt in night's mantle, stole into this manger'. There c[ ] nothing stranger than that God should have implanted his W[ ] speechless baby (the Latin *infans* means, literally, wordless),[ ] he should have prepared his coming by so many signs, and the[n] by stealth.

Many who are exasperated by the weakness and secular[ ] trendy religion have driven themselves into a position where, in[ ] to save their faith from dilution, they have made it antithetical [ ] world. To them, in particular, the Church can give a proper answ[er] Christmas. We are told that 'God so loved the world, that he ga[ve] only-begotten son, to the end that all that believe in Him shoul[d] perish, but have everlasting life'. In these circumstances,[ ] presumptuous to hate the world. Christ's life on earth forbids an[y] to regard his own life as pointless. The moment of his arrival[ ] moment of joy, which is what Christmas, however debased,[ ] remained. It would be nice if the sermon on Christmas morn[ing] simply said, 'eat, drink and be merry, for today we live'.

18 December 1982

* *Unsigned leader by Charles Moore*

MPs are reserving most of their indignation for those newspapers which offered witnesses large sums of money and even larger sums in the event of a conviction – in effect, payment by results. Isn't this tantamount to the obstruction of justice and ought not the law to be changed? Well, either one or the other, but not both, as Sir Michael Havers, the Attorney-General, points out; if it is obstruction of justice (or contempt of court, a more straightforward matter), then the law doesn't need to be changed and Lord Hartwell and his editors could be standing in the same dock where lately Mr Thorpe *et al* stood. One raises an eyebrow to see the *Telegraph* mob occupying the pillory usually reserved for more vulgar practitioners.

I can't see much merit in the defence advanced in the *Daily Telegraph* and *Sunday Telegraph* editorials after the trial, namely, that the contract with Peter Bessell was signed only after his evidence had 'crystallised', to use Mr Justice Cantley's term. Surely this is just the moment when the newspapers ought to stay aloof from witnesses. For if the witness steps into the witness box with the ink scarce dry on the cheque, the temptation to improve and embroider his evidence in order to earn a second cheque will be all the more immediate. By contrast, it might conceivably have been legitimate to pay Mr Bessell for his life-story well *before* Mr Thorpe's arrest; after all, there might never have been any arrest and thus no course of justice to have been interfered with; it might even have been defensible to pay for Mr Bessell's life-story, *after* the end of the trial when the course of justice had been exhausted. But to operate an incentive scheme in between does seem to be the sort of practice which would give the *News of the World* a bad name.

If newspapers are to be criticised, though, it should also be pointed out that without their investigations and the lubrication of these dubious payments the prosecution might never have been launched: if the *Evening News*'s dealings with Andrew Newton were among the most dubious, they also produced the most relevant if not the most reliable evidence. One or two MP's have argued that the prosecution should never have been launched, apparently solely on the grounds that the defendants were acquitted. By this criterion, the Director of Public Prosecutions would be expected to clock up a one hundred per cent record of convictions. As Sir Michael Havers pointed out, the fact that the jury deliberated for two-and-a-half-days does not suggest that the truth was easy to arrive at.

In reality, the DPP, Sir Thomas Hetherington, has behaved in copybook fashion. He took great care before the prosecution was launched, he publicly assumed personal responsibility for the decision, rightly consulting Mr Sam Silkin, the Attorney-General of the day, who equally rightly decided to take no part, seeing that Mr Thorpe was a parliamentary colleague and that the case might have general political repercussions, specifically, that it might dish the Liberals to the advantage of the Tories.

The last resort is to blame the Liberal Party or certain Liberal MPs. Mr David Steel has been criticised for going out of his way to make it clear that he wanted Mr Thorpe to make a new life anywhere except in the Liberal Party. Some say that Mr Steel was ungenerous or premature to invoke Mr George Carman's closing remark to the jury that the ordeal had 'destroyed' Mr Thorpe's parliamentary career. Had not Mr Thorpe suffered enough? You should not kick a man when he is down.

But Mr Thorpe is not down. He is fifteen foot up on a balcony, waving and holding a celebration party. He has expressed no contrition for the embarrassment he has caused to lifelong friends and colleagues. Nor has he expressed the slightest wish to return to private life. He speaks only of a 'short period of rest with my family away from the glare of further publicity'. Who can tell where he will pop up next?

Sympathy with private agony is one thing; encouragement to resume a public career is quite another. There is an endearing but misguided refusal in this country to recognise that public service is a privilege not a right and that it is possible for a man to disqualify himself permanently for public office of any kind. Mr Thorpe's acquittal makes it necessary and possible to say certain things about him which it would have been cruel and unnecessary to say if he had been found guilty and which it would have been contempt of court to say while the case was *sub judice*.

His behaviour over the £20,000 he received from Jack Hayward was indefensibly casual and high-handed. His behaviour towards his parliamentary colleagues throughout has been ruthless, evasive and deceitful. Consider only the personal undertakings which are said to have been given to Mr Steel. Originally Mr Thorpe had promised to resign his seat if the allegations became public. He did not resign. Then he said that if he was charged he would not stand for re-election. He stood. Then he told Mr Steel he would not be coming to last year's Liberal Assembly at Southport. And he came – gosh, how he came.

The question of his guilt or innocence of the criminal charges was not the point. The fact of being on a charge of conspiracy to murder does not licence you to break every undertaking you give to your colleagues.

I have in the past been critical of certain leading Liberals such as Mr Steel himself and Lord Byers for their handling of the affair, particularly in its early stages. Perhaps they were a little naive and indecisive. But they had a great deal to cope with and only a partial understanding of the man at the centre of the business. And if Mr Thorpe has behaved badly towards his fellow Liberal MPs, his behaviour towards the voters of North Devon in standing for re-election while charged with conspiracy to murder was shameless. Indeed there is about his whole conduct since the beginning of the business this absence of any sense of shame – this *anaideia*, if you want to dignify it with a touch of Greek.

I emphasise that none of these aspects of Mr Thorpe's behaviour is against the law or indicates that he was other than entirely innocent of the criminal changes laid against him. But it does suggest that he might benefit from a rather longer rest.

30 June 1979

'Some of us find it possible to be down and out without being ostentatious.'

Mrs Thatcher
Germaine Greer

The Crusade has begun. The Blessed Margaret, already beatified by her lieutenant, Norman St John Stevas, is mounted and riding into battle. This crusade might, like those against the Saracens, turn into a series of bloody disasters, and without the excuse of rescuing the Holy Land, for entered on Mrs Thatcher's standard is the single word, 'Pelf'.

The pursuit of profit is for Margaret Thatcher a holy undertaking, for her religion is that of the rise of capitalism. Capitalism is good for people, good for those who suffer privation and are rewarded with jam tomorrow, just as good for those who suffer privation and never get any jam at all, and no better for those who suffer no privation and have jam whenever they feel like it.

This is the ideology of the United States where, on any day and on almost any television station, you may find Garner Ted Armstrong and his cohorts preaching, in much the same terms as Mrs Thatcher, the gospel of success. Failure, whether of businesses, marriages or health, is explained by evil: success in all fields is positive evidence of virtue. If you are getting richer, you are becoming happier, for you have God's personal assurance that you are on the right path. Witness the millions that Armstrong has made out of preaching. God is served by Mammon, through Mammon and in Mammon.

Much has been made of the diamond-hard head of Mrs Thatcher, her incisive intelligence, and so forth. What few have grasped is that Mrs Thatcher's undoubted capacity to swot and slug her way through the thronging tedium of parliamentary life springs from deep passion and conviction. She has no more ability to assess her actual position or weigh opposing arguments than Joan of Arc, and she may meet the same end, at the hands of her own countrymen and of her own party.

There are fewer women in Mrs Thatcher's parliament than in any since the war. None occupies an important position besides Mrs

Thatcher, who downgraded Sally Oppenheim's appointment from a Cabinet post, leaving her anachronistically isolated and freakish, the only treble raised in a chorus of many voices. She ought not to imagine, however, that she will thereby muzzle the basic misogyny of this nation and in particular her party. Amid the storms of schoolboyish ribaldry at a Tory election night party, one decaying gentleman contributed his opinion that Denis Thatcher looked like a farmer whose cow had unexpectedly won first prize.

British chauvinism is not only sexual. In their triumphant announcements of Mrs Thatcher's election, commentators raved that a major historical precedent had been set, in that a 'major Western democracy' had got itself a female leader. Golda Meir, Mrs Bandaranaike and Mrs Gandhi were supposed to pale into insignificance beside a woman whose personality is so negligible that she is still trying out new images on the public which has already elected her. Compared to those three, Mrs Thatcher is a Head Schoolgirl talking down interruptions in Assembly.

Mrs Thatcher cultivates an image of lone womanhood to go with her Joan of Arc posture. Mrs Gandhi and Mrs Bandaranaike both came from societies with distinct and powerful female components. They were first women among women and then women rulers of men. Mrs Thatcher has not one female adviser or confidante, except, of course, the Queen, who does not like women any more than she does. Neither of them has ever espoused a female cause or concerned herself with the problems of women as a group. It is only a matter of weeks before cartoonists begin to indulge in rich visions of the country ruled by a tea-party of two middle-aged ladies, one of whom has never made a joke and the other never a good one. Their ascendancy is no indication of the status of women in this society. It is simply a freakish circumstance for which women will eventually be expected to pay dearly although it is not at all to their advantage.

Our new leader is committed to spurring the country on to prosperity through a series of hazards. The screaming will begin quite soon when the average man realises that the quality of his life is not improving: the Health Service will be just as unusable, the schools as chaotic, law and order as illusory, his newspaper undelivered and his telephone as unlikely to function properly. Arabs will continue to spit copiously all over the pavements of London, and Mrs Thatcher will not appear to sweep up and give the offenders a whack with her broom.

Once her broken-winded steed has run his head into the stone wall of world recession, Mrs Thatcher has no alternative but to continue spurring it, though blood courses down its torn flanks. Whatever the galled jade may do, Mrs Thatcher's withers must remain unwrung. Although her supporters race off in other directions, she will continue to drive the nation into the wall, out of a crazy certainty that it will eventually gather strength and fly over it. She has actually been elected out of a mad optimism, as irrational in its way as her own conviction that free enterprise is the system designed by God for men to live in and she its prophet.

Her terrifying obtuseness was never better illustrated than by her choice, as her Introit to office, of the words of St Francis of Assisi. If it was her token Catholic who suggested it to her as a way of colouring her rule with the tint of paternalism it so obviously lacks, he was indulging in some of the pixyish perversity which has made him so sought-after an after-dinner speaker. If Mrs Thatcher had not simply found St Francis in her Dictionary of Quotations she would know that he was a ne'er-do-well, a layabout, a class traitor. He gave up the life of a prosperous merchant for the love of Lady Poverty. He dressed in the single garment of the peasant with no hose to his legs and begged for a living, and made of that a rule of life.

St Francis, who may be allowed to have been more intimate with God than Margaret Thatcher, certainly did not think that the free enterprise system was the best way to serve Him.

12 May 1979

Mrs Thatcher
Ferdinand Mount

'There is a splendid lack of coherence about this government', a Treasury Minister observed last week. And what's more, observed it with a chuckle. For not merely is this government developing an unexpected reputation for being rather footloose; the Prime Minister herself is developing a reputation for being A Bit of A Character. Less and less do her colleagues see her as an inflexible, narrow and somewhat dull woman. Far from her being an iron-willed female centurion, in her relations with her Cabinet there seems to be remarkably little Go-and-he-goeth or Do-this-and-he-doeth it. Often it is more a case of Go-and-he-stayeth-put and Do-this-and-he-diggeth-his-heels-in.

Among most ministers up to and including cabinet rank, Mrs Thatcher continues to be regarded with awe, not to say terror. But among senior ministers of the baronial class, she is regarded more as a kind of semi-detached figure, to be treated with tact but spoken of in private irreverently and not without amusement. From outside, she may look like the most purposeful and decisive British Prime Minister since the war, from inside she does not.

Time and time again, it seems, she starts off in one direction and the Minister responsible for taking the decision ends up in another. She appears to be won round, frustrated or overruled with amazing frequency. To the most spectacular examples – Rhodesia, interest rates, Mr Prior's Employment Bill, the boat people, MP's salaries, sanctions against Iran, and now the quasi-recognition of the PLO – one could add that Geoffrey Howe weaned her off the idea of a mortgage subsidy, that David Howell persuaded her out of the denationalisation of the British National Oil Corporation; Mark Carlisle managed to restrict the education cuts and Francis Pym did the same with the defence budget.

For a full catalogue of these reverses, I recommend Hugh Stephensons's *Mrs Thatcher's First Year* (Jill Norman), one of the handiest instant histories of the internal workings of government since Mr Peter Jenkins's account of Harold Wilson's surrender to the trade unions.

Why does she not get her own way more often? Do all these reversals mean that she is a weak Prime Minister? Who is in charge, if anybody? Is Mrs Thatcher losing ground?

Perhaps the best place to start is by considering how this phenomenon looks from the inside – since, after all, it is from the inside that all these leaks and counter-leaks come. And from the inside, the complaint is phrased differently. Ministers don't complain that she lets herself be overruled too easily; the trouble, as they see it, is that she refuses to stick to the doctrine of collective responsibility for Cabinet decisions. Prime Ministers do not usually detach themselves so blithely from the policy of the government they lead. Sometimes, you feel her Cabinet ground-rules paraphrase Lord Melbourne to read, 'I can say what I like, but mind, *you* must all say the same.'

All Prime Ministers lose one or two arguments with their Ministers or don't bother to fight them out to a conclusion; even know-alls and bullies don't have enough time or energy to get their way on every issue. The most natural way to keep your dignity and conserve your energy is to form a settled, early view only about the things that really matter to you; and, for the rest, you suck at your pipe and issue non-committal grunts until a general consensus is reached or until somebody says something which strikes you as sensible.

This is not Mrs Thatcher's way. She likes to speak out publicly before, during and after Cabinet discussion. In her interviews, new wheezes bubble up from her unconscious in an effortless stream, as though the Conservative Party manifesto were being rewritten by Molly Bloom: wouldn't it be nice if interest rates came down? Why don't we have a referendum on what to do about the trade unions? We are being rather swamped by immigrants, aren't we?

She frequently does this on *Weekend World*; something about the twinkle in Mr Brian Walden's eye appears to inspire her to make up government policy as she goes along. But she is also capable, as no other recent Prime Minister, of inventing policy on the floor of the House of Commons, which adds to the stock of public pleasure too, as you see her colleagues wincing.

Sometimes, she detaches herself from government policy only in private. While on the Employment Bill she has used every possible channel, direct and indirect, to counter Mr Prior's equally energetic propaganda machine; on foreign affairs she does not attempt to publicise her displeasure so much. It is more from Lord Carrington's camp that we hear how hard he had to work to persuade her to accept the EEC Budget deal. Indeed, the Foreign Office seems to take a sadistic delight in forcing the most unpalatable stuff down her throat: after Mr Mugabe, she has to say hullo to Mr Arafat. What next – bring back Amin, resurrect Bokassa?

By examining the timing of her upsets and outbursts, we can see more clearly the diverse reasons for them. *First*, but less often these days, sheer ignorance. She arrived with far less experience than any other Prime Minister of modern times. Several times she has simply changed her mind on reflection. Rhodesia is the prime example.

Second, a calculated use of public occasions to rally public and party support over her Minister's heads without having any clear idea of what concrete action is to follow. Her 'swamping' broadcasts and her appeal to the building societies to keep down mortgage rates were low politics at its most basic.

Third, and most important, the use of public occasions to mobilise public and party opinion against her own ministers. It is often a matter of taste whether you regard the end result as victory or defeat for Mrs Thatcher. On the EEC Budget, she may have secured a lot less than she wanted but she did secure a great deal more than the Foreign Office was prepared to fight for. Ditto with Mr Prior and the Employment Bill.

It's a rum way to run a government. But the basic reason for it is unmistakable and, I think, unavoidable, *viz* the original weakness of her position. She seized power by a guerrilla raid; two thirds of her own Cabinet, virtually the whole civil service and most of the establishment press were and still are unregenerately opposed to her. In office, she has been forced to continue this guerrilla warfare. In fact, it is impossible to think of any other way of foisting sound money and the free market on a Parliamentary Conservative Party which remains for the most part doggedly Keynesian and paternalist.

If she had tried to get her way on every point, she would by now have had a couple of Cabinet resignations and probably a Dump Margaret group hard at work. Better to keep your opponents on a loose rein than on no rein at all and have them running wild on the back benches. If your economic strategy can be kept intact only by populist methods, well, better populism than unpopulism.

But this unremitting struggle has led to a quite different form of weakness which is only now being clearly identified: the weakness not of being overruled but of never having ruled properly at all.

The central organisation of this government *has* suffered because the Prime Minister has had to spend so much effort fighting on her flanks, principally against the crafty and resourceful Mr Prior, but also against the Foreign Office. Hence the lack of any coherent policy on wages in the public sector. Who, after all, was primarily responsible for sending teachers' pay to the Clegg Commission? The Prime Minister, Sir Keith Joseph as chairman of the Cabinet's public sector pay sub-committee, and Sir Geoffrey Howe as Chancellor of the Exchequer – the leading hardliners. It was one of the first acts of the Tory government.

That error is now history. We are told that unflinching policy for public sector pay is now in hand. We shall see. The crucial test is yet to come. Is Mrs Thatcher really a weak Prime Minister? Come back this time next year and I'll tell you.

21 June 1980.

Lord Rothschild is innocent
Auberon Waugh

About ten years ago a man called James Cameron – no relation to the doyen of left-wing newspaper correspondents who sometimes rejoices in the witty if obscure nickname of Lunchtime O'Boccaccio's Decameron – was murdered in nasty circumstances in Islington. I had never met or even heard of this second James

Cameron until that moment. His death was just another of those sad events recorded daily in the newspapers.

A few days later I was dining with some people in Wiltshire when one of the company said he had known this Cameron, who was employed by a well-known firm of pill manufacturers and made frequent trips behind the Iron Curtain. In fact these trips were of a frequency which made my informant doubt whether they could be entirely explained by his pill-pushing activities. Perhaps, like Harold Wilson's sorties behind the Iron Curtain on behalf of the timber firm of Montague Meyer before his election as party leader, they were also of use in providing Mr Cameron with background information about conditions and attitudes in Eastern Europe, contacts with important people in the pill world and a rounding of his knowledge and experience in accordance with the general concept of Renaissance Man. But my informant was of the opinion that he probably worked for the FCO's Secret Intelligence Service.

If so, his murder became more interesting. Like so many others who worked in that dangerous trade, Cameron was an active homosexualist. Might he, perhaps, have been compromised in some way by the Moscow authorities and subjected to blackmail? Was he rather the victim of some lover's tiff within the hot-house atmosphere of MI6, or had he been murdered as a security risk by someone from the equally susceptible but opposed ranks of MI5? The possibilities seemed endless, but it was not a line of inquiry one could usefully pursue within the hysterically secretive corridors of our Intelligence and security establishments so I contented myself with writing a concerned but not entirely serious paragraph in *Private Eye* urging our Intelligence and security services to concentrate on their jobs and stop wasting tax payers' money murdering each other in this way.

A few days later the telephone rang in the country and I found myself summoned to the Murder Inquiry Headquarters at Essex Road Police Station. A friendly exasperated Detective Chief Superintendent asked me if I had anything to add to my information; he had spent many hours of his time checking my allegations, he said. I had the uneasy impression that his inquiries may have taken him as far as the head of the Secret Intelligence Service whom I had rashly named as the Guilty Man in my article. No, I said, I had nothing to add. I did not really know why I had written that paragraph; it seemed a good idea at the time.

I tell this anecdote at such enormous length because it seems to provide an important insight into Andrew Boyle's cryptic revelations of last week that among those questioned by MI5 after the defection of Burgess and Maclean was a hereditary peer who worked in Intelligence during the war and who later rose to great eminence. I am not in Mr Boyle's confidence, but nobody who has followed the Blunt case at all closely can be in any doubt that this refers to Lord Rothschild, the immensely distinguished spermatologist who sits as a Labour peer in the House of Lords – nothing wrong with that! – and who was appointed by Mr Heath as the first Director General of the Central Policy Review Staff when the august body was formed in the Cabinet Office in 1971. It would be most surprising if Lord Rothschild had not been asked by MI5 to help in their investigations into the disappearance of Burgess, since he was not only a colleague of Burgess's at Trinity College Cambridge, like everyone else, but also something of a personal friend, in whose London house Burgess lived at one time. It would be equally true to say that I was questioned by police investigating the murder of James Cameron, and there would be nothing untrue in the statement that police investigating the murder of James Cameron had found no evidence against me. Both these statements may fail to convey the full extent of my uninvolvement, but where murder is concerned, in my experience, people generally give one the benefit of the doubt. It is only in the hysterical world of espionage that people are prepared to lose all sight of common sense.

Any suggestion which might be implied that Lord Rothschild could even have been under suspicion by MI5 as a Soviet agent or witting concealer of Soviet agents is so preposterous as to belong to the world of pulp fiction. Quite apart from anything else, Mr Heath would scarcely have been able to appoint him to a position in the Cabinet Office where he had instant access to any government information he required. It is true that Mr Heath was not always as careful in security matters as he might have been, as the sudden resignation of two Ministers in 1973 brought home. After the first 1974 election he offered Jeremy Thorpe a senior position in the

Cabinet while in a position to suspect that Thorpe was being actively blackmailed by a former homosexual acquaintance. Although we may never know whether Thorpe was offered the Home Office, as I heard at the time, or the Foreign Office, as the *Sunday Times* later claimed, both are highly sensitive posts, and it seems curious that Mr Heath was so concerned with his own continuation in office that he should have been prepared to take such an obvious risk. But no such consideration swayed his appointment of Lord Rothschild to the Cabinet Office, and as a civil servant, Rothschild would have been subject to a very thorough security vetting.

It is only within the conventions imposed by our murderous libel laws, where nothing may be discussed except obliquely, with a nudge and wink, that such absurd inferences are likely to be drawn. We should also, in my view, be on our guard against attempts to smear the hereditary peerage. Only this week, in the *Sunday Times*, there was an extraordinary reference to some human excrement found in a grave in the Valley of the Kings which dated from the 1920s, with the unmistakable suggestion that it had been left there by my august great-uncle, Lord Carnarvon. There was not so much as a tittle of evidence in support of this innuendo. Those who knew him and his extraordinarily scrupulous habits will affirm that the idea is preposterous, but there the smear remains in the *Sunday Times* Colour Magazine for any of its gutterish, proletarian readers to pick up if they choose.

My purpose in raising this matter was not simply to reaffirm what anybody who has given the matter any thought will have decided long ago, that Lord Rothschild is innocent. So is Lord Carnarvon, of defiling the Royal Tombs of Egypt. So am I, of murdering James Cameron, although it is true I am not a peer of the realm, so my innocence is of less importance. My real purpose is to appeal for a general amnesty on all Fifth, Sixth, Seventh, Eighth and Ninety Ninth Men who may still be lurking as venerable septuagenarians around the portals of the Athenaeum.

At one time socialism might have been a good idea. Its inspiration, in those days, was generous and humane. Nowadays, it can appeal only to those whose social maladjustment might otherwise push them into the criminal classes, or whose intellectual inadequacies make them hungry for a dogmatic system in which they can hide their inability to think for themselves. Socialism, as anyone can see, has turned out to be a thoroughly bad idea. Is it not time to allow those who made a mistake in their early years, when conditions were so different, to admit it quietly to themselves and quietly retire? Then we can concentrate on the sad rearguard of this intellectual movement, the intellectual runts of our universities and technical colleges, the rooting hogs of the trade union movement and the psychopathic opportunists of the Labour Party who still hope to impose – whether by trickery or brute force – a system they cannot hope to recommend by ordinary persuasion. There *are* Soviet agents still active in our cosy little world of makebelieve.

14 June 1980

Mr Benn's cups of tea
Alexander Chancellor

Last February the *New Statesman* published a story claiming that the late Airey Neave had been involved in conspiratorial discussions with former secret service agents about 'the possibility of violent action if necessary to prevent Tony Benn becoming Prime Minister'. On Sunday, Mr Adam Raphael, the *Observer*'s political correspondent, wrote that doctors treating Mr Benn in the Charing Cross Hospital suspected that he might have been a victim of arsenic poisoning. Never in recent times has a politican been so flattered. Mr Benn, so it was reported on both occasions, was sceptical about these allegations. As well he might be; for, as Ferdinand Mount pointed out in the *New Standard* this week, there is nobody on the Right in politics who would have any interest in seeing him dead. Mr Benn is the stuff of which Tory victories and Social Democratic triumphs are made. There is, however, another possible explanation for Mr Benn's unfortunate illness, which is his extraordinary addiction to tea. He normally drinks about seventeen pints of tea a day and has sometimes admitted to drinking as much as twenty-five pints. According to our medical advisers, this is a dangerous amount. Eight large cups of tea are enough to give a person an overdose of caffeine, with the following possible consequences: increased excitement, trembling, difficulty in sleeping, faster heart beat, ringing in the ears, and flashes in front of the eyes. A London professor of pharmacology says that excessive consumption of caffeine can even lead to 'maniacal behaviour', for there is evidence that it restricts the blood vessels in the brain. Tea is often given to racehorses as a stimulant, but never in the quantities consumed by Mr Benn. 'If he were a racehorse,' says a vet, 'he would foam at the mouth.' But there is another facet of Mr Benn's tea addiction which could be even more important. Our professor says that if a person constantly fills his stomach with enormous amounts of liquid of any kind, there is a risk that he will not get the vitamins and minerals he needs. This, he adds, can cause polyneuritis, the very complaint from which Mr Benn is suffering. Why, therefore, were the nurses allowing Mr Benn to make cups of tea in his hospital bedroom?

20 June 1981

Crossman
Alan Watkins

The Crossman Diaries: Selections from the Diaries of a Cabinet Minister 1964-70 Introduced and edited by Anthony Howard (Hamish Hamilton and Cape)

The following story does not appear in the *Diaries*, either in their original or in their new, admirably edited form, but the late Hugh Gaitskell was once staying the night with the parents of a friend of mine. My friend's mother arrived at breakfast saying she had had an extraordinary dream about Dick Crossman. Gaitskell expressed polite though perfunctory interest. 'Yes,' she went on, 'he was dressed in a short white coat. I was sitting in a dentist's chair and he was going to take my teeth out or something. "But Dick," I said, "you know perfectly well you're not a dentist." Dick replied: "Of course I know I'm not a dentist, you fool, but I can work it all out quite easily from general principles." ' Gaitskell expressed the view that, for once, this was a useful and instructive dream which, among other things, illustrated one reason Crossman would not find a place in any future Labour Cabinet presided over by him.

This was a view Crossman himself took (that Gaitskell would not give him a job, I mean, not that he could extract teeth at will: in fact, Crossman rather paraded his lack of physical skills). But Mr Howard has an interesting footnote, derived from an interview with Lady Gaitskell, to the effect that Gaitskell would indeed have given him a Cabinet post. This, however, is not the immediate point, which concerns not Crossman's prospects under Gaitskell or anyone else but his attitude to reasoning, to action and to truth.

His grounding in ancient philosophy produced contradictions. Perhaps it always does. On the one hand, it made him suspicious of mystery-mongering whether in government or in other areas. He could reduce economists to silence (and sometimes close to tears) by asking them why precisely, on what evidence, they claimed that people were going to behave in such-and-such a fashion; he, for his part, intended to behave in exactly the opposite way as far as the financial administration of his Banbury farm was concerned. On the other hand, his philosophy – or it may have been his natural cast of mind – led him into paths of speculative reasoning which had the most tenuous connection with the real world. Empiricism was called in aid or not, as the case might be, according to the mood of the moment or his general predilections. Thus he would never countenance the view that constituency Labour parties were unimportant when it came to winning or losing elections.

His attitude to truth was adversarial or Socratic. You could not say 'It's a nice day, Dick' without starting an argument. Though his opinion both of lawyers as a class and of the law as a concept or an ideal was a low one (of which more later), in this, if in no other respect, he was at one with the English legal system. Once, when he was editor of the *New Statesman,* he had travelled to London as he frequently did with his local Conservative MP, Mr Neil Marten. Mr Marten had informed him of some new procedure for selecting Conservative candidates. Crossman arrived at the office in an excited condition, summoned me (as his political correspondent), said Central Office was assuming dictatorial powers which would change the nature of the Conservative Party and suggested I write a column on the subject. As it was a thinnish week, I agreed readily enough. On making a few inquiries, however, I discovered that, though changes were indeed being made, they were neither so simple nor so fundamental as Crossman had supposed. He perused my column with evident distaste.

'But this wasn't what I told you,' he said.

'But Dick, what you told me wasn't true.'

'Never said it was true,' Crossman replied huffily, 'only interesting.'

In fact Dick's approach to political journalism was always that of the politician – or, as he once put it in relation to another journalist, of 'someone who is part of the political process'. It was not exactly that he imposed his views on his contributors, though sometimes he tried hard. It was more basic than that. To him it was eccentric, aberrant, for anyone to write to entertain (though he himself could be highly entertaining); to earn money; to tell the truth; or just for fun. He did not advocate untruth. He simply believed that the object was to influence people, whether politicians, readers of the *NS* or voters more generally. This was clear when the paper first urged and then supported Sir Harold Wilson's apparent change of line on Europe in 1970-72. Crossman's aim was to keep Britain out of the Common Market. He responded violently whenever anyone suggested, as I sometimes tentatively did, that Sir Harold might not in fact do what Crossman hoped. This was one of my few predictions that have turned out to be correct.

There was another aspect of Dick which affected truth. This was his desire to shock. He was once a guest at dinner of Mrs Peggy Jay. The hostilities in Cyprus were in progress. Mrs Jay's son Peter was doing his national service in the vicinity. 'I shan't mind,' Crossman said, 'if that beautiful son of yours gets killed by the Cypriots. In fact I *hope* he gets killed.' Whereupon he was ordered from the room – presumably from the house too – by an understandably distressed

Mrs Jay. Such, at any rate, was Crossman's own version of the episode. In later years he was the kindest of men where other people's children were concerned. The interesting thing, however, is not only that the Jay incident presumably occurred but that Crossman chose to boast of it afterwards.

This story is not told by inadvertence. For Crossman's desire to shock went with his wish to expose shams and fictions; and the one acted upon and reinforced the other. If he discovered a political fraud, he would first exaggerate its extent. He would then, almost imperceptibly, come near to lauding the 'reality', dismissing all else as moralising humbug affected alike by the Establishment and by canting dissenters. I will give two illustrations. More could be produced.

Like Orwell, he hated international utopianism of the Bertrand Russell or H. G. Wells kind. Nationalism was the powerful of all political forces. But unlike Orwell, he then came perilously close to approving the uglier manifestations of nationalism. Not only would the thugs win: it was correct, in an odd way, moral, that they should win, in Northern Ireland as much as in Cyprus or Palestine. Might, in the last resort, was right. Likewise with the law. The law was an upper-class conspiracy based on fear, force, fraud and mumbo-jumbo. Not only was it normal for democratic politicians both to despise and to abuse the law: it was proper, anyway inevitable, for them to do so. No doubt this disposition of his, in regard to both international relations and domestic law, could plausibly be re-presented intellectually as typical English positivism of the Hobbesian variety. But there was something else. There was a sense in which Crossman took a delight not only in human frailty but in human wickedness.

The purpose of all this is not to controvert Mr Howard's view of Crossman as a writer who admirably wished to reveal the truths of government in a democracy – to expose shams. Still less is it to dispute the essential accuracy of the *Diaries* as a record of the events of 1964-70. It is to point out only that there were several aspects to Dick's quest for truth. Nor are we quibbling, Wilson fashion, about his abilities as a reporter. Those who wish to learn more should read not merely the *Diaries* but also Mr Howard's valuable Introduction which, among other merits, provides much new biographical information about the man.

7 April 1979

The SDP
Colin Welch

No sooner had I dispatched my last piece to the printer than I realised that the balance was wrong. Support them or not, most of us *do* think the Social Democrats a good thing or better than what most of them left. We value the fundamental decency of what they stand for. We may even envy them bits of their platform – on the unions, for instance. We wish them well, sincerely if perhaps with reservations.

Of all this to my regret I wrote nothing. Why? Well, I took much of it for granted. Nor can anyone claim that the beauties of the Social Democrats have gone unserenaded. Furthermore, a party which calls repeatedly for the rigorous examination of every problem, a party which indeed often seems to regard such examinations as a substitute for a clear guiding philosophy, can hardly object to being rigorously examined itself. So much has been written about its prospects, its ups and recently downs, its effect on the political scene, its personalities, so little about what it actually says. Not that Mr Rodgers actually said to our senior citizens 'drop dead' or 'fly for your lives'. Last week I just interpreted him freely so.

Doubtless I was unjust to his benevolent intentions. But his benevolence does express itself in a chillingly patronising way. Diffidently he offers a Minister for the Elderly – not a reassuring start. Less diffidently he asserts that the elderly may no longer need bigger pensions in cash but rather cheaper and convenient public transport to improve access to family and friends, as also better housing, heating, 'leisure' and health. He further proposes 'positive discrimination' for the elderly as also for blacks, the disabled, large poor families and 'the very frail'.

Some of the elderly might be passively grateful for all those boons. Others might think it grossly illiberal in Mr Rodgers to offer them what he thinks they ought to have rather than the means of buying what they actually want, thereby denying them the dignity of choice. Convenient transport, for instance, is not much use to 'the very frail', frightened or bedridden. It may only bear the mugger more swiftly to and from his prey, the hooligan's brick to the window. Nor does 'positive discrimination' always makes its beneficiaries respected and loved. Dare I say that many elderly people, lonely, unhappy and unattractive as they feel themselves to be, might like above all, say, an occasional drink or smoke, even to be able to offer some such cheer 'to family and friends'? I do not see Mr Rodgers bringing any such comforts (of which, with Dr Owen, he vehemently disapproves), nor yet the cash to buy them. If they are unattainable now, they will be more so when he has doubled the price of tobacco and liquor, as he clearly desires to do, if too shy precisely to say so. 'No to smoking. No to alcohol. Yes to seat belts' is a favourate slogan of his. Should we add 'No to freedom'?

Mr Rodgers and his friends would angrily object. What *they* call freedom they value highly. Dr Owen quotes Mill twice, once to the effect that 'men would learn by being free', that freedom produces morally better people because it forces them to develop 'their personalities'. He even speaks highly of 'the individual's right to self-direction'. Fine: but what does he mean by freedom? Two things, it seems, combined to form a panacea for all ills: decentralisation and democratic participation. In the army we were taught, 'If it moves, salute it. If doesn't move, polish it'. From Dr Owen we learn, 'If it exists, decentralise it. If it *is* decentralised, participate in it'.

Nowhere does he recognise that the individual's right to self-direction may be far less restricted by a central authority which governs loosely than by a host of regional, local and functional authorities which direct and interfere as much as he would wish.

Only very intermittently seems he aware of the fact that many people find participation a frightful bore and would rather cultivate their own gardens than argue ceaselessly with hordes of busybodies. He favours participation partly for our own good. He slily quotes Mill again on our duty to free even slaves who like being slaves, 'because only free men are wholly human'. But democratic participation is *not* freedom; nor can eager participators alone be regarded as 'wholly human'. Gardeners are human too.

Other boons to be expected from participation are various and bizarre.

Most improbably Dr Owen hopes that an industrial system mastered and controlled by 'individuals coming together freely' will be more rather than less friendly to 'the new technology' and its attendant disturbances, less keen to sustain old industries, 'to refuse robots', to preserve 'the traditional office' and so on. Has Dr Owen not read Sir Henry Maine who, unless memory errs, doubted whether universal suffrage would have permitted the supersession of the stage coach and the handloom?

Mrs Williams's own notion of participation is odd in a revealing way. As an example of it, she cites the regional conferences she held as Education Minister. To these 'a wide range of people was *invited*' (my italics), including 'representatives' of teachers, parents, trade unions, local education authorities and pupils. Before these carefully selected studio audiences, the Minister explained her 'problems and priorities', and created 'a more balanced and friendly atmosphere', favourable to 'reform'. In other words, she participated like billy-o and the stooges meekly approved.

Nowhere does Dr Owen let the cat so naively out of the bag. But he does waffle opaquely on about the need for a decentralised society 'to develop a counterbalancing sense of interdependence', about identifying first 'with' the 'community' and then 'to' the nation, and about 'building up through democratic involvement a sense of community in order to rediscover a responsibility from the individual to the state' – phew! So far as I understand this stuff at all, I discern a misty vision of the dethroned state reappearing like a ghost and reasserting itself by supernatural means.

Now some of the defects of decentralisation will strike whoever watches regional TV. In Wiltshire we are Southern. We are thus assumed, quite wrongly, to be more interested in what goes on in distant Brighton and Southampton than in what goes on in London or elsewhere, and to prefer dull regional programmes to good

London ones. Regions, in other words, are mostly bogus, marrying like to unlike, subjecting minorities to bigger minorities, assuming a regional homogeneity and separateness which hardly anywhere exists. Why then should regional or local tyrannies be more tolerable and efficient than a national one?

Perhaps for one reason, some might say: that decentralisation could, for good or ill, permit local innovation and experiment. But how will such initiatives fit in with Dr Owen's national planning, which will apparently burgeon and preponderate, decentralisation or no? Are we not here again at the very heart of Dr Owen's dilemma, of that strange sentimentality to which I referred last week? How on earth can decentralisation and participation be combined with all the other things he and his friends want?

With a statutory incomes policy, for instance, actually reducing some incomes? With national jehads against tobacco and alcohol, against private health and education? With a switch of national resources to 'preventive medicine'? With 'an integrated transport policy', 'an overall energy policy', 'a coherent industrial strategy'? With a massive redistribution of wealth and incomes (a process which Dr Owen most misleadingly regards as making no 'claim on the nation's real resources'. If it transfers funds from the more productive to the less so, from the investor to the consumer, it thereby reduces our resources; so does whatever vast sum is spent or wasted in the bureaucratic process of redistribution)?

If not all, most of these desiderata demand increased coercive

'I want something that will repel a man at fifty feet.'

powers for the central state. What will our decentralisers do about that? How will they square this circle? Or will they alternately centralise, decentralise and recentralise, like a man playing an accordion? Watch this space.

11 September 1982

Arthur Scargill and Robin Hood
Christopher Booker

Reading the other day through the definitive scholarly history of the Robin Hood legend (*Rhymes of Robyn Hood* by R. B. Dobson and J. Taylor, Heinemann 1976), I was fascinated to learn that most of the earliest references to the Great English outlaw placed him not in Sherwood Forest but in the district known as Barnsdale, over the county border to the north in what is now South Yorkshire. Whether or not such a figure ever actually existed, Hood conducted his legendary forays against the wicked authorities from an area somewhere to the west of Ferrybridge and to the east of Barnsley. It was at that point that a strange latter-day parallel began to suggest itself.

Clearly the explanation of that somewhat strange and enigmatic figure Mr Arthur Scargill is that he has been possessed by some ancient *genius loci* of the South Yorkshire coalfield. His persistent playing with fantasies of being 'the great outlaw', of robbing the rich to feed the poor, of defying the wicked Establishment in all its forms, derives not from burning the midnight oil over the sparkling prose of Karl Marx but from a much more ancient and acceptably traditional source altogether. Lord Denning and Sir Derek Ezra have simply become for him latter-day incarnations of the Sheriff of Nottingham, and his efforts to 'build a power base' in the Barnsley Labour Party and the South Yorkshire branch of the NUM are nothing more than attempts to re-create the magic of old Sherwood Forest in the unlikely shadow of the Ferrybridge power station.

What makes Arthur Scargill in fact such a fascinating figure is the way in which, like his great outlaw predecessor, he is so ambivalent. On the one hand, he is the great rebel, the libertarian who believes that laws should not come before people. Last week, for instance, he won huge headlines by his defiance of Lord Denning's short-lived judgment against the private sector steelworkers' desire to strike. In a startling interview with *The Times*, Mr Scargill seemed almost to be comparing himself with Andrei Sakharov, when he defended his right to speak out 'against laws that are oppressive, anti-democratic or against basic freedoms'. 'People who condemn me', he went on, 'applaud Sakharov for his stand against Soviet law. I support Sakharov, I don't agree with the Soviet Union.'

Here spoke the great champion of liberty and basic human decency who, after a celebrated visit to Bulgaria some years ago (his first visit behind the Iron Curtain) said, 'if this is Communism, they can keep it'. But it should not be forgotten that a couple of years later Mr Scargill made another visit to a communist country, when he led an official delegation to some vast international jamboree staged by Fidel Castro. And on this occasion he took a very different line, going out of his way to praise the 'magnificent achievements' of Cuban socialism, and expressing the hope that the kind of society he had witnessed in Cuba would be brought about in Britain as soon as possible.

The great difference between the two Scargills on these occasions was that, on his visit to Bulgaria, he had merely been travelling on a private package tour, as an ordinary, underprivileged underdog. On his visit to Cuba, however, he had been fêted as a distinguished visitor, and treated by senior members of the regime as a fellow socialist over-dog. In other words, faced with the horrors of totalitarianism to however marginal an extent as a *victim* (having to endure a package tour to a Bulgarian Black Sea resort has got *some* connection, however vague, with Gulag), he reacted as a libertarian. Whereas treated to a taste of the delights which totalitarian regimes hold out for their élite, he could not wait to impose such a state of perfectly-ordered political perfection on as many people as possible.

What we have here in short is a fine example of that only-too familiar political phenomenon of our time, the man who sees himself as a fearless libertarian in his ceaseless battles with overweening authority, until such moment as he enjoys any kind of authority himself, when, as Mr Scargill himself has already embryonically shown in the way he runs his little 'political empire' in South Yorkshire, he becomes far more dictatorial than any authority he has replaced.

Eighteen months ago I explored this phenomenon at some length in the course of a series of articles on the question: 'Why does socialism always lead to tyranny?' I argued then that we could derive the most profound illumination on the whole drift of politics in our time from a study of that cycle of political development laid out by Plato in Book VIII of *The Republic* in which he shows how the natural tendency of states and civilisations is to move from Monarchy through Oligarchy to Democracy and then finally to Tyranny. I sought to discuss the prevailing political momentum of our own culture over the past few centuries in this light, and to show how psychologically it can be seen to make perfect sense. And in many ways, psychologically the most interesting moment of the entire cycle is that when the excessive libertarianism of the last days of the Democratic phase is just about to give way to the totalitarianism of the last phase. At such a time, some of the loudest voices in a society will be those who consciously speak like libertarians, in attacking the exploitation and injustices left over from the decay of the Oligarchic phase, while unconsciously they try to force society back into a parody of that lost state of wholeness from which it has become estranged. Society as it stands, they argue, has become intolerably divided and corrupt. It must be made whole again, it must be born anew. Alas, the kind of society which results bears little resemblance to any that might have been commended by Robin Hood, let alone to one in which Andrei Sakharov would feel much at home. There Mr Scargill's fantasies are shown in their true light, as nothing more than the most infantile self-deception.

9 February 1980

4 Abroad

Rolf Schild
Alexander Chancellor

Poor Mr Rolf Schild, who, it seems cannot even raise the measly £1 million ransom which the Sardinian bandits are reported to be asking for the release of his wife and daughter, has concluded that he must be a victim of mistaken identity. 'Why me?' he asked a *Daily Telegraph* reporter, 'there are so many wealthy people in the area.' Why him? The answer has been obvious to many of us for some time. It must, indeed, be a case of mistaken identity, but not one involving anybody resident on the Emerald Coast. To bandits, who are simple folk, the name Rolf Schild must have recalled a far more illustrious name, the fame of which will have penetrated even the wilderness of central Sardinia – the name of Rothschild. If this were so, it would explain the whole tragic affair, and it would perhaps be helpful of the Rothschild family if they were somehow to convey the facts of the situation to the bandits. Or even the money.

22 September 1979

Brain death in the US
Nicholas von Hoffman

Washington

It is fitting in this land of churchgoers that the soothsayers on the Council of Economic Advisers should look to Christmas to rescue the world's mightiest republic from the doldrums. More analysts have been watching the department stores than there have been

Christmas shoppers in them.

America goes into the holiday season and ends the year in confusion. Whereas two years ago they blamed the bad times on inflation and a lack of savings – we were accused of buying too many consumables and not saving to invest – now the *Wall Street Journal* says the fault is stable prices, people saving instead of buying.

Buy a Christmas present for your child and help your country! Senator Paul Laxalt, President Reagan's closest and oldest political friend, the man he recently appointed head of his re-election effort two years hence, wants the boss to get on the air waves and sell, as he did when he used to advertise on TV for General Electric. 'I've discussed this with the President', he said, 'What's lacking out there is consumer confidence. Millions of people are waiting to buy a car or appliance or home because they think they can get a better deal later. I think the President should address the people and say, "You're part of this. The programme can't move forward unless you have the confidence to go out and buy that TV or car or home." '

Whatever may be lacking out there, what is lurking is fear. With fourteen million people out of work, the rest are not buying because they are afraid they will be next and will need the money. The television drives home the idea that the worst may happen to you even if you are not a black teenager; there are many stories on the air about formerly prosperous white families from Michigan and Ohio who moved to the Sun Belt to find work and now live in tents in the park.

On the air and in the papers this is a Christmas with heavy emphasis on child and spouse 'abuse' by unemployed workers, alcoholism and climbing suicide rates. It's a credit to the orderliness of most out-of-work Americans that they turn the gun on themselves and don't wave it at bank tellers, something which gets harder to do as the tellers are replaced by computer terminals which take your deposits and cash your cheques with robotic efficiency. If the red suicide line on the graphs catches up and crosses the black unemployment line, we will have found a new and altogether creative way of disposing of joblessness.

Who will pay for the funerals has yet to be worked out. Most workers lose their medical insurance and such when they lose their jobs; they also lose their self-confidence. They will be staring at their

Christmas trees thinking it is somehow their fault that they got dumped. The disposition to blame oneself is encouraged by the television programmes on which job experts, whatever they may be, expatiate on how to write a CV (new jargon for Curriculum Vitae), how to dress and how to grovel. Having the right attitude is stressed, a flashy subservience, an eagerness, a willingness to work until you drop while looking like you're grateful. It also helps to indicate no task is too low, vile or disgusting, and the women can crank up to make coffee for the men again. No more talk about sexual harassment. They say that in his heyday every morning at MGM, Louis B. Mayer had a starlet kneeling between his legs while his barber gave him a shave and he read *Variety*. This year in Washington, not a heyday period for anyone, the bailiffs are working evicting people for non-payment of rent. There is a backlog of 4000 such families. You can see them on the sidewalks with their lampshades, their scratched TVs, sitting on stained sofas, asking themselves what comes next. It is worse if the family owns a parakeet.

We are a perky nation, however depleted we may be. Many communities have summoned their strength to renew the war on incest, a war which I bet you didn't know we were fighting. Persons denominated as 'counsellors', often hirsute, hefty women, have been coming on the television to encourage children to report their daddies to the police or their teachers if Pops 'abuses them sexually'. It is not safe to be the father of a daughter in the United States and show affection in any manner other than by expensive, economically stimulative Christmas presents. Why this war is waged exclusively against fathers leching unnaturally after their daughters is not discussed. A mother can do thing to her children that would make a Greek playwright retch, and nothings is said about it. As for brothers and sisters fooling around, the mental health community has no interest whatsoever.

We enter 1983 with a high-tech heart, preferably an artificial one. Our science temporarily stumped by the spread of Acquired Immune Deficiency Syndrome, or AIDS, among homosexuals, haemophiliacs and most recently, new-born infants, has successfully implanted a plastic heart in the breast of a human being who, at this writing, lives a not altogether satisfactory life as a comatose zombie.

We follow Barney Clark's story every day, every hour, as the government's centre for disease control issues communiqués concerning the newest reports of AIDS' progress in killing us. It is like America to invent so many diseases. We will not go routinely to our graves, dead from old-world afflictions. We want our own and we mean to have them.

We have our ways. We who invented the disposable society, the throw-away container, the junkable everything, we are on the threshold of making obsolete the old ways of taking care of sick people. Nursing them back to health is too expensive and it entails too much dirty work that only Haitians or other illegal immigrants care to do but don't even do well. When a human part is diseased, we replace it in the same way we fix broken computers or television sets. We pluck out the defective module and slam in a new package. We can do the same thing with hearts and kidneys, livers and spleens. It's less time-consuming and more up-to-date than preparing barley soup.

Even in our economically depressed state, we are our old selves – trying, inventing, coming up with the new and the better. Only the other day we passed another socio-cultural landmark (we like to coin compounds beginning with socio – it sounds scientific). We married medicine and criminal justice with the first execution of a condemned murderer by hypodermic injection. This happened in Texas, and everyone's excited about the possibilities of combining these two American obsessions, punishing the guilty and high-tech, stainless steel medical procedures. We think it is the beginning of new life styles for some and death styles for others.

We have a public relations problem. It kinda sneaked up on us. We have 1,115 men on the nation's various death-rows. That's a lot of chicken to fry at once, the smell of which might offend foreign nostrils, nostrils attached to noses attached to heads less dedicated to the endless and relentless war against crime than us. The proposal is to inject these persons with a fluid that will only cause brain death. Then, they will be stored until their organs, hereafter referred to as modules, are needed by persons whose own original factory equipment has broken and needs to be replaced.

Hereafter persons convicted of capital crimes will be called 'donors'. Capital punishment, as we have known it, will be abolished.

The world will admire and love us. Our judges, instead of condemning murders to death as we have done in the past, will announce, 'The State has decided to give you the opportunity to realise your true, human potential and fulfil yourself by an act of sharing and togetherness that will put you in the most intimate contact with others. You are being given a chance to participate in a pro-life programme and to give yourself in a unique and uniquely satisfying way.'

Better to give than receive, eh, Mr Scrooge? A merry and generous Christmas to all you dear English people.

18 December 1982

Sweden and *Exit*
Andrew Brown

'People talk about the horrors of war, but what weapon has a man invented that even approaches in cruelty some of the commoner diseases?' Modern medicine can prolong these cruelties almost indefinitely, and in Sweden it is widely believed to do so. 'RTVD', the Swedish equivalent of EXIT, is twenty times as large as the English organisation in proportion and population; and Ms Berit Hedeby, one of the founders of RTVD, was recently released after serving six months of a twelve-month prison sentence for killing a friend whom multiple sclerosis had weakened so much that he was no longer able even to feed himself the pills that would end his life. Ms Hedeby did not mean to become a martyr: assisting a suicide is not a crime in Sweden; but after her friend's death had passed unnoticed she wrote a book about what she had done. It seems that she expected her readers to feel nothing but admiration for her perseverance – she had to make three attempts on her friend's life before her efforts were successful – but she was arrested and tried. The court, greatly to Ms Hedeby's surprise, decided that her efforts had gone beyond what was allowable, and she was found guilty of homicide, though not of murder.

The other leading member of RTVD is rather less flamboyant in his advocacy. He is Ingemar Hedenius, for many years Professor of Philosophy at Uppsala University. Hedenius started to write on the subject more than twenty years ago, when he discovered that some doctors denied both that euthanasia was ever practised in Sweden, and that it ever ought to be. Anyone who does not die unexpectedly will, in Sweden, be taken to die in a lavishly equipped public hospital, and all these places tend to be run as if the patient were the least important object in the building. During the late Sixties and Seventies, when the necessary equipment became widely available, it became common practice in these hospitals to feed patients who had become too weak to swallow with a tube thrust through the nose and down into the stomach. Fed in this way with gruel and antibiotics, people could be kept alive for at least five years, though they were, of course, incapable of speech and movement, and as far as anyone could tell, incapable of thought or feeling also. You cannot hope for a personal dispensation in Sweden: anyone anxious to avoid dying like that had to try to change the whole system, and Hedenius set out to prove that the assumption that it is a doctor's ineluctable duty to prolong life under all circumstances led to far great cruelties than would an open acceptance of euthanasia.

Hedenius argues that there are four possible ways to shorten a patient's life: you can fail to provide certain forms of treatment – such as drip-feeds for patients who can no longer swallow; you can stop providing such treatment – pulling the plug out of a respirator; you can give humane, though dangerous treatment – sufficient quantities of painkiller to remove all pain, even though this may shorten the patient's life; and you can give humane, though fatal treatment – a deliberate overdose. The difference, he explains, between these last two forms (for the last dose must, logically, always be an overdose) is 'like getting drunk, there's always one glass too many, but it makes a difference if it is part of a course of treatment'. But all these forms of euthanasia are ethically identical in as much as they all involve a deliberate decision to shorten the patient's life, taken by someone who is in a position to understand the consequences of the decision.

If we are going to distinguish between them, we cannot do so on the grounds that some are murder and some are not.

Hedenius distinguishes between them by the effects they have on the people who must carry them out. He no longer believes, for instance, that the health service should be asked to give fatal injections 'because it would put too great a strain on the staff, and we must strike a balance between the suffering of the patients and that of the staff'. But at the same time, if hospital staffs were to accept Hedenius's idea that all forms of euthanasia are ethically the same, then they would undergo the same distress whatever they did to ease a patient's death. Doctors and nurses, whose long training and sense of professional standards give them a certain distance from their work, may be able to appreciate the subtleties of Hedenius's position; but most of the disagreeable work in geriatric nursing is done by untrained 'auxiliaries'.

Hedenius's assumption that the opinions of the enlightened will determine the moral standards of the whole country is not shared by the people who run the medical profession; and some doctors are worried by the fact that the mere existence of a vocal pressure group that advocates widespread euthanasia will tend to undermine the certainties of the auxiliary staff. There was a case two years ago when a youth employed by a job-creation scheme in the geriatric wards of a large hospital in Malmoe found that the human vegetables in his care were more than he could bear to contemplate. He stole disinfectant from a cleaning cupboard and mixed it into the orange juice he fed the patients. The victims were apparently unable either to taste the difference or to protest. More than twenty of them were poisoned in this way over a period of months before any doctor noticed what had happened. The young man was of course a psychopath, who should never have been let anywhere near the dying, and there was a note to this effect on file at the hospital when he was given the job; but so long as the auxiliary staff in hospitals are partly recruited from the otherwise unemployable, it is virtually certain that some of them will crack under the almost unimaginable strain of the job. If such people were to suspect that doctors and nurses are already helping patients to die, the possible consequences do not bear thinking about.

This irony is that, although neither the auxiliaries nor the RTVD realise it, the Swedish national health service has in fact *already* introduce a comprehensive programme of passive euthanasia. The practice of keeping people alive at all costs has secretly ended. Nurses are nowadays trained to give two sorts of drip: one, used for patients who are to recover, contains all the necessary nourishment; the other contains nothing but glucose, water and salts. This mixture administered intravenously will keep a healthy man alive for six weeks; a sick patient will last five weeks at the most; and in at least one large Stockholm hospital the drip is not even placed directly in a vein, but subcutaneously.

The nurses know very well what they are doing, but, as one nurse said, 'The best thing about nursing is that it is the doctor who makes all the decisions', and they have no doubt that this form of treatment is officially sanctioned. At one nursing school the pupils are simply taught that 'this is the way things are done nowadays'; at another, they are given two weeks' intensive teaching about terminal illnesses and then encouraged to draw their own conclusions. No directives, either for or against euthanasia, are given at this second school. Someone educated in this way told me that 'a non-existent directive is far more effective than anything in writing might be'; but this tacit agreement obscures the complete reversal of official policy towards the dying which has taken place since 1974.

Professor Gustav Giertz is chairman of the committee which determines the official attitude of the medical profession to ethical questions. The papers produced by this committee have passed straight through parliament and become statements of the government's attitude as well; and Professor Giertz explains his view of

'All the bomb sites in the world, and you have to walk into mine.'

euthanasia by saying: 'There are a lot of extremists in RTVD, people who feel personally threatened by the health service, but when you analyse what they are saying, it is very similar to my position – except of course that they think active euthanasia is desirable . . . One should not have to make an effort to keep alive the dying with exceptional methods of treatment – operations, force-feeding, and so forth. The important thing is to care for them well: to see that they are as comfortable as possible, and to make it easy for them to die . . . we disagree with RTVD about the means to be employed, but not about the ends.'

14 February 1981

Dwarves and Mr Begin

Sir: I must take vigorous exception to Mr von Hoffman's revolting turn of phrase (20 June) when he dealt with the Israeli premier Mr Begin, to wit that the man was a 'homicidal dwarf'. This is an entirely unjustifiable, gratuitous, discriminatory and unacceptable slur upon dwarves who by and large do not blow up hotels, hang British army sergeants, massacre 200 Arabs at Deir Yassin, or bomb other people's power stations.

Nigel Ash, British Board of Diminutives, Orde Hall Street, London WCI

4 July 1981

Gallipoli
Murray Sayle

When I was a young lad at school in Sydney, and knew a lot more than I know now, we had the Great War, as we called it, pretty well sized up.

The day to remember was 25 April 1915, probably the most famous date in all military history. Early on that fateful morning two divisions of Australian soldiers, the toughest in the world, assisted by their faithful New Zealand bearers, had stormed ashore at Gallipoli, a place lying somewhere north and well to the east of Brisbane. The Day and The Landing were as well known to us as Waterloo is to English schoolboys, or Washington Crossing the Delaware to Americans, but with a difference. The others had been triumphs. Ours was a disaster.

Our men had, indeed, got ashore, we learnt, rather in the manner of the US Marine Corps minus, of course, the deodorants and after-shave lotion. Waiting for them, machine-guns at the ready, was the entire Turkish Army, supported by numerous Germans, just as our side were being helped by the British and French. What they actually encountered was, in fact, far worse: the Australian attack fell on a rugged part of the Turkish coast defended by an obscure colonel named Mustafa Kemal, *dit* Atatürk, one of the more brilliant and resourceful military commanders of the twentieth century. The Turkish 57th Regiment he commanded were not, it appears, exactly sissies either.

Our men fought with the courage expected of them, we learnt, the same *élan* and readiness to take a sporting chance which have subsequently made Australians the proprietors of the Ashes, the Davis Cup and the London *Times*. But they had been sent to fight in a waterless wilderness of cliffs and ravines, everywhere overlooked by Turkish guns. The campaign settled into hopeless trench warfare, a foretaste of the Somme slaughter the following year. Some 16,000 Australians and New Zealanders never came home from Gallipoli, or at least not in one piece, a heavy blow for two small countries but light compared with what was to come. 'We are with you to the last man and the last shilling', Australian Prime Minister Andrew Fisher telegraphed the Cabinet in London on the day the war began. It looked as if we were being held to the offer.

Who were the guilty men? Again, no doubts. The folks who brought us Ypres and Passchendaele had designed the disaster in the Dardenelles. British generals, monocles screwed into myopic eyes, brass hats jammed firmly down on heads of oak, had ordered these suicidal attacks against impossible objectives, unable to conceive the possiblity that their strategy might be mistaken, until the flowers of the forest, yours and theirs, were a' wede away. What's more, they operated from the comparative comfort of dugouts, châteaux and, on Gallipoli, the wardrooms of battleships lying far offshore, pink gins at elbow.

Behind these homicidal idiots stood an even more sinister figure, one Winston Churchill, a hare-brained amateur strategist who had dreamed up the whole disastrous operation. He had, it was true, somewhat redeemed himself later by appearing in the trenches in person, but had since faded into a well-merited and, for sure, permanent obscurity.

My dad, a soldier in the same war, declined to discuss the matter with his children. However, as Anzac Day rolled round every 25 April, he would put on his ribbons and his RSL badge (the Returned Soldiers' League, the most potent pressure group in Australian politics) and take the day off for The March, the remembrance, by thinning squadrons and ships and regiments of both world wars, of fallen comrades. Later the Old Man would arrive home with his boozy mates, well ahead of the day, as Scott Fitzgerald used to say, their chests covered with (British) decorations. For hours the house would be awash with gushing bottles and toasts to 'Pommy bastards', 'thieving Gyppoes' and 'good old Johnny Turk, the gamest fighter in the world'. These alcohol-fuelled sentiments would, as often as not, be spiced with jokes along the lines of 'Poor old Poms, no flag of their own, had to pinch the corner out of ours'. Or, 'Do you know how to rescue a drowning Pom?' 'No.' 'Good.' Guffaws, and a new beachhead opened on another crate of ale. My long-suffering mother put up with this because, in the title of a beautiful Australian play, it's *The One Day of the Year*.

Such attitudes, in some ways critical of the Mother Country are not, it should be stressed, really directed at the lower orders, or members of the British working class, regarded as brave, goodhearted, simple-minded, cap-touching fellows capable of being Australianised and, indeed, the ancestors of the Australians themselves. The targets are the officer class, or upper classes, the higher up the worse, always excepting the radiant beacon shining from the summit. If the reader has also noticed a certain eagerness for British approval running underneath, as a kind of counter-current to this robust disdain, then he/she is beginning to penetrate some of the mysteries of the Australian national character – always assuming, in these enlightened days, there is any such thing.

The ambiguous legend of ANZAC (Australian and New Zealand Army Corps, for those wholly ignorant of the art of war – it also means 'almost' in Turkish) was not the only tradition conceived on the crumbling cliffs of the Dardanelles. On 2 September 1915, an Australian cub-journalist named Keith Murdoch, aged twenty-nine, managed to get himself ashore on Gallipoli. Murdoch had failed to get accreditation as an official war correspondent but wangled a pass out of the British Commander of the expedition, General Sir Ian Hamilton, with a letter pleading that 'my anxiety as an Australian to visit the sacred shores of Gallipoli, while our Army is there, is intense'. Giving him twenty-four hours, Sir Ian apparently missed the implication that they might not be there long.

A day ashore was quite long enough to give young Keith, gifted with the family nose for news, the basic picture. It was confirmed by talks in the press bar tent on the offshore Greek island of Imbros with Ellis Ashmead-Bartlett, disgruntled war correspondent of the London *Daily Telegraph*. (As usual, elements of Oz-Brit collaboration persisted, even in unpromising circumstances.)

Ashmead-Bartlett proposed a daringly disobedient plan. An experienced reporter from the Russo-Japanese war, he judged that the entire Dardanelles expedition faced disaster, with winter approaching, the Turks digging in, and fresh supplies flowing down from Germany. Any reporting along these lines from the front was, however, censored as 'defeatist' by the British GHQ, who insisted that victory was at hand, if only two, three, four or more divisions could be rushed out to Gallipoli. Or, why not make it the round dozen?

Ashmead-Bartlett was under military discipline, but his new friend Murdoch was not. The British journalist proposed that Murdoch hand-carry the story to London ('pigeon', we say in the trade). Their conversation was overheard by another correspondent, Henry Nevinson of the *Guardian*, who patriotically shopped the pair to GHQ. Murdoch was arrested by British military policemen in Marseilles and the offending dispatch taken off him. Of course, he still had the facts in his head. Stepping to a typewriter at Australia House in the Strand, young Keith hammered out a story that, years later, his boy Rupert would have been proud to print on page one of any of his many newspapers.

After preliminary praise of Australian troops Murdoch *père* addressed himself to the heart of the problem. 'The General Staff of the British Army', he wrote, 'are unchangeably selfish.' He had seen, he reported, a staff officer 'wallowing' in a bath cooled with ice, while wounded men were dying of heat a few hundred yards away.

'General Sir W. P. Braithwaite' (British), wrote Murdoch, 'is more cordially detested in our forces than Enver Pasha' (his Turkish opposite number). As to the soldiers of the New Army, hastily recruited in Britain and rushed out to the Straits, 'they are merely a lot of childish youths without strength to endure or brains to improve their condition'. It was hard to believe that these were British soldiers at all, their physique and training being so much below that of the Turks. 'After the first day at Suvla', reported Murdoch, 'an order had to be issued to officers to shoot without mercy any soldier who lagged behind or loitered in an advance. From what I saw of the Turk, I am convinced that he is . . . a better man than those opposed to him.'

This passionate and, possibly, slightly overstated piece of Pombashing was, in principle, intended for the eyes of Australian Prime Minister, Andrew Fisher, the one who had offered the last man and the last shilling. It soon found its way, however, into the hands of Asquith-basher Lloyd George, who circulated it to the War Cabinet. Ashmead-Bartlett, meanwhile expelled by GHQ from Imbros, returned to London, and he and Murdoch blew the whole story in the *Sunday Times*.

The Dardanelles campaign was abandoned in time for the survivors (and six more Australian divisions) to be sent to France. Incidentally, British Generals Sir Charles Monro and Sir William Birdwood, who got them off Gallipoli without losing a single man, are remembered fondly in Australia to this day. Not all Poms are irremediably evil.

Gallipoli made Keith Murdoch. He went on to great things in

Australian journalism, and died, full of honours, as Sir Keith, in 1952, owner and part-owner, of a string of posh newspapers. But death duties cut deep 'down under', too. All his son, known universally as Young Rupert, inherited was a stodgy little paper called the *Adelaide Advertiser*, just as widely known as 'The Old School Tizer'.

Sir Keith put his lad to the family trade – he seems never to have considered any other – sending him first to Oxford, and then to the *Daily Express*, where, aged twenty, Rupert tried to borrow £1 million from Hugh Cudlipp to start a new London newspaper. Back in Australia, the young proprietor hired a brilliant editor, former war correspondent Rohan Rivett, and with a commendable series of campaigns on such worthy subjects as the injustices dealt out to Australian aborigines, soon made a great success of his patrimony. His first big acquisition (and step, some think, down the slippery slope) was the Sydney *Daily Mirror*, an old paper of mine, the prototype for both the London *Sun* and the New York *Post*, tit, tinsel and all. Employing speed, surprise and deception – military tactics as old as war or business – young Rupert, energetic as ever, has gone on to build an empire on which the *Stars*, *Posts*, *Timeses* and *Suns* never set. Let's hope not, anyway. An awful lot of people will be out of work if they do.

But, like the rest of us, Rupert Murdoch seems Gallipoli-haunted. I made my own private pilgrimage in 1965, on assignment wangled from the *Sunday Times* to cover the fiftieth anniversary. The local Turks were, naturally, astonished to see the 'Almosts' return, grey in the jowl, cheerfully re-enacting one of the greatest cock-ups in all military history. Sure enough, the boats were once again carried a half-mile down the coast by the treacherous current, and the second landing, too, took place at the wrong spot. One Australian old soldier beat a New Zealander with his crutch in a dispute over which of them had hit the beach first. Another died of a heart attack in a Cairo brothel, a late casualty of the campaign. As for myself, like many before and since, I paced the tiny pebbled cove, still littered with rusty buckles and spent bullets, looked up at that appalling cliff and the Turkish machine-gun positions on top, and thought that there, but for the grace of God . . .

A decade later Peter Weir, one of the new crop of Australian film directors, made his own sentimental landfall on Gallipoli. 'I found something unknowable about the place, a national myth developed through failure,' he recalls. Back in Australia, he teamed up with David Williamson, Australia's foremost playwright, in a film script on the campaign. Unknown to the writers, another partnership was forming about the same time in London. Two men of substance were interested in taking a punt on the burgeoning Oz film biz. One was Australian entrepreneur, Robert Stigwood, who has made an immense bundle out of *Grease* and *Hair*, Olivia Newton-John and *Jesus Christ (Superstar)*. The other was Rupert Murdoch. They arrived in Sydney asking for scripts. Weir/Williamson submitted theirs, already rejected by a dozen prospective backers. Next morning Stigwood was on the 'phone. 'Rupert and I were up all night, reading', he said. 'This is the film we want to make.' As Americans say, it figures.

It was indeed in New York that I saw *Gallipoli* on its first release, only last week. The film is playing to packed houses, twenty-four hours a day, in a smart cinema on the Upper East Side, under a tremendous banner reading 'A Story You'll Never Forget, From a Place You've Never Heard Of'. I must say that even a hardened cosmopolite like my good self was a little put out by this proposition. 'Who was this George Lincoln?' I asked an American neighbour. 'Didn't he deliver the Ginsberg Address?'

But back to the film. Weir and Williamson are, on this showing, men of formidable talent. I am not, however, a member of the dreaded Murrumbidgee Mafia of Australians praising up each other's work. I have strong reservations about the way they have handled their subject.

The first thing that struck me was how exquisitely Weir handles the Australian landscape. The film was, apparently, all shot in Australia, except for sequences of training and brothel-crawling in Cairo, the rebuilding of the Sphinx and the Pyramids apparently being beyond even the resources of Messrs Murdoch and Stigwood. One can see, too, a certain commercial canniness joining with artistic enterprise in the heavy use of scenery. The Outback, after all, is highly photogenic, relevant to the Australian character, appears for nothing, and never gets drunk or asks for ten per cent of the box office, unlike, in all these respects imported American film stars.

The next point that struck this customer, almost at curtain-up, is how much Australian ideas of what an Australian looks like have changed. Twenty years ago the part of the hero, Archie, would certainly have gone to my friend Quentin Goffidge, later Slabs O'Mulligan and finally Chips Rafferty, tall, lean and perpetually looking as if he could use a beer (actually he once kept a wine bar). *Gallipoli*'s hero is played by newcomer Mark Lee, short, golden-haired, handsome to the point of prettiness. A runner in training when the war breaks out, he is, what's more, strictly TT. Oddly enough, quite a few of the real Australian soldiers playing parts as extras in the film look quite like Chips Rafferty.

Archie and his mate Frank go off to war as the Big Sporting Event they can't afford to miss. The idea of war as a kind of athletic meeting is, historically, undoubtedly one that Pom and Oz share, as witness the North of England footballer who dribbled a football across no-man's-land on the first day of the Somme, or the Australian on Gallipoli who shouted to the Turks, after a heroic failed bayonet charge, 'Play youse again here next Saturday!'

What the war might have been about gets only a brief glance. 'If we don't stop them over there, they'll be coming here next', says Archie, in what sounds like an early version of the Domino Theory. 'They're welcome to it', says a grizzled oldtimer, taking in the desert with a wave of wrinkled paw. Clever, but to be absolutely, meticulously fair, chaps, the Dardenelles Campaign was an attempt, bungled beyond doubt, to use British seapower to shorten a ghastly war. And, if it hadn't been for the same saltwater Pompower there'd scarcely be an English-speaking Australian available to buy up the London *Times* or finance anti-war movies.

One of the saddest things about wars is that, like weddings, they often seem a good idea at the time. To point out that passions often cool later is not, really, all that profound.

'I'm going to run like a leopard', Archie promises his athletics trainer, who has a shrewd suspicion the young man is in fact getting into shape for the war. This is supposed to be taking place in Western Australia, whose capital city is certainly a quiet town ('in the midst of life we are in Perth') but might, nevertheless, well have had a leopard in the local zoo. The plot, however, makes clear that Archie has never been there. Australian stockmen in the far Outback, in other words, get their imagery out of books, just like Australian writers. We still have some way to go in matching up our language and our landscape.

The story line, from this point, pretty much follows the historical picture we learnt at school. Archie and Frank go off to Egypt for training, where they find the local shopkeepers and working girls distressingly dishonest. They land by night at Gallipoli, and come under shellfire for the first time the next morning, underwater, while swimming in Anzac Cove (both dazzling sequences).

In the whole film we only see two Britishers, both English officers, with monocles. They haughtily point out that they are entitled to a salute from other ranks, even Australians, and when they get the two-fingered variety they gasp in tones of shock/horror something about 'undisciplined Colonial rabble'. I did not actually catch the word 'convict' but the thought, clearly, was there.

Inevitably, the Big Push is ordered by (British) GHQ. The Australians are to undertake a suicidal diversion in broad daylight against a Turkish position which makes the Siegfried Line look like a children's playground. The idea is to enable British reinforcements to land without too much discomfort. Two waves of Anzacs are cut down by Turkish machine-gunners almost before they are out of the trenches. Just as we learn that the British are actually lolling on the beaches drinking tea, the third wave is put in, and our hero, still trying to run like a leopard, stops a burst full in the chest, in a freeze-frame ending which exactly duplicates Robert Capa's famous photo of a Spanish Civil War soldier caught at the instant of death (or was he? See Phillip Knightley's excellent *The First Casualty*, pp 209-212).

Admittedly, it is an Australian brigadier who gives the fatal order, being, apparently, unable to set his watch to a simple time-signal, but he is a highly Pommified one, and clearly a gormless idiot to boot, part of the same familiar syndrome.

Audiences in Australia, I understand, are standing in their seats and cheering *Gallipoli*. The film is doing big business in America, too – the best ever, for the first weeks of a foreign film – despite the fact that no one has heard of Gallipoli or, possibly, Australia. I suspect, too, that it will do very well here, the view of the ordinary British soldier about the brass hats being not all that different from the Australian one if expressed, perhaps, a trifle more deferentially.

Gallipoli (the place and the movie) go far, too, to explain why Sir Keith Murdoch's lad might want to own the London *Times*, despite the hairy financial risks involved, and why he might well stand a chance of getting along better with members of the British working class, such as printers, than some of his more gently-bred predecessors. Murdoch *fils* does, after all, speak something quite like the same language. But what are we to make of his film?

In my view *Gallipoli* is, like its namesake, a gallant failure. Seeking to say something profound about the Australian character, it instead rakes up old resentments, making the chief merit of Australians the fact that they are not Pommies, rather than examining the better qualities which some of my friends assure me we possess (and share with Poms, quite often, too).

Weir and Williamson have made a beautiful and moving film. The endless, Hollywooden credit list at the end, everyone from Key Grip to Best Boy, suggests that we have another masterpiece like *All Quiet on the Western Front* here, and so does the stunning closing shot, a clear challenge to Milestone's hand reaching out for a butterfly, and the terminal, ghastly crack of a rifle.

But *Gallipoli* has, for me, a whinging, petulant tone, something resentful and masochistic and (I know I'll have the women's movement down on me here like a ton of feather dusters) fussily feminine. What I miss is the note of grief beyond expression, of Bugles calling for them from sad shires. But perhaps that came later in that gruesome war, and Gallipoli still had some of the flavour of a sporting occasion, a day out for the boys which turned a bit nasty in the end.

People who make anti-war films, worthy as their intentions are, always seem to me to be making their case too easy by picking a lunatic attack in a failed campaign of a war whose cause was not clear at the time, and is now a matter for experts to argue over. When is someone going to make a film against war which says that the conscripts who kept Australia out of the Japanese Co-Prosperity Sphere should have burnt their call-up papers? Or the British and

American soldiers who broke open concentration camps should have stayed at home and practised passive resistance? Much as I respect the pacifist and conscientious objector, there is one intellectual Gallipoli our gallant Aussie lads have still to storm.

10 October 1981

The Pompidous
Sam White

Almost everyone involved in the events of May 1968 was at one time or another touched with madness. There was de Gaulle himself raging impotently as control of the situation slipped away from him; a cross between Lear and the emperor without any clothes. There was Malraux jibbering away about a crisis of civilisation; there were ministers who were bracing themselves to tell de Gaulle that he should go; there was Giscard advising that on the contrary de Gaulle should stay on as some kind of totem figure and that it was Pompidou who should resign; and finally in the wings there was Mitterrand proclaiming in the best putschist manner that he was ready to form a provisional government, seemingly quite oblivious of the fact that there was a legal government in office which still enjoyed a parliamentary majority.

Only Pompidou, in an atmosphere of panic absurdly reminiscent of 1940, seemed wholly sane as he bore alone the heat and burden of the day. Yet he too, at a critical point, had committed an act which he later regretted. Returning in haste from Afghanistan he ordered the reopening of the Sorbonne which his Minister of Education had closed because of the rioting, and the release of arrested student rioters. This provided the students with a heady victory and the workers quickly took the point – a spontaneous wave of strikes began.

Built into this larger psychodrama, as Raymond Aron called it, was another psychodrama based on de Gaulle's relations with his Prime Minister. This is the subject of a recently published book by

Pompidou himself and consisting largely of notes he took at the time. The book, entitled rather menacingly *To Establish a Truth*, was authorised for publication by his widow and is in a sense as much an act of vengeance on her part as it is of posthumous vengeance on his. It deals with two events which poisoned Pompidou's relations with de Gaulle: the General's disappearing act at the height of the May troubles and the attempt to involve Mme Pompidou in the so-called Marcovic affair. De Gaulle, who tired of prime ministers as lesser men tire of mistresses, had long been at loggerheads with Pompidou over an issue which he called 'participation'. He was suitably vague about what it actually meant but to him it represented the half-way house between capitalism and socialism – a kind of combination of profit-sharing and a worker share in management. Pompidou, a pragmatist who was then presiding over a period of unprecedented prosperity, scoffed at the whole idea, pointing out that neither unions nor employers would have anything to do with it.

It was then that de Gaulle decided to replace Pompidou with the more pliant Couve de Murville. Unfortunately there were two obstacles to that: the first one was that the government had a majority of only one in the National Assembly and the second was that Couve, try as he would, could not win a parliamentary seat. Then came the May events and it was easy for de Gaulle to conclude that they were the result of his warnings about the need for social reform not being heeded. The decision to replace Pompidou with Couve after the Gaullist triumph at the 1968 elections was therefore not a sudden one but one which had been maturing long before the student troubles.

The other matter of contention, however, sprang directly from them: de Gaulle wanted to resolve the crisis by holding a referendum while Pompidou insisted on general elections. In the end Pompidou won both the argument and the elections, only to be sacked almost immediately after. As though this were not hard enough to forgive, there was the wholly unforgivable affair of de Gaulle's disappearance which preceded it. He left the Elysée Palace on 29 May after taking the most minute precautions to indicate that he was leaving for good. His stated destination was his country home at Colombey-Les-Deux-Eglises but instead he turned up four hours later at General

Massu's headquarters at Baden-Baden.

There the great actor put on his greatest act. Everything he announced was *foutou*, while Massu administered first aid in the form of a pep talk and Mme Massu busied herself preparing beds for visitors who had only given a few minutes' notice of their arrival.

Pompidou believes that de Gaulle had decided to quit when he left Paris that morning and that it was Massu who persuaded him to return. So too, understandably enough, does Massu. There is one piece of evidence, however, provided by Pompidou himself which suggests that he never really intended to resign and that the whole performance was a consummate piece of play-acting intended to test reactions to his departure. Shortly after de Gaulle left Paris Pompidou told the head of the television news department, Edouard Sablier, that he would like to go on the air that evening to address the nation. Sablier, whose first loyalty was to the Elysée, passed this request on to de Gaulle's secretary-general, Bernard Tricot, who promptly banned the intended broadcast.

This strongly suggested that de Gaulle anticipated such a move on Pompidou's part and had instructed Tricot to block it. It would be interesting to know what Pompidou intended to say in his broadcast but of this there is not a clue in his book. Two other points, however, are satisfactorily cleared up. It is now clear that, contrary to general belief at the time, de Gaulle did not discuss or even mention the possibility of army support if he should decide to return, nor the supposed price of that support – an amnesty for former OAS officers like General Salan.

We now come to the second high point of the book, the Marcovic affair. There is no doubt that a deliberate attempt was made to involve the Pompidous, and especially Mme Pompidou, in this affair by claims that she had attended orgies organised by Alain Delon's former bodyguard who was later murdered. Fake photographs were circulated to back up this claim and a Jugoslav pimp in prison on a charge that had nothing to do with the affair offered evidence that he had seen the Pompidous on such occasions. Pompidou was the last to learn of these rumours as he was the last to learn that the Pompidou name figured in the Marcovic dossier. The Minister of Justice at the time, René Capitan, was an old enemy of Pompidou and clearly relished the possibilities that the case opened up for destroying him. De Gaulle too, with his deep cynicism, possibly thought that there might be something in it, but he did give instructions that Pompidou should be informed. The task was given to Couve de Murville, who funked it.

Finally someone did summon up the courage to tell Pompidou but by that time every dinner table in Paris had been buzzing with the story for three weeks. De Gaulle tried to make amends by inviting the Pompidous to a dismal little dinner at the Elysée when the non-existent scandal was at its height, but the damage had been done and Pompidou remained unbending and unforgiving for the rest of his life. There is no need to dwell on de Gaulle's behaviour in both cases: it was quite simply disgraceful. One other extraneous point might be mentioned here, for it demolishes another legend. In interviews which Mme Pompidou has given in connection with the publication of the book she makes it clear that her husband did not die of cancer of the marrow as has been generally assumed, nor did he die in agonies of pain as has so often and vividly been described. He had, she says, developed a rare blood disease named after its discovered Waldenstrom, which was kept under control by heavy doses of cortisone. This treatment could have prolonged his life by several years had it not been for a heavy attack of septicaemia brought on by piles.

10 July 1982

Iceland
Peter Ackroyd

Reykjavik

The moon was like an arc-light, so close you could brush it with your hand, as though it had been attracted to that land on earth most like itself and had come to guard it. The medical student was walking beside me. 'There are ghosts in every corner of Iceland.' Did he

believe in them? 'I will not say "I do not" because then I may see one.
We are not really Christians here. We do not believe in the Devil. We
do not really believe in God.' He said it in a half-ironic manner,
which was characteristic – as if to say, foreigners are not really
interested in us, so why should you be?

The editor of the largest newspaper in Iceland stared out of the
window, at the small red and blue houses stretching down to a lake. 'I
ask myself, what is dream and what is reality? My three best friends
are no longer alive, but they are still with me. Who is living and who is
dead?' He was a poet; there is a tradition in this country of poets
becoming editors.

The President of Iceland, Vigdis Finnbogadöttir, was telling me of
the many dreams that had foretold her election. 'One woman
telephoned me to tell me her dream. She was looking down upon a
beautiful green valley – that is a typical sight for a dream here – where
she saw three men holding a parchment. Suddenly a fair lady
appeared and snatched the vellum from them, and then ran very
lightly up the hill. There were three male presidents before me and,
so you can see, she was right.'

Dreams; ghosts; trolls. Iceland is an island of spirits, haunted by its
dead and by the primeval powers of the land. It is the central mystery
of this place, the first thing to understand. The belief in such matters
is not whimsical or merely decorative; it is rooted in the Sagas, which
are the living literature of Iceland, and plays a powerful role in the life
of the race. In the cinema near my hotel, the auditorium had been
filled with people; not to watch the latest American film, but to
participate in a seance. Mediums were on the stage, trying to invoke
the wandering spirits of the Icelandic dead. There were Lutheran
ministers among the congregation. These people believe – not in
Christianity, not in the pagan gods, but in an amalgam of the two.
Their religion represents a sense of continuity, a kind of spiritual
lineage, a line with which they are entrusted and which they keep
unbroken through even the most perilous circumstances.

The subscribers in the telephone directory are listed under their
Christian names (if that is the right phrase) – as if the surnames did
not fully belong to them. And, in fact, they do not. By law, each
Icelander is named 'son of . . .' or 'daughter of . . .'; only first names

are used, in parliamentary reports, in newspapers, in conversation. The last name, the social foundation, is unchanging and in a sense anonymous. It is another way of asserting the continuity of these generations, springing directly from the first Viking settlers – generations which foreign conquest, terrible disease and privation, and the no less terrifying forces of this volcanic island, have been unable to change or to destroy.

In order to explain themselves, the Icelanders continually revert to their history: the Vikings arriving in the ninth and tenth centuries, the epidemics and famines which so devastated the land that there were twice as many Icelanders in 1000 as there were in 1800, the coming of a printing press in the fifteenth century. In conversation, the centuries chime like distant bells. Old legends and ancient myths have accumulated around this history of privation – stories of hardship endured, of the spirits of the mountains.

These stories, these sagas, are born out of wonder and isolation; out of the need to wrench human significance and human shape from a landscape which seems actively to repel life. Even the language in which these sagas are written is itself seen as a kind of legend, an historical force which has acquired its own identity. It has not changed markedly in the last nine hundred years; the books now written use the same language – syntax, grammar and vocabulary – as those composed in 1300. It is as if we wrote and spoke in the language of *Piers Plowman*, or John Gower; as if our newspapers used similar words and constructions to those of Chaucer. One must not, of course, exaggerate this remarkable fact. New words are continually entering the vocabulary. 'If I was speaking to a thirteen century poet,' the newspaper editor suggested, 'it would take us half an hour – no, let us say one hour – to understand one another clearly.' The dead writers of England are precisely that – dead, as distant as sky-writing which we read once before it vanishes. But the Icelandic language, and the culture which shines within it, lives on in its original form. It, too, has survived.

I went to see President Vigdis, in order to discuss such matters. She began by describing the origin of the Icelandic elves and trolls, as a polite prelude to serious conversation. I asked her about her presidential campaign. 'I was like the ogre of the old legends. I crossed Iceland in three steps.' She was piloted around in a tiny plane to each small community; her hosts would put her up in the children's room. She would make a speech in each place. First, she would begin seriously by quoting the sagas. 'I always speak of the sagas. That is what we are, and how we are. And then I spoke of daily life. I was not the candidate, I would say, it is you. There is something in me which is them. We are all the result of this particular past. We live in Iceland, with ancestors who never gave up, who never accepted that life was hopeless. We conquered the land, otherwise clearly we would not have survived.' And now? 'In the same way, we will conquer inflation. For me it is a problem to think of a problem. I am an optimistic person; what I experienced in my journeys was great warmth, great understanding among the people. What makes you think we cannot do it?' She brushed cigarette ash off her dress. 'I have quite a lot to say, as you can see.'

The wind was coming up, and whistled around the old house filled with bound volumes of the sagas like a monastic library. 'And before, you asked me what is power? My ambition is to be what I am. Perhaps I am now a proper person, a warm person, but that came late in life. So what is this ambition to prove myself? I do not want power. I want inspiration, to inspire people with the thoughts I have, with the thoughts that have inspired me. That is all. When you get back to England, you must read Njal's saga. You will not believe the complexity of these stories we have.' Then she put on her raincoat, and took me back to Reykjavik.

On the 'plane back home, I was sitting next to a twelve-year-old Icelandic boy. As we approached London by night, the clouds parted and one part of the city was lit up to the horizon. The little boy clapped his hands, and sucked in his breath. He turned to me. 'That is beautiful', he said. 'It is a revelation.' This was the word he used. In a way, it catches the heart. It tells us of what the Icelanders have never had, what history and what possibilities have been denied them. And yet what have they raised in its place – what intensity of longing, what affirmation of themselves, what willing embrace of the land and the spirits of the land. Who could say where the advantage lies?

6 September 1980 (abridged)

India
Shiva Naipaul

The dark green plain, sliced through by a broad, orange-coloured arc of the Ganges, was dissected into shining rectangles by fields of rice which stretched as far as the eye could see. Scattered across that sodden verdancy were the brown-tiled roofs of huddled villages. Here and there, casting graceful reflections and breaking the monotony, were palm trees. But they were few and far between. For, over the centuries, the plain had been relentlessly surrendered to one of the chief obsessions of its inhabitants – the cultivation of rice. From the air, it was a vision of order, fruitfulness and peasant contentment. This was a deceptive first impression: I was looking down on Bihar, ancient but degenerate heartland of Hindu culture.

Bihar, home of at least sixty million Indians (it is the second most populous state in the Indian Union), is nowadays notorious for its squalor, its backwardness, its gross corruptions. It has become a byword for all that is most hopeless and terrible about the Indian condition: the subcontinent's heart of darkness. The mere mention of the name in the intellectual circles of Delhi or Bombay or Calcutta (even Calcutta!) calls forth shrugs of despair. In the drama of progress many Indians justifiably enjoy painting for visitors there is no place for Bihar. Bihar, it was often implied, had degenerated so far that it was now beyond the reach of the usual panaceas of social and economic reform. One of the seed-beds of the glorious past had decayed and the heirs of the men who had made that past had decayed with it and slipped beyond redemption. Best, perhaps, not to think about it. Let nature take its course. Bihar, it seemed, defied reason and alienated compassion.

It excelled in virtually all the negative indicators. It had the highest birth-rate, the highest level of illiteracy, the highest number of college dropouts. Its politics were the most caste-fettered. A model of political instability, Bihar, since 1947, had run through nearly two dozen Chief Ministers. With roughly thirty per cent of its population landless, it had become a reservoir of the semi-slavery known as bonded labour. Brigandage was rife: dacoity was a favourite pastime of the college dropouts and of jobless graduates. Many were 'students' by day and brigands by night. The educational system was disintegrating. For one whole year the University of Patna had remained closed after rival groups of students, organised on caste lines, had begun to murder each other.

From one year to the next, Bihar generated more tales of atrocity than any other region of India. Massacre had become almost a commonplace in its more remote villages where caste warfare articulated the struggle between the landed and the landless – or, as the Marxist ideologues like to put it, between 'kulak' and 'serf'. Typically, it was Bihar which caused a furore in the New Delhi parliament when news broke that the police, as a matter of course, had been blinding scores of common criminals in their custody. It has been estimated that probably fifty people are killed every day by politically motivated acts of violence. The horror is obscured because many of these incidents go unreported in both the local and national press. 'People ask how long Bihar can carry on as it is without the society breaking down completely,' a civil servant who knew that state well said to me. 'The answer is that the society has already broken down.' Acts of God compound the Bihari tragedy. The people lurch between the threat of drought and the threat of flood: too little or too much water. In Bihar, famine is always just around the corner.

'You want to know if there is anything *good* that can be said about Bihar?' The Punjabi editor of one of Patna's English-language newspapers was amused by my question. 'The truthful reply is no. I cannot think of a single good thing to say.' His office, tidy and dark and cool, kept at bay the over-heated glare and chaotic ugliness of the Patna morning through which I had ventured to come and see him. He had many problems trying to produce his paper. His staff, most of whom were equipped with degrees in English, did not really know the language and refused to accept that they did not know it. English was a dying language in Bihar. 'To be frank with you,' he said, 'this so-called paper of which I'm editor is fit only for toilet paper. I'm quite ashamed of it. But what can I do with these people? What can anyone do with them?'

He lived the life of an exile in Patna. It had proved almost impossible for him to create a social life in that debilitated environment. If, for instance, he invited a Bihari to his home, it was more than likely that the invitation would not be reciprocated; and if by some chance it was, his host's womenfolk would be carefully locked away from his gaze. The Bihari suffered from an eerie lethargy. Such energy as there was came from imported individuals like himself. The locals who were desperate enough and ambitious enough often emigrated to other states: Bihar was a major exporter of raw labour power. 'What we are faced with', he said, 'is a human problem, a *personality* problem. How do you solve the personality problems of sixty million people?' And he too had shrugged despairingly.

The businessman who had come from Delhi to set up a factory making pump machinery for tube wells was equally discouraged. He reckoned that roughly twenty-five per cent of his original investment had been eaten up by bribes to politicians and bureaucrats. 'You have to grease palms at every stage. To push even the littlest piece of paper up the ladder costs you money.' He had not yet come across an honest politician or bureaucrat. Yet he was a realist. He was not against bribery as such. To do business anywhere in India, bribes usually had to be paid. What upset him, what he found 'unfair', was that after paying your bribe nothing much happened. 'That is the astonishing thing. That is what I still can't get over. *Nothing* happens. They just wake up enough to hold out their hands for the envelope and then go straight back to sleep.'

Like the editor, he was perplexed by the Bihari character. They signally lacked what he called a work ethic. Mostly, they were apparently quite content to take home the two or three hundred rupees a month they earned for doing next to nothing. The idea of working harder or earning more did not appear to have any appeal. Without notice, his employees would disappear for days at time – to attend the wedding or funeral of some distant relation; or to take part in some lengthy and obscure religious ritual. He had concluded that the Bihari was almost devoid of ambition in the conventional sense. At any rate, ambition was not associated with productive, disciplined labour. Its place was taken by a fatuous greed. If his factory managed to produce anything at all that was only because half of his work-force had been recruited from non-Biharis.

After autumnal Delhi, the Patna air was disagreeably vaporous and clammy. My taxi-driver was an unshaven, sullen-faced man, mouth bloodily discoloured by over-indulgence in *pan*. We proceeded slowly, carefully dodging the cows which reclined by preference in the middle of the road, showing not the slightest tremor of anxiety at our approach, serenely contemplating their ramshackle world. 'That tranquil, far-off gaze [of the Indian cow]', wrote a business-like American observer in the 1920s, 'is, indeed, often remarked and acclaimed by the passing traveller as an outward sign of an inner sense of surrounding love . . . after examining the facts, one is driven to conclude that the expression in the eyes . . . is due partly to low vitality.' We crawled along dusty, pot-holed lanes crowded with pedestrians and cycle rickshaws and lined with the stalls of petty merchants. Ceaselessly, the driver honked his horn. I stared at the meagre limbs of the rickshaw wallahs, haunches angled off their saddles, effortfully pumping the pedals of their cumbrous vehicles as they toiled their human cargoes homeward. India, even today, offers a still more elemental mode of public transport: in Calcutta I saw people being carried about in hand-pulled rickshaws.

We were halted by a religious procession. Gaudily coloured idols, bedecked with tinsel and garlands of marigolds, were riding on the open tray of a lorry. A shabbily uniformed band walked behind the lorry, their trumpets and drums filling the steamy air with strident discordancy. Patna, as I was to discover, was a pious town, much given to exhibitions of Hinduism's polytheistic zeal. Hardly a day passed without my seeing processions similar to this one. Dusk was falling when I got to the hotel.

The hotel, owned by a state-controlled corporation devoted to the development of tourism, was a gloomy place, so dimly lit that it was painful to the eyes: the electricity was running at about half-power. After filling in many forms, I looked for the bar.

'Bar is closed,' said the receptionist.

'What time does it open?'

'Bar is closed permanently.' He spoke, I felt, with satisfaction.

The bar had been shut up during the Janata era, a victim of Morarji Desai's prohibitionist fervour. Despite Janata's demise and Indira Gandhi's more tolerant attitude towards the consumption of alcohol, no steps had yet been taken to reopen it. If I wanted anything to drink, anything either hard or soft in a bottle, I would, the receptionist explained with intensifying satisfaction, have to send 'outside' for it. Indeed, he pointed out, if I wanted cigarettes I would have to send 'outside'; if I wanted matches I would have to send 'outside'.

'What about food? Do I have to send outside for that as well?'

He laughed. 'Food you can have inside,' he said. 'Restaurant is in operation. But if you want anything else . . .' He spread his hands resignedly. 'If you wish, I'll send a boy right away. Of course he'll require a little extra . . . it is not, properly speaking, his job, you understand.'

I was beginning to understand. It was not in the staff's interest to provide too many facilities within the hotel. Sending 'outside' was a much more rewarding exercise. Desai's attempt at moral revolution had coincided neatly with self-interest.

As I stood there meditating on these matters, the lights went out altogether. A peon was summoned. He arrived, bearing a lighted candle, and escorted me to my room. After about an hour, the lights came on again, spreading their painful glimmer. I went down to the restaurant. Young men in red trousers and black jackets lounged listlessly. The only diners apart from myself were a taciturn Bihari family and a Japanese woman of middle age – come to Bihar, I assumed, to see Buddhism's sacred places. During dinner the lights went out again. Candles flamed into life.

'Does the electricity go on and off like this all the time?' I asked my red-coated attendant.

'Every day, sahib.'

'Why?'

'Power shortage, sahib.'

'Why is there a power shortage?'

He simpered inanely and shrugged.

The shortage of power in a state that accounts for more than half of India's coal production had ceased to be strange. It had become one more unalterable fact of life to be endured. Later, I discovered one cause of the shortfall: the private contractors licensed to transport coal from the nationalised mines had fallen into the habit of siphoning off substantial quantities into the black market. Bihar was as powerless before the doings of men as it was before the doings of nature.

I watched the wavering reflections of the candles in the panes of the windows and doors; I listened to the murmur of voices penetrating from the lightless road. The Bihari family departed. So did the Japanese woman. I called for my bill. My waiter bent over me, whispering the amount into my ear.

'But where's the actual bill?'

He looked embarrassed; he signalled over one of his colleagues.

'You have a problem, sahib?' asked the newcomer politely. He was dressed in a less flunkeyish style than the others and seemed to be in a position of some authority.

'I would like my bill.'

My original attendant skulked away, vanishing into the candle-lit gloom.

'Naturally, sahib, we'll provide a bill if you want one . . .' He hesitated, his soft eyes exploring my face. 'May I be frank with you, sahib?'

'By all means.'

He explained succinctly the system of petty embezzlement engaged in by himself and the rest of the staff. The loot, he explained, was shared out equally among them. It was all very democratic, all very co-operative. 'Sahib,' he murmured, assuming a piteous expression, 'we cannot live on what they pay us. If we tried to do that, we would all starve.'

He paused. I watched the reflections.

'Do you really require the bill, sahib?'

'Forget it.' I felt weary, infected by a sudden apathy.

He smiled. 'I can see you're a good man, sahib. I'll invite you to my house. You will see how I – a *chef de rang*, sahib . . . a *chef de rang*! – you will see how I live, in what conditions I must raise my children. Would you like to visit my humble home, sahib?'

I said I would. The *chef de rang* led me through the candle-lit gloom to my room. 'Take care to lock your door, sahib. Patna has many bad, anti-social characters.'

I promised I would take every care. Bowing solicitously, he retreated. Sleep did not come easily in the overheated darkness.

One sultry evening I am led by the *chef de rang* down a meandering, muddy lane. He goes before me, lighting my way with a torch whose beam traces the outlines of fetid pools. We leap across a gutter. He says, 'We're here. Welcome to my house.' A young woman appears in the doorway. She draws the edge of her sari foward so that it veils the lower half of her face. Twittering, she scuttles off into the darkness. 'That is my wife,' says the *chef de rang*. 'She is shy. You must excuse her. It is not our custom for women to talk to strange men.' He takes me into a white-washed room about ten foot square, roofed with corrugated iron. The lingering warmth of the day continues to soak through the metal. 'Sometimes,' he says, 'in the hot weather season the heat is so great that the skin of the children is blistered by it.'

Most of the space is taken up by a bed. On it his three children, two girls and a boy, lie sleeping. He switches on the ceiling fan, the only noticeable item of luxury I can see in the room. Gaudy icons decorate the walls: gods and goddesses with faces tinted mauve, pink and blue; multi-armed, elephant-nosed, monkey-faced divinities. On a shelf there is a shaving mirror, some tattered Hindi paperbacks and a collection of medicines. A folding table is set out before me. He covers it with a white cloth, arranges a knife, fork and spoon and offers me a napkin. All of these refinements are stamped with the monogram of the hotel. His wife, head lowered, brings in a bowl of curried chicken and scuttles out. The *chef de rang* squats on the bed, using his fingers, swallowing with noisy relish.

'You think,' he says when we have finished eating, 'that I am a wicked man to cheat my employers.'

'I haven't said that.'

'Will you please tell me how a man can live on 450 rupees [about twenty-five pounds] a month?' His rent alone consumed one hundred rupees. How could he survive on what was left? How could he feed his family? It was not possible for him to live honestly on what he earned.

Yet the *chef de rang* could consider himself a fortunate man. By the standards of Bihar his salary was almost princely. If the most humble post in the hotel where he worked fell vacant there would be literally thousands of applicants for the job.

'If I did not cheat a little, sahib, my children might not be alive today. The Ganga would have taken their bodies a long time ago. When big men cheat, sahib, they take lakhs, they take crores. What do I take? Ten rupees here, five rupees there – so I can put food in the mouths of my children. It makes me sick at heart to do it, sahib.' He pauses, massaging the region of his heart. 'There are some who do worse things. Some sell the bodies of their daughers, their wives. Our mentality is no good, sahib. No good at all. I do not care for my own country or countrymen.'

His confession is becoming oppressive. What prompts it? The hope of a handout? Sympathy? It is likely that he himself does not know. He has probably lost touch with his own motives. The *chef de rang* is obscurely ready for any eventuality – compassion, money . . . anything.

'We have thought of sterilisation. Even that we have thought of.' He falls silent, staring at his sleeping children.

'What stopped you?'

'I have only one boy child. He may sicken and die tomorrow. Who can say? Girl children do not really belong to their father. Boy children look after you in your old age. They alone can perform certain rites. What would happen to me if this one son of mine should die? I have bad dreams about that, sahib. It worries me a great deal.'

I sit in the hot cell, looking at the gods and goddesses, listening to his complaints and the chorus of the frogs; I sit there until the power fails and I begin to sweat. The beam of his torch guides me back through the malodorous darkness to my room.

'Peaceful Exam at Hajipur,' announced the headline in the newspaper. 'The Intermediate examinations in Vaishali District,' said the accompanying report, 'were being conducted peacefully at RN College and Jamunilal College centres . . . Strict police arrangements have been made to maintain law and order on the campus . . .' Elsewhere was reported the tragic end of a 'notorious criminal' who had been mysteriously drowned in a river, a misadventure the police were at a loss to explain. As if to compensate for that, the body of a murdered policeman had been found lying beside the railway tracks in Forbesganj. I read on, confining myself to the same page. Saharsa District had, for many days past, been cut off by floods from all other parts of the state and the rest of the country. The District had no prospect of immediate relief. In Nawada there had taken place a protest march by teachers who wished to voice their opposition to the rampant corruption of the District's education office. A 'sugar famine' was raging in the town of Khagani. In the Kolhan region, noted one of the more cryptic dispatches, the people were 'in distress' – no cause was specified. A small item repeated allegations about the mass torture and killings of Adivasis – the tribal folk who make up about ten per cent of Bihar's population. In Araria a gang of bandits had attacked the house of a local high school teacher. Electricity flowed in the district of East Champaran for only one or two hours a day. This meant, among other things, an acute shortage of drinking water. 'Moreover,' continued the item, 'the Public Health Department and the local municipality have not yet installed any power-generating set specifically for water supply in the town. It has become nobody's concern here.' Between Bagaha and Narkatiaganj train services had been 'paralysed' because of mass casual leave. The residents of Khagaria had not received promised flood relief and, like the people of Kolhan, were in distress.

But in Bihar that morning there was some good news too. Bhagalpur University announced its intention to establish a diploma course in Gandhian Thought.

4 December 1982

'*Come along you two, it's no time to have a row*'.

Russian policy

Sir: I am surprised that Russia has not taken advantage of the strange moral position over Vietnam taken by the Western governments and their odd interpretation of the Helsinki Agreement. Western governments protest against the USSR for refusing to let certain of their people immigrate; they protest against the Vietnamese Government for allowing 'the boat people' to go. They even demand that Vietnam close its frontiers. (And of course they protest against the invasion of Cambodia which put an end to the genocidal regime of the Khmer Rouge. Apparently it would have been acceptable if Hitler had confined his massacres to Germany and not crossed the frontier.)

Why hasn't Russia taken this superb opportunity to grant visas to the West to anyone who asks for one? It is highly unlikely that there would be a mass immigration of the proletariat – and that in itself would be a good propaganda point. As for the intellectual dissidents, many like Solzhenitsyn have complained at being forced to leave their country, so perhaps the exodus of the middle class would not be very spectacular. But suppose even the exodus were spectacular . . . the Security Services of the West would be overwhelmed by the numbers they had to vet; our unemployment figures would soar, and what a triumph for the USSR when the Western governments very soon had to plead to Russia to close her frontiers as now they plead to Vietnam?

Graham Greene, Antibes

22 September 1979

'How do you spell "trajectory"?'

Female circumcision
Richard West

Who could have guessed, even as little as a year ago, that female circumcision was to become the latest liberal cause? Until recently one would have thought that abortion and sex education (for) with smoking, alcoholism and South African rugby (against) were still the campaigns to rally the good and true. Then, in Paris, early this year, I noticed that *Le Monde* was running a series of front-page articles on the subject of female circumcision, complete with maps showing the prevalence of the custom in different parts of Africa. A few months ago, our contemporary, the *New Statesman*, carried a long denunciation of female circumcision, followed later by 'Living', the women's page of the *Observer*. I would hazard a guess that similar or the same articles may have been published as well in the United States.

Since clitoridectomy is a gruesome practice sometimes resulting in death, one should I suppose welcome these articles on simple grounds of humanity; but I could not suppress some puzzlement at finding this cause advanced in the liberal and left-wing press. The custom of female circumcision has long been referred to by white people in Africa as an example of black barbarity and therefore of unfitness to govern. I have heard it described on innumerable occasions – in Kenya where female circumcision is widespread, in Rhodesia and even in South Africa, where such a salacious topic is mentioned only in private, and not in front of the opposite sex. But they talk about it all right. 'Ach man, do you know what the Kaffirs do to their women to make them faithful?'

The arch-negrophobe, Richard Burton, wrote about female circumcision in *Two Trips to Gorilla Land*. Regretting that the 'delicacy of the age' did not allow him to be explicit, Burton nevertheless gave a vivid account of the customs in Pongo-land, which he visited in 1861: 'The operation is performed generally by the chief, often by some old man, who receives a fee from the parents: the thumb-nails are long, and are often used after the Jewish fashion:

neat rum with red pepper is spurted from the mouth to "kill the wound" '.

In his commentary on the *Arabian Nights* and other banned and salacious books, Burton described the practice of female circumcision in Africa and elsewhere. With the relaxation of laws on obscenity, the custom has once again proved useful to writers. In *Call it Rhodesia*, published in 1966, Mr W. A. Ballinger kicks off with a lurid account of the goings-on in the Bundu Bush. The hero, Strong, one of the Pioneers of Rhodesia, spies on the initiation of two dozen girls: 'The slender, coppery bodies were quite naked save for a single string of cowrie shells around the waist. The young breasts were ringed brightly with concentric circles and about the pubis a triangle in red . . . each body was a moving text-book of sex. And this was the lesson that the girls had been learning in the long house. How to attract men and then to hold them.' The Bundu mother approaches with a phallus stick. And so on. The girl whom Strong rescues explains that in the operation 'the clitoris, the prime sense organ of pleasure, was cut out to ensure the faithfulness of wives.'

Books like *Call it Rhodesia*, which also contain some raping of nuns in the Congo, appeal to the prurience of the white reader, while leaving him with the thought that Africans are violently sensual and cruel. This mixture of fascination and fear in connection with sex, explains much of the attitudes of the whites in Rhodesia and South Africa. Female circumcision, because it revolts our sensibilities, has long been an obsession.

The present campaigners against clitoridectomy may not know of the much wider campaign that was waged exactly fifty years ago, in Kenya, then a British colony. The Kikuyu tribe who had lost much of their land to the whites were then in a state of some unrest, which was to explode twenty years later in Mau-Mau. To make matters worse, the Scottish missionaries in Kikuyuland, although popular for the schools which they had established, had tried to suppress the custom of female circumcision. Their main objection, it seems, was not so much to the physical operation but to the very erotic dancing and lessons in love play that went beforehand – the sort of things described in the Ballinger novel. As early as 1914, in Thogoto and Tumutumu, several girls had been encouraged to have the circumcision performed in a mission hospital, under the eyes of European doctors. The doctors objected and so, of course, did the Africans who disliked this clinical version of what to them was a holy rite.

About 1919, the missionaries started a new campaign to prevent the ritual of circumcision. They claimed it was dangerous, that the wounds could fester and cause the girls' death. The custom also discouraged the girls from becoming Christians and getting married in church to one of the numerous male converts. The young Kikuyu political leader, Jomo Kenyatta, travelled in the same year to London to win support for his land reform programme, but he found that people were much more interested in female circumcision. His biographer, Jeremy Murray Brown, writes: 'In London, female circumcision, or clitoridectomy as the fastidious called it, became the talk in advanced circles, and Kenyatta was sought after by hostesses at tea-time discussions.'

Early in January, 1930, all Kenya was horrified by the news that a woman missionary in Kikuyuland had been murdered by persons unknown who had forcibly circumcised her, and smothered her with a pillow in the attempt to stifle her screaming. This crime is still part of the sinister folk-lore of all whites in Africa, although it is no doubt forgotten in Britain. The present Dame Margery Perham arrived in Nairobi a few weeks after the murder and gallantly spent a night in a hut in Kikuyuland in order to demonstrate to the whites her faith in the Kikuyus. But the clitoridectomy rumpus continued throughout 1931 when a conference was held in Geneva under the auspices of the Save the Children Fund. *Plus ça change* . . .

The campaign died away, largely because Jomo Kenyatta defended the practice of female circumcision in *Facing Mount Kenya*, an anthropological study of his own Kikuyu people. (This simply and beautifully written book, incidentally, shines by comparison with all the insensitive jargon-ridden guff on Africa by modern sociologists.) Kenyatta's chapter on circumcision explains how the actual operation is only a ritual part of the preparation of girls for marriage and motherhood, and how the Kikuyu sexual instruction, far from encouraging licence, teaches young men and women how to control their passion. He denies that the operation is cruel: 'A woman specialist cuts off the tip of the clitoris . . . no other part is affected.

She has been doused with very cold water ... It is only when she awakes after three or four hours of rest that she begins to realise that something has been done to her sexual organ.'

Some of the modern feminists, especially in America, believe that the clitoris is the sole organ of sexual pleasure, a theory proclaimed in a famous book, *The Myth of the Vaginal Orgasm*.

Kenyatta did not believe that clitoridectomy robbed women of sexual pleasure, and he spoke with authority on that matter; nor did he have much time for the sexual habits of some of our women's liberationists: 'Masturbation among girls', he wrote, 'is considered wrong ... It may be said that one of the reasons, is probably the motive for trimming the clitoris, to prevent girls from developing sexual feelings around that point. Owing to these restrictions, the practice of homosexuality is unknown among the Kikuyu.'

Clitoridectomy may be brutal and possibly dangerous. That it degrades women, I doubt. The Kikuyu may have something to learn from Western feminists but I think that the opposite also applies. I put more trust in *Facing Mount Kenya* than in *The Myth of the Vaginal Orgasm*.

15 December 1979

'One mouse making it doesn't mean we have equality'

Richard West's memory

Sir: I have a high regard for Richard West but an even higher regard for my friend Bruce Beresford, whose film about Australian Rules football is called *The Club*, and not, as Richard West twice has it (6 February), *The Game*. The film is based on a play by David Williamson, although it is perhaps a blessing that Richard West did not try to say so, else we might have heard about a new Australian playwright called William Davidson. It is also worth pointing out that *The Angry Odd Shot* is really called *The Odd Angry Shot*, unless I, too, am suffering from an inability to words get the in order right. But it is nice to hear that Richard West likes Australia, which needs a few more dyslexic immigrants in order to thicken the racial mix.

Clive James, Observer, 8 St Andrews Hill, London EC4

13 February 1982

Ile-de-France
Richard Cobb

The Companion Guide to the Ile-de-France Ian Dunlop (Collins)

Paris is the most fortunate of capitals, because despite the new line *(voie-express)* from Boissy-Saint Léger, the industrialisation of the valley of the Lower Seine up to Mantes, the steady invasion of the wide plains of the Pays de France, due north of the city, the degradation of much of the valleys of the Orge, the Yvette, the Bièvre and the Marne, it is still within reach of a great deal of unspoilt countryside and of calm villages. The Ile-de-France is the most beautiful region of France, partly because it is the most varied and, if one excepts the great show-places, the most unassuming. It offers the contrast between the rolling gorse-covered slopes of the Hurepoix and the open country south of Houdan (Landru territory), the sandy woodlands round Etampes, the lakes and ponds of the Yvelines, the huge wheatlands of the Brie with their gigantic perspectives lovingly cared for, the naked country of the Parisis and the Pays de France, an invitation to barbarians and invaders and a contradiction in terminology (no *doulce France* here in this flat and threatening plain), the high plateau of the Vexin Français, crossed by the old *route haute* from Paris to Rouen, and running down towards the Seine, in a series of sheltered valleys and winding dusty roads, the peculiar rock formations and grottoes of the Forest of Fontainebleau, the *désert de sable* of Ermenonville, the secret villages of the Mantois, the bracken and heather of Saint-Nom-la-Brétêche, on the edge of the forest of Marly, and the shady villages of the valley of the Oise.

It is an area of streams and small rivers: the two Morin, the Ourcq, the Aubette, the Yvette, the reedy Loing, the Orge, the Bièvre, the Rémarde, the Essonne, the Troesne, the Beuvronne, the Yerre, the Avon, the Yvron, the Lunain, the Mauldre, the wonderfully peaceful Epte, once a sanguinary frontier dividing France from Normandy, its churches and castles flaming in the night: mostly gentle, feminine names, as inviting as they would imply, and, two hundred years ago, covered in watermills and busy with the transport of wood and wine. Only due south, towards the grim Beauce (*la steppe beauceronne* as Max Jacob called it) is the country waterless and totally forbidding. The rivers – the Seine, the Oise, the Aisne – and streams give to the Ile-de-France a variety of gentle contours that shelter clustered villages around their churches, the towers of which so often mark out from a great distance the welcoming presence of water. The open and rather alarming Brie is bordered by the sheltered valleys of the Ourcq, the Valois rolls on the periphery of the flat Pays de Gonesse and the Goële; and the naked Brie itself secretes comfortable and enclosed little market towns like Brie-Comte-Robert and Rozay.

The greatest wealth of the Ile-de-France resides in its wonderfully varied countryside, in its avenues of poplars, in its orchards and forests, its gentle hills and its largely unspoilt villages and, above all, in an abundance of country churches, unassuming, and in a mixture of styles: a few Romanesque, but most of the twelfth and thirteenth centuries, a great many of them largely rebuilt in the second half of the fifteenth century, after having been burnt and sacked by the English, especially in the Brie, the Valois, and the valley of the Epte, resulting in a concentration of Flamboyant, and, in the Montmorency family country north of Paris, Renaissance.

Canon Dunlop has provided above all an excellent guide to rural churches: Richebourg, near Houdan, Saint-Sulpice-de-Favières and Villeconin, in the Hurepoix; Voulton, Rampillon, Saint-Loup-de-Naud, Donnemarie-en-Montois, in the Brie, near Provins; Champeaux, La Chapelle-sous-Crécy, Autheuil-en-Valois (a Romanesque church used as a barn); La Ferté-Milon, Crépy-en-Valois (the ruined Saint-Thomas, dedicated to Thomas-à-Becket, and still bearing on its outer wall a revolutionary inscription of 1794 dimly denying, in fading black letters, the immortality of the soul); Pontpoint, Othis, Luzarches, Le Mesnil-Aubry, Groslay, on the very edge of Paris, and Taverny.

There are Notre-Dame-des Ardents of Lagny, Saint-Maclou, of Pontoise, the fine church at Gisors, the lovely Sainte-Anne-de-Gassicourt, a jewel in a factory suburb of Mantes (no longer la-Jolie). The coverage is so good that one is surprised at the omission of the splendid churches of Etampes, the first stop on the way to Compostela, of the exquisite Saint-Ouen-l'Aumône, just outside Pontoise, and of the little church of Auvers, a tortured painting, torrid, as if moving in the waves of heat, by van Gogh, who is buried in the churchyard. One would have liked too some mention of the churches of the villages of Paris: Charonne, Montreuil, Vanves, Ivry, Choisy, Chaillot.

For those – and they do not include myself – whose taste is for royal châteaux and hunting lodges – Renaissance and Louis XIV – Canon Dunlop is a guide as enthusiastic as he is learned. Even the tiniest and most ruined *gentilhommière* is included and we are taken room by room through all the big *pièces montées*. I do not share his enthusiasm for Versailles (where I preceded him by two years as *assistant* at Hoche), which I think is the saddest town in Western Europe, and the long Boulevard de la Reine, the most hopeless street in France. The Parc, he considers, is best seen in October; I think it is even better in the utter stillness of February, when the long avenues dissolve in mist and the frozen silence is only broken by the distant sound of the woodcutters' axe. But even at the height of summer there are little unexpected principalities of quiet in the valleys of the Epte and the Troesne, the Ourcq and the Rémarde; even in August, one can walk for hours in the Forest of Dourdan or in the woods round Etréchy without meeting anyone on a weekday, and especially on a Tuesday.

This guide is a labour of love. It is a key that will open many tiny, hidden, forsaken places, a ruined keep in a farmyard, the remains of an arch in a field, an escutcheon, forlorn and heralding nothing but desolation and an old Revolution, a marine monster in flaking stone, lost in enveloping greenery, strange props for *Orphée*, a triumphal entrance leading to emptiness, a stone stag in an autumnal forest that has heard the French horn for two hundred years: and the infinite sadness of the Petit Trianon, which, as the author says, is the most beautiful building in Europe.

5 May 1979 (abridged)

Poland
Tim Garton Ash

Soviet tanks advanced through the streets of Cracow last month. No fighting broke out. The Poles greeted the Red Army with amused curiosity, not Molotov cocktails. The only shooting was done by cameramen. The tanks rolled in a replay of the Soviet 'liberation' of Poland at the end of the Second World War, which Karol Wojtyla, now better known as Pope John Paul II, lived through in the beautiful city whose Archbishop he later became.

The co-operation of Party and State authorities in making a feature film about the Pope's life is just one example of Poland's new front of national unity against the threat of a second 'liberation'. The three greatest forces in the Polish nation today are the Catholic Church, with the loyalty of some thirty million souls, the 'Solidarity' organisation of independent trade unions, with the support of over ten million workers, and the Communist Polish United Workers' Party, with a dwindling membership now probably around the three million mark, one million of whom are also in Solidarity. The question is: how can these three work together?

In one sense, the party-church relationship is the easiest because both, in contrast to Solidarity, are highly centralised, authoritarian organisations. The Episcopate works out a 'line' in private consultations about which we learn as little as about the discussions in the Politburo. Its representatives are then obliged broadly to adhere to it, at least in public. Since the two-day meeting of the Episcopate in early December, the Church has spoken out more clearly than ever before in the interest of the government. Now the Church has traditionally regarded itself as the guardian of national sovereignty since the days when the Primate governed as interrex. Cardinal Wyszinski is clearly convinced of the present danger to that sovereignty. He appeals for order and responsibility, as he did in the crises of 1956 and 1970-71. An official spokesman of the Episcopate has gone even further by publicly criticising two opposition groups, the right-wing Nationalist Confederation for an Independent Poland (KPN) and, more important, the Social Self-Defence Committee (KOR). 'We live in a concrete system and a concrete geopolitical situation', he said. 'Everybody must accept it and get on with it.'

Here he was not really speaking for the whole Church but for one faction within it. The labyrinthine internal history of Polish Catholicism since 1945 has revolved around the difference between 'accepting' and 'getting on with' the communist system. Inauspiciously, the story of Catholic collaboration with the communist government was started by a fascist. Facing death in a Soviet prison cell, the leader of the pre-war Polish Falanga, Boleslav Piasecki, made a personal pact with the devil in the guise of General Serov, subsequently head of the KGB. Piasecki returned to Warsaw a free man in the summer of 1945 and set about organising a Catholic lay organisation, 'Pax', which he led with considerable skill until his death in 1978. Piasecki and his colleagues accepted seats in the Polish Parliament (the Sejm). By and large, they had responsibility without power – the fate of the collaborator through the ages.

In the wake of the 'Polish October' in 1956, a more independent group of Catholic deputies emerged, sharing the name 'Znak' with a broad grouping of Catholic intellectuals. But in 1976 Znak was split. After some manoeuvring behind the scenes by the Politburo member responsible for the Church, one Stanislaw Kania, more amenable lay Catholics were hoisted into the parliamentary seats of Znak where they compliantly voted for the much-disputed revised constitution. It is a member of this splinter group (sometimes known as 'Neo-Znak'), Jerzy Ozdowski, who last November was appointed by his old party patron to be the first Catholic deputy prime minister in the history of the Soviet bloc. As such, he is a symbol of Kania's attempt to build a government of national unity: as also is the new prominence given to state as opposed to party authorities (this year, for the first time, the Head of State, not the Party leader, delivered the New Year address to the nation), and the recent changes in the leadership of the umbrella organisation of parliamentary parties – aptly enough called the Front for National Unity.

Yet there are many Catholics who feel that the Church has gone too far in its 'acceptance' of the system. The Episcopate, they say, is supping with the devil, and there is a shortage of long spoons. The Church has traded its moral authority for material concessions: permission to build new seminaries in Koszalin and Szczencin, for example. Moreover, some of the more powerful bishops are not averse to playing a direct part in politics, and are decidedly averse to the kind of politics represented by opposition leaders like the Democratic Socialist, Jacek Kuron.

Nonetheless, the fact is that over the last ten years the weight of the Church has been thrown more often behind the opposition than against it. Far from 'accepting' the system, Cardinal Wyszinski has at times attacked its most sacred symbol. In 1978, for instance, he advocated 'simply pensioning off all the censors'. Even at the height of its euphoria, Solidarity did not go so far as this. It was mindful of the consequences of the total abolition of censorship in Czechoslovakia in 1968. The Episcopate came out strongly against including the 'leading role of the Party' in the 1976 revision of the constitution. The Church has consistently supported the 'flying university', from whose ranks Solidarity's most influential Catholic 'experts' came.

Thus there is a sense in which the Church itself has sown the wind, and is now endeavouring to forestall the whirlwind. Of no one is this more true than of the man whom Lech Walesa calls the 'greatest of Poles'. As Archbishop of Cracow, Karol Wojtyla opened his churches to the opposition after the mysterious death of the student Stanislaw Pyjas in 1977. As Pope, he unmistakably, if discreetly, distanced himself from the 'Neo-Znak' and Pax collaborationists during his visit in summer 1979. Yet last November he received Jerzy Ozdowski in private audience at the Vatican one week before the announcement of his appointment as deputy prime minister. At Christmas the Pope could be seen and heard on the state-controlled media extending his greetings to 'everyone in Poland without exception' and using the Communist Party's own current catchword *odnowa*, 'renewal'. This is as near to a blessing as Mr Kania could possibly hope for.

More directly, the Church has over the last month visibly re-established its authority within Solidarity. One must recall that when Cardinal Wyszinski preached his first cautionary sermon during the occupation of the Lenin shipyard last August, the workers not only ignored his warning but hung out a placard with the memorable text 'The Madonna is on strike'. Four months later at the restrained and moving ceremony to inaugurate the monument to workers killed in the 1970 riots, Lech Walesa himself preached a sermon more cautionary than any the Primate had delivered: more Catholic than the Pope's. In fact, the text was largely written by his parish priest. The union's promised weekly paper will have a moderate Catholic intellectual as its first editor.

It remains to be seen whether Walesa and his ecclesiastical counsellors will be able to hold in check the more radical members of Solidarity's national leadership. The latter look to KOR, not to the Episcopate, for their advice; they consider it vital to sustain the pressure on the regime, which means further strike threats; and they are deeply sceptical about collaboration with the party at any level. One Central Committee member had drily remarked that the struggle for Solidarity is now between Christians and Social Democrats: the Communist Party can only watch and pray. Ironically, they must be praying that the Catholics win out.

In the short term this could improve the chances of establishing the farmers' Solidarity without the kind of cliff-hanging which accompanied the national union's registration in November. It would be wrong to underestimate the militancy or politicisation of Poland's peasant farmers. In 1937 the country saw a phenomenon which must be almost unique in European history: a peasants' political strike. Yet nowhere is the Church so powerful as in the countryside. Most Polish villages are like Clochemerle, but a Clochemerle in which the communist mayor has lost all credibility. It is surely in the power of the clergy to persuade their peasant parishioners of the fateful consequences of any serious interruption in food supplies to the cities (and private farms account for some eighty per cent of domestic food production).

Undoubtedly the Solidarity-Party relationship is the most problematic part of the new political triangle. One view of the nature of this problem was given by Professor Mario Nuti in a recent article in the *New Statesman* (published with a title which must have strayed from the competition pages: 'Poland and the dangers of Scandinavian Socialism.' Readers are invited to invent more improbable combinations . . . 'New Zealand and the threat of Islamic revival', 'Kampuchea and the pitfalls of Monetarism' . . .) 'The Government', writes Professor Nuti, 'has now revealed to the public the full extent of current economic problems,' whereas 'the new political force [i.e. Solidarity] has displayed a worrying poverty of ideas.' He writes as if the Communist Party had begun to tell the truth of its own free will, from the goodness of its heart; as if the demand for full and truthful information about the country's economic position had not been one of the unions' 'ideas' all along. Nuti continues: 'The Party and Government bodies are discussing a reform of economic planning and institutions for introduction after the normalisation of economic and political life, presumably in a few years. Solidarity has nothing to say about it, except that its expert advisers will criticise government proposals when they are made public.' A good word, 'normalisation'.

The fact is that the unions have every reason to be cautious about becoming directly involved in government decision-making. The changes in the Party leadership may be worrying for Moscow, which sees its few remaining trusties like the old hard-liner Werblan being eased out of power. That does not mean that they are reassuring for Solidarity. 'Normalisation' on the lips of men like Stefan Olszowski, not to speak of General Moczar, means a return to Leninist norms (which, incidentally, precluded full information for the general public). The Party has yet to show what is new in 'renewal'. Thus far concessions have had to be wrung out of the leadership at every turn. The Politburo has not acted; it had reacted. Moreover, as the Warsaw Solidarity leader Zbigniew Bujak, pointed out to me in October, the pictures of Walesa driving around in a government car and spending his time in Party luncheon rooms were deeply offensive to his members. Indeed it was the risk that the union leadership would be compromised and finally held responsible by its members for their economic misery that he singled out as the greatest single danger to Solidarity over the next few months.

The union leaders point out that it is not their business to run the economy. Only in view of the present catastrophic state of affairs are they prepared to co-operate with the government on a temporary basis. There is a real danger of a simple breakdown of the basic economy, leading to the kind of elementary chaos and hunger which prevailed in Russia in 1917, with each peasant for himself and the devil take the cities. That is something which the Soviet Union could not tolerate. But a danger which is, if anything, even more immediate is the collapse of the Communist Party. At the moment the Party is burning from the bottom upwards, like a haystack. More than half a million members have turned in their cards. Another million or more have joined Solidarity. To be sure, in the last few weeks the Party has actually instructed them to: on the principle of the Trojan Horse. The trouble with this Trojan Horse is that Greeks tend to become Trojans the moment they get inside the city walls; they become Solidarity supporters first and Party members only a poor second. Meanwhile, the party apparatus or *nomenklatura* – perhaps 200,000 people appointed by the Party to key positions of the State – is in disarray. The majority dig in their heels against any reform, fearing for their privileges. A minority try to run ahead of the tide, becoming daring reformers overnight, demanding horizontal co-ordination, regular re-election of officials, and other appalling departures from the Leninist canon.

We now have the extraordinary spectacle of the Catholic Church hurrying to keep the Party from falling completely apart. At one point even Jacek Kuron, for fifteen years its arch-opponent, dispatched emissaries to Warsaw factories to persuade their Party committees not, please, to upset the Party any more with schemes of democratic reform from below. Kuron and Wyszinski agree on this, if on little else; the facade of Party unity must be preserved at all costs, like Humpty Dumpty on his wall, pointing towards Moscow. We do not know whether Moscow can be satisfied with a Party façade built into a front of national unity. But an intervention would surely precipitate its final collapse, not shore it up. And then, could all Brezhnev's tanks and all Brezhnev's men pick up the pieces again?

This is just one indication of the kind of explosion that intervention could cause. Workers at the large oil refinery just outside Gdansk, a Solidarity stronghold, have resolved to blow up the whole complex if Soviet tanks appear in the streets. Unlike the Polish army, they don't need weapons or ammunition, only a match or two. They have asked their priest to administer the last sacrament.

10 January 1981

Lebanon's invasion
Christopher Hitchens

Abu Jihad is an Arab name meaning 'father of Jihad'. Jihad means 'holy war'. As a choice of *nom de guerre*, then, it suggests a very serious fellow. And Khalil al Wazir, the man who affects it, is indeed Deputy Commander of Al Fatah. I spent an evening in his flat in Beirut last week (in an area of the town since pounded to rubble) discussing the chances of an Israeli invasion. I suspect him of rather liking the impression he produces on visitors. He receives them in the bosom of his very large and happy family. Jihad himself, the eldest son, turns out to be a polite, plumpish and cheerful youth, with a serious interest in politics. Much time is spent in recounting the sorrows of the clan – the exile from Ramleh in 1948, the wretched years in the Gaza Strip, the indignities visited upon relatives, the second exile and the gradual burgeoning of the Palestinian revolution. Tea is brought, hands are pressed, cheeks are pinched. Presiding over all is the jovial paterfamilias, as if to say, 'What, me a terrorist?'

Yet, when the talk turns to the impending attack, the atmosphere alters. I mention the extreme vulnerability of the Palestinian forces in the south. 'Look,' he says, 'I remember when the Israelis invaded in 1978. General Mordechai Gur was publicly criticised in Israel for not being harder and tougher and for not seizing Tyre and Sidon. He replied that he didn't want to risk his men against fighters who *wanted* to die. So maybe they will kill all our forces there – but we will be back again. See for yourself . . .'

Miles to the south, in Sidon, I carried a dog-eared Hachette guide to Lebanon, published in the early Fifties. Describing the town, the battered volume had this to say: 'Like most of the ancient Phoenician cities, it is built on a promontory faced by an island. It is surrounded by pleasant gardens where oranges, lemons, bananas, medlars, apricots and almonds are successfully grown. It has some 40,000 inhabitants including 15,000 Palestinian refugees.'

Three decades later, that laconic charming description would need a few amendments. The lush crops rot on the ground because thousands of cultivators long ago fled from Israeli bombardment to live, in doubtful security, in the filthy bidonvilles of Beirut. The old buildings and streets are charred and furrowed with the evidence of previous raids. For the surviving inhabitants, Phantoms and Mirages long ago became reality.

The Palestinians who remain there, not just from the 1948 exodus but from many subsequent ones, were as insouciant about the prospect of an invasion as their deputy commander. The only sign of nervousness was a blank refusal to permit a visit to Beaufort Castle, off-limits to the press since 1978. In the event, this shrug at the inevitable has proven militarily deceptive. The Israelis in 1978 were satisfied with driving the PLO forces northward – with forcing them to fold their tents and flee. This time, they have tried to encircle and destroy as many trained Palestinians as possible. Mr Begin may claim that the objective is to create a twenty-five-mile strip between his northern border and the Palestinian positions in order to protect the Galilee. But it's more revealing to attend to General Sharon, who has been saying in public for weeks that the objective must be the physical destruction of the guerrillas and their infrastructure. By this means, he hopes to buy five years of peace and perhaps to drive the Palestinians into their designated Trans-Jordanian 'home'.

So much is becoming clear from the hourly and daily bulletins. But travel a little further south from Sidon and Tyre, and you come to the border of Major Haddad's mini-state: a strip six miles wide garrisoned by a rough militia and armed and victualled by Israel. Here can be seen one of the outlines of the merging partition of Lebanon. Paradoxical as it may appear, there is now a tacit agreement between Israel and Syria on spheres of influence. Ever since Mr Joseph Sisco's 1978 shuttle from Damascus to Jerusalem, it has been understood that Syria holds eastern Lebanon and the vital Bekaa Valley (historic route of invasion thrusts towards Damascus) while Israel controls the southern zone and exercises the right to blitz the Palestinians without Syrian reprisal. There are advantages to both sides in this makeshift, unspoken deal. The principal advantage is that it neutralises and quarantines the PLO – neutralises it militarily from the point of view of Israel, and quarantines it politically from the point of view of Syria. Neither party wishes to see a really independent Palestinian state, though Syria is hampered by having to pretend that it does. This explains the refusal (rather than the reluctance) of Syrian forces to engage Israel during the crucial first few days, even in Beirut airspace. There may be, for the sake of honour, some slight breaking of lances. But the keystone state in the 'Arab front of steadfastness and confrontation' will be sitting this one out.

Numerous considerations, however, make the arrangement precarious. American annoyance at Israel's unilateral annexation of the Golan Heights stemmed from a fear that it would destabilise the unwritten accord by touching Syrian territory. Abu Jihad said rather sarcastically that many Arab countries want to 'protect' the Palestinians – to monopolise and manipulate them. And currently the Syrians are feeling rather frisky because of the humiliation of their Iraqi foes by the Iranians. They make take revenge on American policy in some more indirect way as a salve to Arab pride. Mr Philip Habib, who must fill the shoes of Mr Sisco, represent Mr Reagan, conciliate the Israelis and appease the Arab League, will find his brow getting dewy before he wings gratefully home. The Fahd plan for a Palestinian mini-state, so named after Crown Prince Fahd of Saudi Arabia, was still somewhere near the table a few weeks ago and commanded a certain amount of State Department support. It must be reckoned among the terminal casualties of the Israeli invasion.

Two areas of Lebanon remain outside the 'spheres of influence' compromise. Beirut may be full of Syrian soldiery directing traffic and manning road-blocks, but it is otherwise still the Hobbesian city of the war of all against all. During my stay, the nights were being made late by the gun battle between supporters of Iran and partisans of Iraq. They hardly broke off when Israeli sonic booms rattled the windows. On any other night, it might be any other group. The city has become a free port for every kind of militia and faction. The French Embassy was blown up and nobody knew who to blame because there were so many obvious candidates. A secretary at the British Embassy was raped and told to deliver a warning to the Embassy and speculation was only slightly more concentrated. In a few months a general election is due and a selection by the subsequent parliament of a new president. A poll taken by the excellent Beirut magazine *Monday Morning* found that there were only ninety-two surviving MPs out of the proper complement of ninety-nine. Of those interviewed, only five were imprudent enough to state the name of the presidential candidate they were backing.

The other region of Lebanon which escapes inclusion in the Syrian-Israeli accord is the Christian belt north of Beirut, which has its own access to the sea and its own relative autonomy. The Christians both need partition and reject it. They ruled the country for so long that they cannot ever fully acknowledge the end of their own dominion. But mastery in a kind of Crusader ghetto may be the best they can now achieve. To get to their capital of Jounieh, you have to cross the appalling central belt of Beirut, where for street after street and block after block everything is scorched and desolate. This was the business and banking quarter – Beirut is one of the few cities where a civil war has been fought in the opulent areas rather than in the suburbs and shanty towns.

When you reach Jounieh, you can see where the banks and the businesses have gone. The place is full of semi-chic and pseudo-French effects, with new building and investment in evidence everywhere. The militia of the Phalange Party are always on view, much better groomed than their Syrian or Palestinian counterparts. The craggy face of Pierre Gemayal, the old Fascist leader who has now ceded power to his two sons, glares from large hoardings like some forgotten patriot of the Fourth Republic. In every palpable way, you have entered another country. Here, sympathy for Israel is widespread, but it's unlikely to take, as it once did, the shape of a formal military alliance. As long as the Christians stay well out of regional politics, the Syrians are inclined to leave them alone. Christian spokesmen say privately that the Americans have told them this is a smart policy.

So Lebanon will continue to exist on the map, and Beirut will continue to be a *place d'armes* for every quarrel in the region. But gradually greater Syria is living up to its dream of recovering lost territory, and greater Israel is asserting its sovereignty too. In between are the Palestinians, now loved by almost nobody. I would very much like to know who shot Ambassador Argov. Usually, these things turn out to have been done by the Al Fatah renegade Abu Nidal, who used to operate from Baghdad in his campaign against the 'sell-out' leadership of Yasser Arafat. He has now moved his headquarters to Damascus in the course of the Byzantine feud between the two capitals. You can start to believe anything after a week or two in Beirut, so I will say no more except that I hope Mr Argov will recover and will consider himself properly avenged.

12 June 1982

Mr Mugabe's forthcoming victory
Xan Smiley

Salisbury

The ban on reading Sithole's obscurer scribblings was lifted just last week – nearly two years after his 'internal settlement' with Ian Smith and Bishop Muzorewa, and four years after the white chief's 'not in a thousand years' prophesy. Television advertisements still invite young men to Join the Army (they don't say whose), with encouraging group pictures of eager volunteer striplings – three white to one black. Fresh recruits (also predominantly white) are still being conscripted for military service. Yet there are at least 20,000 professed guerrillas, now also lawful citizens, inside the country, the recipients of hundreds of British footballs to keep them quiet.

Whose country (apart from 'God's own', as Rhodesian whites once called it) are we now in? The television newsreader reports that, by Governor's order, the place must revert to Rhodesia until independence brings plain Zimbabwe (*reculer pour mieux sauter*, presumably), but the same announcer promptly and firmly signs off: 'This is Zimbabwe Rhodesian Broadcasting'. There's no longer a *'Rhodesian'* before the *'Herald'*, but the leading letter to the approving editor proclaims that Rhodesians (i.e. whites) have been fighting 'seven years for democracy'. Few of Smith's tribesmen have ever questioned the justice of the old cause or understand why, if it is still just twitching, it is nigh dead. It must seem bad enough to be monitored by the Commonwealth concoction – Fijians who are even taller and blacker than the 'Mau Mau ters', the Kenyans; the occasional Maori or black cockney guardsman adds extra confusion; the Kiwis and Aussies look uncannily Rhodesian; and 'the poms', popularly depicted as indisputably music-hall British, who have discovered to mild surprise that some of these guerrillas with impossible party nicknames (Zanu, Zapu, Harpo, Groucho) seem 'very reasonable chaps'.

But in a land of oddities, by far the oddest feeling is that there is no longer a war. Hardly less strange, however, is the flavour of the peace. Nobody is quite sure if the cherub-cheeked umpire, Soames, has blown the final whistle or whether, with the umpire likely to be assaulted by rather more than twenty-two ungentlemanly players, there will be another year of extra time for the final battle – after the election kick-about.

Yet the frailty of the peace barely lessens the delight of it. The killing is down from the sixty that were perishing each day as recently as three months ago, to isolated cases. For whites, the smell of near-defeat that has crept up on them, their possible humiliation after independence and renewed black factional bloodshed – all have created an air of suspended belief, mixed, to be sure, with almighty relief and gratitude for survival this far. Is continued war better than Mugabe? Few whites like to ponder that one, but even Smith's hardest core are beginning to wonder. The prospect of peace in a country almost destroyed and utterly degraded by war, but which remains blessed with natural resources, a smiling climate, scenic beauty and a majority of inhabitants who detest violence, brings joy to the rockiest heart.

Furthermore, the momentum of peace is increasing – thanks largely to the excellent performance of the monitors (mostly British), who have been sensitive, courageous and restrained, and are backed by a Governor who is treading warily but weightily, knowing that each liberty accorded to one side inevitably provokes suspicion and anguish from another.

The guerrillas, now corralled into only fourteen assembly camps, are understandably nervous that they may prove irresistibly nice targets for an enemy. Hence their initial reluctance to 'come onsides'. But confidence has been gradually won, and Soames has thought it worth risking guerrilla displeasure by occasionally using Smith's old security forces to enforce the law. But the guerrilla leaders in Salisbury have appeared keenly co-operative, ferociously threatening to shoot those of their comrades who refuse to come into the peace camps.

Yet the possibility of just a handful of incidents constantly menaces the peace, and could destroy it in a matter of days. Assassination of the leaders is the most immediate worry. Relations of the victims of the Viscount air-crash have sworn revenge against Nkomo, and Mugabe is likewise Satan in the eyes of many embittered whites. There is no shortage of people, whatever their race, who are chewed up with hatred.

By the guerrilla leaders' own estimation, there are also probably over 2000 guerrillas, now termed bandits, who are refusing to stop fighting. A white backlash could easily be whipped up. A load of bombs dropped from a private plane onto a guerrilla assembly point could instantly destroy the peace. Many of the bishop's auxiliaries are out of control. South African troops have brazenly infiltrated the Rhodesian army and at least one mainly white show of military muscle (in the small town of Karoi) flagrantly violated the Lancaster House agreement. To try to rule the guerrilla parties out of the election, Rhodesians are insisting that many of the professed guerrillas now in the camps are really *Mujibhas* (the 'eyes and ears' of the guerrillas, their young messengers and porters) who have been handed guns, leaving the 'heavies' to roam the country, electioneering. Most on-the-spot observers reckon, however, that only five per cent of these supposed guerrillas lack authenticity.

It is true that political bully-boys of all types are already at work. People in Salisbury's black townships are increasingly prey to the blandishments of party gangsters. But the real slaughter has miraculously subsided, and the odds are that Soames will steer the country through to a messy election. If the idea of freedom and secrecy once *inside* the polling booth can be instilled in the voting millions, the genuine popular verdict will – despite the intimidation – be clear enough.

For whom will they plump? The whites are praying for the bishop, though Smith is confusing his own party by arguing in favour of a deal with Nkomo, at the expense of the bishop whom the white leader cordially detests. Most whites foolishly assume the bishop will win the most seats. The older blacks, the churchier ones, the women, the more sophisticated wage-earners, and many of those beholden to white bosses, are all said to be likely bishop supporters. The white cry of 'look what happened next door in Zambia and Mozambique' (i.e. economic disaster) will equally, it is said, steal votes away from the radical Mugabe, whose Marxism and fractious guerrillas' in-fighting will allegedly frighten people away. In addition, the bishop's organisation is well-financed and efficient, while Mugabe's badly lacks orchestration.

Mugabe's shortcomings are real, but I doubt they will deter the mass of Shona-speaking voters, who comprise seventy-five per cent of the electorate. The guerrillas are widely and correctly credited with having forced the white surrender. If the tough nuts are supported, the war will stop – so runs the simple but sound logic of the rural villager. And almost every black tells you that the bishop promised peace, which only Mugabe's 'boys' can now bring. The caveats against Marxism and the guerrilla propensity for violent internal intrigue mean little to the many blacks who have no wealth to lose and never enjoyed much freedom. To visit guerrillas in the assembly camps in the tribal trust lands, long since ravaged by the war and abandoned by the white economy, is to visit another planet, where Western 'bourgeois' values and the blessing of 'white efficiency' are irrelevant.

At present, a massive wave of pro-guerrilla enthusiasm is sweeping the country – the towns as well as the villages in the bush. 'Africans are great joiners', say sage white farmers. After the euphoria has died down, Mugabe's wilder men and wilder statements of the past, plus the bishop's dogged sobriety and organisation may – in a month – begin to stem the guerrillas' electoral tide. The next six weeks will be crucial. Mugabe is bound to undergo a sudden conversion to 'moderation' on his return. The white community will be inundated with compliments and assurances. I suspect he will retain the best chance of an election victory, perhaps even large enough to give him and Nkomo's Zapu an outright combined majority. If that occurred, Britain's last-ditch ploy would be to woo Nkomo for the umpteenth time into an alliance of non-Marxists. Many tortuous combinations will be mooted in order to keep Mugabe out. But it is also distinctly possible that Mrs Thatcher may find herself swallowing the bitter pill of granting power to a Marxist.

Many whites say that there will be a mass exodus. Much, therefore, will depend on Mugabe's performance in the coming month. It will be remarkable if he can convince enough whites to remain, in order to hold the economy and security of the country together during the next year, if he wins. But weird things do happen.

12 January 1980

5   The Falklands

Nicholas Ridley
Alexander Chancellor

'For he might have been a Roosian, a French or Turk or Proosian, or perhaps Ital-ian!' But in fact Mr Nicholas Ridley, Minister of State at the Foreign Office, is – greatly to his credit – an Englishman. He happens to be one, just as Miss Clare Francis Wilson, the young woman who was tortured by Chilean intelligence agents, 'happens' to be English. This was how Mr Ridley described her on the wireless the other day, and one wonders what he meant. It is difficult not to place this remark in the context of right-wing talk which seeks to convince people that Miss Wilson is, to all intents and purposes, foreign, that she can barely speak our language, and that she is therefore generally undeserving. Much emphasis is also placed on the fact that her lover, Mr Bernado, is some kind of terrorist, as if her choice of lover were not entirely her own business. Things used to be different. Do you remember Don Pacifico? He was a Portuguese Jew, but because he was born in Gibraltar, was a British citizen. He just happened to be one. He was, however, extremely Portuguese. He was first of all Portuguese consul in Morocco, and then Portuguese consul-general in Greece, until he was sacked for misconduct in 1842. He stayed on in Athens as a merchant, and in 1847 his house was burnt down by a mob. The mob was in a state of excitement because, out of deference to Baron Rothschild, who happened to be in Athens at the time (are the Rothschilds ever out of the news?), it had been forbidden to carry out its annual Easter practice of burning an effigy of Judas Iscariot. Don Pacifico's house was nearby, so it burnt that instead. Because the Greek government was dilatory about paying compensation, Lord Palmerston sent the British fleet to Piraeus and had all the Greek ships there seized. Eventually Don Pacifico received compensation, came to settle in London, and –

feeling rather foreign to the last – was buried in the Spanish cemetery at Mile End. But possession of a British passport used not only to entitle one to this sort of protection. It also carried obligations. One was expected to show allegiance to the Crown. William Joyce ('Lord Haw-Haw') was an American by birth who, before the war, had obtained a British passport under false pretences, but then settled in Germany and acquired German citizenship. Unfortunately for him, his British passport, however illegally obtained, did not expire until 1940, which permitted the House of Lords to have him executed for treason. If Miss Wilson is by any chance a traitor to this country, let her hang; if not, Mr Ridley should stand up for her.

20 September 1980

Naval cuts
Ferdinand Mount

How the Royal Navy ever came to be known as the Silent Service is a mystery. All military lobbies are garrulous, but you can't beat an ululation of admirals for the detail and ferocity of their complaints. The newspapers have been swamped with leaks. Mrs Thatcher, it is claimed, plans nothing less than to destroy the Royal Navy. Her Mr Nott has been got at by the wrong people in the Defence Department. He is new. He does not understand the complexities of high strategy. Why should it be only the navy which has to suffer the cuts to make room for the £600 million-a-year Trident programme?

Because Trident is to be launched from submarines, the non-combatant might think. Shows how little non-combatant knows. Trident is the spearhead of our entire defence effort, and its cost should be shared between the three services.

Curious, is it not, how cuts are always said to be tri-service matters, while any new project is a question of 'fulfilling an essential role which only the Royal Navy can play'? From this, as from all previous defence rows, it soon emerges that the notion of a unified

Department of Defence is as much a polite fiction as ever.

All defence rows have an odd language of their own. These roles, for example. Now in popular psychology, 'role-play' is the term used to jeer at the way people behave in public, pretending to be things which really, in some mysterious inner core of self, they aren't. In defence jargon, though, role-play is all. These days, each service is no more than the sum of its roles. And there is a giddy-making arbitrariness about which roles you pick and which you discard. Take East of Suez. At one moment, essential, Britain's frontier on the Himalayas; the next, outdated imperial play-acting.

Now the role of monarch of the seas, capable of showing the flag in every port, is deemed to be a frivolous luxury; frigates and destroyers are little better than floating gin-palaces for tanning the knees of officers leaning over taffrails (do I mean taffrails?). Admiral of the Fleet Sir Edward Ashmore, a recently retired Chief of the Defence Staff, argues that, although defence of sea and air communications and general air defence are 'two bottomless pits for expenditure', we must 'concentrate on that for which by temperament, experience and geography we of all Europe have become uniquely capable, the maritime effort'. Well, he would, wouldn't he?

Sir Edward also subscribes to the fashionable view that the British Army of the Rhine no longer scares Russians because there are so many more of them than there are of us – or, well, anyway, look at the French who don't even commit their troops to NATO, both of which seem funny reasons for withdrawing a division of your own troops. If outnumbered, does one immediately take steps to be further outnumbered? Another view is that Trident is a dreadful mistake and we should have ordered our own Cruise missiles to be launched from B-52 bombers. Or both Cruise and Trident are dreadful mistakes, because we can't afford them and because they don't frighten the Russians either.

The non-combatant (NC for short) has the distinct impression that while all parties have decided preferences, the arguments they use to support these preferences tend to be less than dazzling. Besides, NC muses, has not defence been 'pared to the bone' half a dozen times already? How come there is so much left of it?

In manpower, the three services are still roughly at the levels planned by Duncan Sandys back in 1957 – 332,000 today with a greatly enlarged support army of civilians, as against an intended 375,000. Unfortunately, the bill for modern weapons and for satisfied servicemen has continued to rise at a far greater pace than the ability of the poor old economy to pay for it. It is a question of constantly running backwards to stay in the same place.

Every Tory government since the war has come to power promising to strengthen our defences, and every Tory government has in practice been forced to make cuts. Even Churchill slowed down the rearmament programme which Attlee had bequeathed.

Historically, the Tory Party has not been noted for its enthusiasm for rearmament, which means higher taxes. Labour governments, by contrast, like Democratic Administrations in the US, having no bias against soaking the taxpayer, often turn out to be surprisingly warlike and are often ready to furnish the means.

But all agree that there are no votes in defence. It is not a subject of much popular interest. Even the feared stalwarts of the backbench Conservative defence committee are something of a stage army, and a not entirely united one. While they may share a general view that money spent on defence is well spent, they have their individual quirks. Mr Julian Critchley believes that Britain cannot afford an independent nuclear deterrent. Mr Alan Clark has a complicated admiration for Russia. Mr Winston Churchill is a somewhat unreliable light tank gun, merrily swivelling, firing in all directions, occasionally jamming.

Mr Keith Speed may have done himself some good in this somewhat motley fo'c'sle by getting himself sacked as Navy Minister. But in the ward room the view is such a case tends to be that we could all make this sort of flashy gesture but it really doesn't do. The feeling is less 'we need more chaps like him' and more 'we therefore commit to the deep the body of our dear brother Keith here departed'.

Mr Speed delivered a decent resignation speech to the Commons, but his crispness melted a bit during his rhapsody on the roles which would no longer be filled if the frigates were scrapped . . . patrolling in Belize roads . . . keeping a high profile in Hong Kong . . . it all seemed hardly worth £130 million per frigate, or even £50 million if we built the cheaper sort Mr Speed himself had been working on.

Mr Nott clearly outgunned him. Did we really need three different ways of destroying enemy submarines? Tory backbenchers did not have to believe everything they read in the *Daily Telegraph* – neatly ignoring the other papers which were full of much the same stuff. Anyway defence spending has been increasing in real terms at three per cent a year, as promised at the election, and will go on increasing. We ought to talk of changes in capability, not of cuts in expenditure. Mr Nott is coming on nicely at the three-card trick.

The row will no doubt be settled in the usual unsatisfactory compromise as the summer wears on. The admirals will lose a few ships and a few men, but not as many as they presently fear. But what has, I think, not quite come out so far is the *political* advantage which Mrs Thatcher, intentionally or unintentionally, gains in other fields by any concessions she and Mr Nott may make on defence. She will be able to say: look, we have saved jobs in the shipyards and in the navy itself by going to the absolute limit of what the country can afford to spend on defence. But that does leave us correspondingly short of money to spend on the Channel Tunnel and on electrifying the railways.

The advantage of attacking on all fronts at once on public expenditure is that every concession which is forced out of you is a handy argument for saving money somewhere else. Mrs Thatcher's initial – and nearly fatal – error was to come to power with such a huge privileged area of government activity explicitly exempt from

'Of course, Jack didn't know that giants were an endangered species.'

the sweep of her axe: defence, law-and-order, most of health and social security, not to mention the commitment to implement the Clegg recommendations on public pay.

Bringing defence properly into the game will not make nearly as much difference to defence itself as the admirals assert. But it will be a considerable help to the Government's efforts to control public expenditure in general. A more awkward May for Mrs Thatcher certainly, but perhaps an easier October. Mr Nott's campaign therefore deserves the discreet support of all non-combatants – even if NC may still be a little at sea as to which role, if not which pilot, to drop.

23 May 1981

The Débâcle
Ferdinand Mount

A débâcle speaks for itself. All things that inescapably follow – the humiliation, the indignation, the ministers hurrying in and out of Cabinet, the spectacular sitting of Parliament on a Saturday, the calls for the resignation of Mr John Nott, Lord Carrington and anyone else standing in the line of fire – are not only themselves part and parcel of the debacle; they help to explain why it happened.

The Falkland Islanders are the last victims of our refusal to be honest with ourselves; we have clung to the rhetoric of empire long after we have lost the desire or the ability to maintain its reality. The easy refuge in these circumstances is to blame the 'appeasers' in the Foreign Office. It was undoubtedly the Foreign Office which is to blame for the misreading of Argentina's intentions and for Britain being caught napping. Lord Carrington and his juniors had to go, and they duly went – in Lord Carrington's case, with remarkable candour and dignity – providing a respectable herd of scapegoats for a demoralised government. Mr Nott survives, I think rightly, but his survival surely depends on a successful outcome to what may be the last great naval task force Britain will ever launch.

This column has rarely found much to admire in Lord Carrington's style of diplomacy, except in Rhodesia. But apart from the immediate and crucial misjudgment over the Falklands, it would be unfair to pile all the blame on him or even on to the Foreign Office collectively for what has been the undeclared ambition of every British government for the past generation; somehow or other to disembarrass Britain of the Falklands.

Back in 1968, Lord Chalfont, then Minister for Peace and Disarmament at the Foreign Office (one of Sir Harold's masterly fancies), was nearly debagged by the islanders when they gathered the impression that Britain intended to discuss a transfer of sovereignty with Argentina. Under this present government, Mr Nicholas Ridley had a scarcely less frosty reception from the islanders when talk of a 'leaseback solution' was in the air. The islanders were and are determined to stay British, and they know how to shame British politicians into giving pledges which they would rather not give.

After all, didn't the islanders have British public opinion firmly behind them? So they did, and do. But opinion is a relatively painless, cost-free commodity. When it comes to paying for the maintenance of a permanent naval force in the South Atlantic sufficient to deter any invader, British public opinion seems to be less ardent.

Year by year, for twenty years now, successive British governments have given Argentina the impression that they would not be prepared to pay for any major project which would help to secure the Britishness of the Falkland Islands. The runway was never lengthened to take direct flights from Europe. A commercial agreement was signed in 1971 which gave Argentina a virtual monopoly of air and fuel services. Britain gave up her nearest deepwater base, at Simonstown, because of apartheid. Almost more important than the lack of arrangements to secure the islands' defence was the absence of colonial enthusiasm. The Falklands were left to fend for themselves.

Most of the islanders are tenants of the Falkland Islands company. Ultimate control of this company has changed hands several times. Recently, it belonged to the Charringtons Coalite empire; at one moment, it almost fell under Argentinian control, via Sir James Goldsmith. Since the islanders rarely own their own homes, many of them find themselves obliged to leave when they become too old for work; they tend to emigrate to New Zealand or Britain. The young often leave too. The result is that the population has dropped by about fifteen per cent in fifteen years. Whatever the final outcome now, many more will surely leave when and if they can.

Britain's contribution to the islands has been ancestors, a governor, a flag, a few marines, an occasional gunboat – and the rhetoric. Last Saturday it seemed that almost every British MP was personally prepared to shed his last drop of blood for the Falklands. Extremities of heroism were promised by all sorts, from Mr Patrick Cormack, doubtless to be remembered as Boy Cormack by readers of the next edition of the British Book of Heroes. 'The defence of our realm', Mr Edward Du Cann told a hushed house, 'begins wherever British people are.' We should start, I suppose, by bombing Buenos Aires where there are ten times as many British people as there are in the Falklands.

How much would it have cost to protect the islands securely against Argentina in perpetuity? Mr Keith Speed, the Navy minister, who was sacked for disagreeing with Mr Nott, believes that it could be done for £20 million a year – on the analogy of what it costs for three British frigates to patrol the Straits of Hormuz. That sounds like an underestimate for patrolling waters 8000 miles from home.

But even if his figures are correct, the costs of protection would come to £40,000 per island family per year. For half that sum, most of them would be quite pleased to emigrate to New Zealand. But if the safety of the islanders is not the sole concern, if British possession of the Falklands is militarily necessary and commercially valuable, then why have we not lengthened the runway? Why are we not busily drilling and leasing?

But Mr Speed is one of the few people in the whole business who is utterly honest. He believes that the Royal Navy ought to continue to patrol the world and the South Atlantic in particular and that if we will the end, then we must will the means.

The other form of honesty – and I think the preferable one – is to say that if we cannot provide the means, then we had better stop pretending that we can secure the ends. That was the logic behind Christopher Mayhew's resignation from the Navy ministry when Denis Healey – now the most zealous of gaucho-biffers – scrapped Britain's great aircraft carriers. A few years later, the next economic crisis proved Mayhew right by forcing the government to withdraw Britain's frontiers from the Himalayas, where Sir Harold Wilson in one of his most exuberant moments had drawn them, and redraw them distinctly West of Suez.

That sort of honesty comes hard to politicians. The cost of gunboat diplomacy increases at a prohibitively expensive rate. Even for superpowers, it has long lost the cheapness and effectiveness it had in the days of the huge technological gap between the imperial power and the natives, when whatever happens,

'We have got
The Maxim gun and they have not.'

What they have now is our second-hand warships, plus some new French aircraft. In 1833 we gained the Falklands from Argentina with a single sloop. We are attempting to regain them with two thirds of the Royal Navy.

In the case of the Falklands, the moral right is indisputably on our side. Is the British government really prepared to fight to regain its rights? Mr Enoch Powell insistently poses this question as the only one ultimately worth asking. But it is not the only question, and the answer to it is not settled by the dispatch of this great British armada. How much force is to be used? At what point should Britain regard herself as having gained her point and retrieved her self-esteem? When the last Argentinian marine leaves the island? When Argentina begins to negotiate? Mrs Thatcher's undertaking to return the islands to British administration is less specific than it sounds, but it could not stretch to include total failure to dislodge the Argentinians.

The immediate causes of the debacle are of the Government's own making. To dispatch a task force to see what can be retrieved, by blockade or marine landings or both, is the only way to deter similar acts of aggression in other parts of the world. This last British Armada is a quixotic but necessary enterprise. The position of the British Government remains at best a highly undignified one. But then discarding an empire tends to be a succession of indignities.

10 April 1982

No, no, no
James Fenton

The fleet, wrote Mr John Witherow to *The Times* from on board HMS *Invincible*, 26 April, had gone into battle formation for the first time. 'It now presents an impressive sight with the aircraft carriers *Hermes* and *Invincible* surrounded by an array of frigates, destroyers and supply vessels, slicing their way through a curiously leaden and calm South Atlantic.' Leaden and calm? There must be some mistake here, since as everyone in Britain now knows the South Atlantic is at present lashed by hurricanes, with waves of thirty or forty feet, depending on which newspaper you read. We are going to war in order to prevent further sea sickness amongst the Marines.

It may seem surprising that the wind should be used as an alibi for attack, yet the essential development of the crisis has been perfectly straightforward and predictable from the time of the decision to send the task force. If a fleet was sent it would have to be used, in the unlucky event of its arrival before any diplomatic solution had been found. Consequently, the original supporters of the sending of the ships, such as Mr Foot or Mr Healey, are now in the worst possible position to attack the decisions of the War Cabinet. During the whole course of the crisis, outright opponents of the Government's policy have numbered a mere ten per cent of the population, but there were plenty of waverers who did not wish that the threatened force should actually be used. With the recapture of South Georgia, the waverers fell in behind the Government. It was not until that moment that Mr Foot decided to break ranks. His timing could hardly have been worse.

At least, however, we may now hear slightly less of that typical sound of the last weeks, the sound of the Labour politician carefully choosing his words. There is an awful sense that any MP who dares to criticise a military operation lives in terror of public opinion. One sharp word against Rear-Admiral Woodward and the lynch mobs will bear down on Parliament Square. For my own part, I do not think there is war fever in the country, and I do not believe the electorate to be immune to reason. The fundamental case against war over the Falklands was always simple to argue and humane in its assumptions. It should have been put by Labour as a whole.

That Mrs Thatcher lost the Falklands is a matter for regret. Whatever the outcome of the present action, she should resign for that reason alone. A wise man, according to Father Brown, hides a pebble on a beach and a corpse on a battlefield. But we should not let the Thatcher Government hide that particular corpse in this particular way.

Given the Government's initial error, there was an obvious case for economic sanctions against Argentina, together with any other peaceful pressure available. I have not heard a single convincing argument against this course of action. All the objections to sanctions (that they tend to take a long time, that they do not always work, that they are difficult to maintain) apply equally well – indeed famously – to military expeditions. In general, though, sanctions cost fewer lives.

Suppose we had not been able to negotiate our way back to the status quo, we might reasonably have divided the issue into the question of territory and the actual administration of the islands. But the effort of the Falkland lobby has been to prevent, as far as possible, any such division. Thus Mr Rex Hunt was at pains to warn the islanders not to leave their homes even for the duration of the war, since if they left they would never get back. Clearly he was worried that as soon as the kelpers were out of the way, the dispute would begin to look territorial. What Mr Hunt needed, what Mrs Thatcher needed, was for it to look like a mercy mission. The kelpers are to be liberated, even at the cost of their lives. In the end, the Government did offer financial help to those who did wish to leave, but it came late in the day and apparently was not relayed to Her Majesty's Consul in Montevideo.

In the meantime the war got under way – one of the more secret wars of recent years. At least I cannot think of any major engagement about which the public have been so ill-informed. The dispatches from the fleet have been without discernible value, excepting as evidence of the reporters' increasing identification with the military. The Navy's own film reports have been blacked by ACTT. The television studios have been skilfully concocting substitute news footage out of old film that happens to be lying around the office: the landing on South Georgia, says a nervous commentator, may possibly have taken place in the vicinity of this harbour, and might conceivably have been effected with some of these helicopters, or perhaps with a ship looking something like this; there may very well be only one casualty who may only have lost a leg.

I don't believe we will have the first idea about casualties or what is happening on either side until it is far too late to do anything about it. If the Government is lucky losses will be at a sufficiently low level for Mrs Thatcher to continue crying 'rejoice'. We will be treated to all the rhetoric of sacrifice and all the horrors of military pomp.

But it is obvious that such luck will have been bought at the expense of the Argentines and we shall render impossible the only logical, logistical future for the Falklands – namely that they are bound in some way to Argentina. We shall have shed much blood, and we shall not be forgiven for doing so, either by the Argentine junta, or by their domestic opponents, or by their allies in South America. To pursue such a policy is politically foolish; to pursue it when there was an obvious option of economic sanctions and generous recompense, is more than that – it is frivolous, murderous, wicked.

1 May 1982

Last piece
Ferdinand Mount*

Let us see where we have got to.

At the outset, Mr Francis Pym divided the questions to be settled into three areas: short term, medium term and long term. On all three, the original position of the British government has now moderated considerably. Or perhaps it would be more precise to say that the lines of Britain's ultimate, irreducible demands have now been made clear. Some claim that if these demands had been made clear at an earlier stage before bloodshed, while Mr Haig was still shuttling, then Argentina might have been more eager to accept them. This seems doubtful. The nearer in time to the original invasion, the less likely it is that the junta would have been willing to pull back its troops, thus undoing the theatrical impact of the coup.

The correct time and place to unveil the final terms are surely at the eleventh hour and in the last plausible forum of reconciliation, in this case the UN. In the short term, Britain no longer insists on the Argentinians withdrawing their troops first. It is now conceded that the withdrawal could be phased in parallel with the withdrawal of the British task force. In the medium term, Britain no longer insists upon the restoration of exclusive British administration but is ready to concede some form of joint administration. In the long term, Britain no longer insists that the wishes of the islanders are 'paramount', although their wishes and interest must still be consulted; and instead of merely stating that the question of sovereignty is up for discussion, Mr Pym now looks benignly upon various alternatives to British sovereignty, such as UN trusteeship.

These are considerable concessions. And in the truncated form in which Mr Perez de Cuellar is addressing the question at the UN – by leaving out the long-term future as far as possible – they may seem more considerable still. Such terms would be hard, though not impossible, to persuade the Conservative Party to accept. They seem to me the least unacceptable means, both of diminishing further bloodshed and of trying to create some kind of future for the islands which does not involve turning them into an armed camp for the next twenty years. These are the sort of terms I had in mind when arguing in this column last week that it was the prime duty of the government to negotiate a cease-fire. This argument seems to have caused some surprise in the public prints. But what else has Mr Pym been up to, for heaven's sake? Nor, I imagine, are his reasons very different from the ones advanced in this column.

Many Conservatives – both those in favour and those critical of the new terms – are now saying that the Argentinian junta would be crazy not to accept them. Over the next couple of days, we shall see how crazy they are.

The change on the diplomatic front is reflected by an equally important change in the military choices as publicly stated by the British government. Appearing on *Weekend World* last Sunday, Mr Nott seemed – and we must to some extent be guessing here, as no doubt he means the Argentinians to guess too – to step off the escalator, at least for the moment.

For the previous fortnight, we had been led to believe both by the Prime Minister and the Defence Minister that the task force had an unstoppable momentum, dictated largely by the South Atlantic winter. It would be unfair, we were told, perhaps impossible, to keep the task force rolling about in these huge seas for months. The choice was therefore between full-scale invasion and full-scale retreat, between awful bloodshed and abject humiliation.

As from last weekend, this no longer seemed to be the case. Mr Nott told Mr Brian Walden: 'The incoming winter is going to cause horrendous problems for the Argentine forces on the islands, and our troops are relatively well looked-after and provisioned in ships . . . so we do have a range of options and we could extend the blockade for far longer, if we wished.' General Winter seems to have switched over to our side.

Now whether the acceptability of this third choice derives from fresh advice from the task force commanders or from a fresh set of tactics to put pressure on the junta evolved by the inner cabinet, in practice it does amount to an enlargement of the stark either/or which was previously on offer.

For this third choice can shade into a considerable range of other choices – or 'option-mixes' if we wish to sound smart. The islands can be partially invaded. The blockade can be maintained more or less aggressively. British frigates are now patrolling up and down Falkland Sound, blazing away at Argentinian supply ships; a British warship is said to have circumnavigated the island of West Falkland and met no sign of life.

Intensifying the blockade? Preparing to land on West Falkland? Frightening the Argentinians into coming to terms? Or a little of all three? By the time you read this, the question may be decisively answered or it may not.

But what needs to be placed on record is that the government has not been ashamed to proclaim the enlargement of the available choices. Mr Nott seems thereby to have gone some way towards recapturing that freedom of action and reaction which appeared to be slipping last week. That impression was reinforced by the confusing babble of public discussion. From the start, I think there have been two quite different conversations going on: one, conducted by the *Sun*, the *Express*, Mr Enoch Powell *et al*, has been about honour, and race and fatherland, a mixture of El Cid and Sid Yobbo; the other, conducted by the large majority of the British people, not least as measured in the correspondence columns of the popular papers, has been altogether more temperate and many-sided.

The Cid/Sid line is that there is always only one choice: to biff or to run. This is only the obverse of the line taken by Tony Benn. Either don't send the task force at all, or be prepared to go the whole hog and bomb bases on the Argentinian mainland and accept as many casualties as may be necessary to retake the Falklands.

Many people who do not instinctively warm to either extreme nevertheless have a guilty feeling that Mr Benn or Mr Powell must in some way be a superior person because of the highly advertised rigour of his logic.

This kind of intellectual bullying is to be fiercely resisted. If carried into daily life, such crude dichotomising would generate the most extraordinary rules of conduct. Chap treads on your toe. By Benn/Powell logic, either you ought to shoot him dead, or you should apologise for having placed your unworthy toe under his perfectly formed foot. Any reaction lying between these two extremes, we are told, is a pathetic evasion of the logical choice.

Horsefeathers, I say. What logicians call the Law of the Excluded Middle applies only patchily to human affairs, which characteristically pose several different, overlapping questions at the same time. That is why policies have to be compromised and qualified in order to obtain the least bad answers as to as many of the questions as possible. Outcomes tend at best to be smudged.

For most people in this country, the Falklands crisis is neither a joyful crusade nor a mad militarist adventure, and its outcome is one to be awaited with the grimmest apprehension. Let us leave it there.

I had hoped to write a leisured, ample piece this week as a farewell, for the time being, to the *Spectator*. The article would include a ripe assessment of the past five years, an olympian appreciation of the state of the nation and the tasks that lie before us, possibly even a message to the nation's youth. It would be the sort of job requiring a knobbly pipe and a pouchful of St Bruno.

Instead, this has turned out more like a hurried farewell on a draughty station platform, interrupted by the clanking of troop trains. There is time and space only to say how much I have enjoyed writing here and how kind everyone has been – which is what people say after a bereavement which, for me at any rate, this is.

15 May 1982

*After publishing this article Mr Mount left the *Spectator* to become a political adviser to the Prime Minister, Mrs Thatcher.

The instrument of war
Alexander Chancellor

The British task force, dispatched as an instrument of pressure for peace, has become a mighty and unstoppable instrument of war. It will not stop now until the last Argentinian is either dead or captured or on his way home. It no longer makes any sense to talk of minimising the casualties when, as at Goose Green, an attacking British force is heavily outnumbered by an entrenched enemy. The Paras could only do what they did do, which was to attack with the maximum vigour and fire-power. Brilliantly they thus managed to limit their own losses to seventeen, but at a cost of two hundred and fifty Argentinian lives. Nor is the progress of the war conducive to that spirit of magnanimity which, it is felt in Washington, the British must show if any lasting settlement is to be achieved. As Max Hastings has reported this week from the Falklands, the troops are feeling far more magnanimous – 'As casualties and personal anger and hatred of the enemy escalate on both sides, so it becomes more difficult to maintain restraint.' This anger and hatred can only have grown fiercer after the discovery at Goose Green of large stocks of napalm (though, as ITN's defence correspondent bravely pointed out, napalm, horrible though it is, is hardly a more horrible weapon than the British cluster bomb, and neither weapon is in fact forbidden under any international convention). And the anger and hatred of the British troops are not without political implications. Max Hastings also wrote: 'I think the only outcome of this war that would cause great bitterness among those who are fighting, is any peace that gives Argentina a share in Falklands government after we have won.' One has the strong impression that this is just how Mrs Thatcher now feels. She identifies very closely with the armed forces, which is one of her strengths as a war leader, and she is reported to be very impatient with people like Mr Pym who tell her that, however heavy the casualties, negotiations will eventually have to take place – if not with the junta, with its successors in government. Nothing has happened to make an amicable settlement of the sovereignty dispute any less desirable than it was before. And it would be cruelly wrong to suggest that such a settlement would now mean that British soldiers had died in vain. One must remember why the task force was sent to the South Atlantic in the first place. It was to uphold two principles: the first that armed aggression should not be allowed to pay, and the second that the interests of the Falkland Islanders should be

*'He should have been imprisoned in an
empty bottle . . .'*

protected. The first principle has already been more than adequately upheld. The second must be a central feature of future negotiations. Whatever solution is eventually arrived at, it is surely improbable that the Falkland Islanders would voluntarily choose to live in a permanent state of Argentinian siege. But the time may come when it will be for the Government – not the islanders – to decide how these interests should be best protected.

5 June 1982

The final day
Max Hastings

Port Stanley

I awoke from a chilly doze on Monday morning to find a thin crust of frozen snow covering my sleeping-bag and equipment in the dawn. Around me in the ruined sheep pen in which we lay, a cluster of snow-covered ponchos and rucksacks marked the limits of battalion headquarters. The inexhaustible voice of Major Chris Keeble, second in command of 2 Para, was holding forth into a radio handset as decisively as it had been two hours earlier when I lost consciousness. All firing in front of us, where the battalion's rifle companies had stormed a succession of enemy positions in the darkness, was ended. Desultory Argentinian shells were falling on untenanted ground some 600 yards to the right. We could hear heavy firing of all calibres further south, where the Guards and the Gurkhas were still fighting for their objectives.

Might I go forward, I asked? By all means, said the energetic Major. He pointed across the hill to the new positions of the rifle companies, and detailed a soldier from the defence platoon who had crossed the ground during the night to show me the way. We left the headquarters group huddled around their radios and bivouacs dusted with snow, and began to stride across the frozen tussock grass, my guide chattering busily about men he knew who had been hit during the night, and the amazing helicopter pilot John Greenhalgh who flew in his Gazelle without benefit of night vision aids to bring up ammunition and recover the wounded in the midst of the battle.

We began to pass the abandoned enemy positions, strewn with weapons and ammunition, clothing and food. 'Not short of much, was they?' said the Para. 'So much for the navy's blockade'. We reached 'A' Company, a few hundred yards frontage of unshaven scarecrows surrounded by arms and equipment, their positions dotted with flickering flames from the little hexamine cookers on which they were brewing hot chocolate and porridge from their arctic ration packs. Nearby stood the Scorpion and Scimitar light tanks which had supported the battalion in the attack. The delightful Lord Robin Innes-Ker, who had seemed at times less keen than some of his more homicidal comrades about passing the summer soldiering in the South Atlantic, had at last entered into the spirit of the thing. 'Did you see us?' he enthused. 'It was tremendous. We fired a hundred and fifty rounds. Once we saw somebody light a cigarette in front of us and that was it . . .' Everybody agreed that the night had been a huge success, not least because those doing the talking had come through it alive. I sat down in an untenanted bivouac – a poncho flapping uneasily above a peat hag – to write a dispatch. The obliging Blues and Royals had carried my typewriter in the back of a Scorpion from San Carlos Bay to Wireless Ridge, complaining somewhat that it was taking up precious ammunition space. At last it came into its own.

A forward gunnery observation officer came and sat beside me. He asked in vain (as every soldier asked every correspondent throughout the campaign) if I had the faintest idea what was going on. I said I only knew that I was due to join 3 Para late in the afternoon, in time to see them launch the next – and everybody hoped final – attack of the war that night. A cheeky eighteen-year-old private soldier put his head under the poncho and demanded a cigar, which I was not cheeky enough to refuse him. 'We did pretty good, didn't we? You get paid extra for doing this? Why does BBC always tell everybody where we're going to attack? How many more days do you reckon?'

Suddenly we heard men calling to each other in the snow shower outside: 'They're running away! It's on the radio! The Argies are running everywhere!' The Company Commander, Major Dair Farrar-Hockley, shouted to his platoon commanders to be ready to move in five minutes. I pulled my dispatch from the typewriter, ran over the ridge to where I had heard a helicopter engine idling, and thrust it, addressed optimistically to Brigade Headquarters, into the pilot's hand. Then I began to gather up my own equipment.

'Do you want a lift?' called Roger Field of the Blues and Royals. One of the most pleasant parts of this war was that, after so many weeks together, so many people knew each other. I climbed clumsily on to his Scimitar, and clung fervently to the smoke projector as we bucketed across the hillside. We halted for a few moments by one of the enemy positions captured during the night. The men picked a path through the possible souvenirs. We speculated about the identity of a sad corpse covered with a poncho, its feet encased in British-issue rubber boots.

We clattered down the ridge to meet the long files of 2 Para who had arrived before us. As we approached the skyline, we saw soldiers lying, standing, crouching along it, fascinated by the vision below. Jumping down from the tank, I walked forward to join them. They were looking upon the wreckage of a cluster of large buildings at the head of the estuary, perhaps three hundred yards beneath us. It was the former Royal Marine base at Moody Brook. Two or three miles down a concrete road east of it, white and innocent in the sudden winter sunshine, stood the little houses and churches of Port Stanley. Suddenly in a few minutes of the morning, the climax of all our ambitions, apparently as distant as the far side of the moon at breakfast, lay open for the taking. The soldiers, three nights without sleep, began to chatter like schoolboys. The Battalion Commander, David Chaundler, was giving his orders: '. . . I'm not having anybody going down that road unless that high ground is covered, so I'm getting 'B' Company up there. The tanks will stay here and provide a firebase . . .'

The first men of 'B' Company were already threading their way through Moody Brook and up the opposite hillside. The Blues and Royals took up position down among the rocks from which they could cover the entire road into Port Stanley. 'A' Company was to march straight up the road. I trotted after Dair Farrar-Hockley. We crossed Moody Brook amidst orders shouted down the line to stay rigidly in file on the track because of the danger of mines. With disgracefully selfish professional ambitions in my mind, I started to reflect aloud on the risk that 45 Commando might already be approaching Stanley from the other flank, that if negotiations started our advance would be stopped in its tracks. The word was called forward to quicken the pace. Dair Farrar-Hockley, signaller and correspondent trailing in his wake, began to hasten past the files of the leading platoon to take position among the point section, each man praying silently for the radio to remain mute.

We passed a building burning opposite the seaplane jetty, abandoned vehicles, loose ammunition littering the road like sweet papers in Hyde Park. Then we were among the first demure little bungalows of the Stanley seafront. 'We've got to stop, sir, and wait for the CO!' shouted a signaller. There was a groan, then reluctant acquiescence. The men dropped into a crouch by the roadside, peering ahead towards the town centre. Then an NCO at the point of the Company called: 'I think I can see a Panhard moving in front'. The soldiers hastily adopted tactical positions on either roadside, searching the distance for the threatened armoured car. A man with a rocket launcher doubled forward, just in case. Nothing happened except that a trawler began to move out across the harbour, showing a white flag. Through binoculars, I began to study scores of men, evidently enemy, standing idly watching our progress from the hillside perhaps a mile across the bay.

Then there was more excited chatter around the signallers: 'The Argies have surrendered! No one to fire except in self-defence'. Men called forward. Up the road behind us strode a knot of officers led by the colonel. 'Get in behind the Colonel's party, "A" Company', ordered Dair Farrar-Hockley urgently. 'Nobody but "A" is to get in behind the Colonel.' Every man who had not lost his red beret was wearing it now, passionately conscious that a unique opportunity for regimental glory was within their grasp.

The Battalion's officers had advanced perhaps two hundred yards beyond our initial halting place when a new signal was brought to the

Colonel's attention. No British soldier was to advance beyond the racecourse, pending negotiations. There was a bitter mutter of disappointment. Where was the racecourse? Beside us now. There was a brief chorus about Nelsonian blind eyes, rapidly stifled. The Colonel ordered 'A' Company to turn aside on to the racecourse. Suddenly, the tiredness of the men seeped through. They clattered on to the little wooden grandstand and sat down, still draped in weapons and machine-gun belts, to cheer one of their number as he clambered out on to the roof and, after some technical difficulties, tore down the Argentinian flag on the little flagpole, and raised that of 2 Para. At their urging, I took a group photograph of this memorable gathering of desperadoes on the stepped benches. Then, inevitably, men began to brew up and to distribute a few cases of Argentinian cigarettes they found in the starter's hut, first booty of the battle.

I wandered down to the road. It stretched empty ahead, the cathedral clearly visible perhaps half a mile away. It was simply too good a chance to miss. Pulling off my web equipment and camouflaged jacket, I handed them up to Roger Field in his Scimitar, now parked in the middle of the road and adorned with a large Union Jack. Then with a civilian anorak and a walking stick that I had been clutching since we landed at San Carlos Bay, I set off towards the town, looking as harmless as I could contrive. 'And where do you think you are going?' demanded a Parachute NCO in the traditional voice of NCOs confronted with prospective criminals. 'I am a civilian', I said firmly, and walked on unhindered.

Just round the bend in the road stood a large building fronted with a conservatory that I suddenly realised from memories of photographs was Government House. Its approaches were studded with bunkers, whether occupied or otherwise I could not see. Feeling fairly foolish, I stopped, grinned towards them, raised my hands in the air, and waited to see what happened. Nothing moved. Still grinning and nodding at any possible spectres within, I turned back on to the road and strode towards the Cathedral, hands in the air. A group of Argentinian soldiers appeared by the roadside. I walked past them with what I hoped was a careless 'Good morning'. They stared curiously, but did nothing.

Then, ahead of me, I saw a group of obviously civilian figures emerging from a large, official-looking building. I shouted to them: 'Are you British?' and they shouted back 'Yes'. Fear ebbed away, and I walked to meet them. After a few moments conversation, they pointed me towards the Argentinian colonel on the steps of the administration block. I introduced myself to him quite untruthfully, as the correspondent of *The Times* newspaper, on the basis that it was the only British organ of which he might have heard. We talked civilly enough for a few minutes. He kept saying that most of my questions could be answered only after four o'clock, when the British General was due to meet General Menendez. Could I meanwhile go and talk to the British civilians, I asked? Of course, he said. I walked away towards that well-known Stanley hostelry 'The Upland Goose' down a road filled with file upon file of Argentinian soldiers, obviously assembling, ready to surrender. They looked utterly cowed, totally drained of hostility. Yet I did not dare to photograph their wounded, straggling between comrades. It was only when I saw officers peering curiously at me from their vehicles that I realised that my efforts to look civilian were defeated by my face, still blackened with camouflage cream.

Forty minutes later, I walked back into the British lines from 'The Upland Goose' with the sort of exhilaration that most reporters are lucky enough to enjoy a few times in a lifetime. Around one of the bungalows by the racecourse, a throng of British officers had gathered, waiting impatiently for the order to move into town. Brigadier Julian Thompson, the delightful star of the British High Command throughout the campaign, was instantly sympathetic when I asked about transport to the fleet. After a frenzied half-hour wait during which I ran in vain to three helicopters whose pilots shrugged and flew away on other business, the Gazelle that the Brigadier had summoned for me pitched in. It was a few minutes before 8 p.m. London time on Monday evening when we landed briefly on HMS *Fearless* to collect one of the Ministry of Defence public relations men without whom no correspondent throughout the campaign could contact his newspaper.

From the earliest days of the passage on *Canberra*, these men from the Ministry had showed a genius for obstructionism that suggested talents seconded from the Department of Health and Social Security or the VAT inspectorate. Ignored by the military high command, they were unable to exercise any positive force for good. Their energies could be directly solely towards enforcing restriction. For weeks, it had been our punishment to work through the night to gather a story, only to discover that the Ministry men, devoted alike to their beds and three square meals a day, had filed it to London hours (or sometimes days) after the broadcasters had transmitted their voice reports.

Now, at last, the men from the MoD enjoyed one final triumph. I ran headlong into their cabin to seize one bodily and take him with me to a ship with transmission facilities. But I blurted out the essentials of my story to a disinterested audience. 'I am afraid that there is a complete news blackout', declared the most senior of their number, a Mr Martin Helm. 'You cannot communicate at all until further notice.' Could he, I asked after an initial seizure, contact the ministry to demand the lifting of the ban? No, such a call was covered by the ban itself. A bitter argument followed, in which it was put to him that Argentinian radio was already announcing a ceasefire, and that it was quite impossible to conceive what injury to British security might be done by a dispatch reporting my visit to Port Stanley. Mr Helm and his colleagues were unmoved. I went miserably to bed, to lie sleepless with rage towards the system which had so effortlessly thwarted me.

The ban was lifted at 3 a.m. London time. It later emerged that its original imposition was the result of a misinterpretation of a signal intended to achieve quite other results. Looking back, of course, it

'I can never remember whether we change into frogs or princes.'

was a trifling moment that pales into insignificance. It seems absurd to have allowed oneself to be so selfishly preoccupied with one's own affairs at a moment of national importance. Sitting in Port Stanley cathedral for the thanksgiving service for victory on Sunday afternoon, the struggles of correspondents and public relations men seemed very small beside the great events that we were so fortunate to witness. As with all these things, it is only after the moment has passed that we see that we have been allowed a small share or a small view of history being made. And as with all the moments, one will no doubt waste many hours for the rest of one's days thinking about how much better one could have done things, said things, written things, if only one had known.

26 June 1982

Losing your nerve?

Sir: As your readers are painfully aware, and as the archives will indelibly confirm, the *Spectator* lost its nerve over the Falklands war. I imagine that accounts for the cover showing an inane lion teetering ridiculously on a lump of rock, and for the unpleasantly snide tone of the leader column (19 June). The next week you quoted, sympathetically and at considerable length, an Argentinian lady's views on the conflict.

I wonder if you will permit me to offer some of the obvious comments you so carefully refrain from making on her letter?

1. It is not too difficult to achieve a bloodless conquest when you send an overwhelming force against a token handful of Marines.

2. Our professional fighting men spent weeks in hazard under the attack of the very professional Argentinian air force, during which time that Thatcher government which 'has no respect for life' refrained from striking at the bases from which the planes were launched.

3. The analogy she draws between people like herself and

possible Argentinian emigration to the Falklands would only be valid if such emigrants were prepared, as she was, to take on the customs and eventually the nationality of the host country; rather than, for instance, attempting to enforce their own language in education of native children, and a fundamental change in traffic regulations.

The Falkland Islanders chose to remain British, despite considerable discouragement. This lady's grandfather chose to abandon his native land and settle in a foreign country. Had we acquiesced in the takeover she would, I am confident, have preened herself on being a citizen of a confident thrusting nation rather than poor old decadent Britain.

I am glad she understands she is an Argentinian. She is, in any case, stuck with it; just as you are, sir, stuck with that failure of nerve. But in both cases I feel a decent silence would be a better reaction to being confounded than sniping.

John Christopher, La Rochelle, Rye, E. Sussex
10 July 1982

Frivolity

Sir: Your coverage of the Falklands episode has cleared up one small point: whether you run a fairly responsible journal for the libertarian Right or a fairly entertaining magazine. You run a fairly entertaining magazine. However, there are so few of these about nowadays that I am probably justified in keeping up my subscription, though I suppose it is a bit frivolous of me.

Kingsley Amis, *186* Leighton Road, Kentish Town, London NW5
28 August 1982

6 Class

The upper classes and urination in public
Alexander Chancellor

Members of the upper classes have long had the rather unattractive habit of urinating in public. They do it ostentatiously in front of gamekeepers and beaters, though not very often, it must be admitted, in front of women. But what happens when a seventeen-year-old boy from Stepney relieves himself against a wall in Southend? He is fined £450. Passing sentence, the chairman of Southend magistrates court declared: 'We are not going to tolerate people coming to Southend and upsetting visitors or anyone else who is here to enjoy themselves.' Just because a magistrate is anxious about the Southend tourist trade, there is no reason why he should impose such a preposterous fine – nine times the normal rate for unruly football hooligans.

21 June 1980

Roger Hollis
Auberon Waugh

When I came down from Oxford in June 1960, after only a year there and without a degree, my father said there were only two possible professions for young men in my situation: teaching or spying. Since I was under no illusions about my suitability as a teacher I wrote off, at his suggestion, to his old friend Sir Roger Hollis, who was then

Director-General of the Security Services. He replied, civilly enough, that I was too young for his branch of the Service, but recommended me to the Foreign Office people from whom I heard in due course.

The history of my attempts to join MI6 must await another occasion. Suffice to say that although I was reasonably convinced I had spotted a Soviet agent on the selection committee and still feel bitter, when I think of it, about a former friend who testified to the investigators that my chief characteristics were my indiscretion and irresponsibility, I do not feel, in retrospect, that the Secret Intelligence Service was making one of its gravest blunders when it declined my offer.

I remember one incident with particular shame. Whatever may be claimed about subsequent developments, it was quite plain in the autumn of 1960 that the Foreign Office was already looking for candidates who were both classless and left of centre. Accordingly, that is what we were all desperately trying to be. During a committee discussion about Africa, I had expressed misgivings about the future prospects of a newly independent African state. Afterwards the invigilators asked me if this meant I thought Africans were innately inferior. Not at all, I replied cleverly, just that they were better at different things. What things in particular, asked one of my tormentors – probably the Soviet agent – did I think Africans were better at? My brilliant young mind raced. A mental seizure. I could think of nothing. 'Well, climbing trees', I said weakly.

I had no further contact with Sir Roger Hollis until, in retirement, he came to live fairly close to us in Somerset and supported the wicked scheme for building a golf course in the Quantocks, which I was instrumental in frustrating, but I often saw his brother Christopher – one-time Conservative Member for Devizes and resident poet of the *Spectator* – who was my godfather. From my father's *Diaries* Roger seems to have been quite a convivial fellow – 'a good bottle man', as he is described on his first appearance with Roger Fulford, Tom Driberg and others at a lunch in Worcester. It was at the Hypocrites on that memorable night in December 1924 when 'a poor drunk called Macgregor . . . turned up having lain with a woman and almost immediately fell backwards downstairs. I think he was killed.'

There is an account some years later of the two of them being turned out of the Swan in Wells and another pub in Farringdon Gurney, ending up in a field.

Not the sort of person I would expect to be much impressed by the Soviet Union. True, Burgess was a bottle-man, too, but there is all the difference in the world between an Oxford bottle-man and a Cambridge bottle-man. Nobody who knew Tom Driberg at all well could have been in much doubt that he was a Soviet agent. Tom was not a man who liked being laughed at but he always pretended to be immensely amused whenever I accused him of spying for Russia. It never seriously occurred to me that he was drawing money from MI5, too, although rereading the reference to him in my introduction to *The Last Word: An Eyewitness Account of the Thorpe Trial*, (Michael Joseph) I see I must have guessed subconsciously. In any case, one had only to reflect on his sexual preferences to spot that he was an obvious candidate for one or other of the British Intelligence Services. It is my contention that what caused Roger Hollis's downfall was an inability, in dealing with 'people like ourselves', to distinguish between those who came from Oxford and those who came from Cambridge. But before pursuing this argument, I must repeat an anecdote which acquires a certain poignancy in the light of last week's revelations, that Sir Roger was – and in some quarters still is – seriously suspected of having been a Soviet agent.

About fifteen years ago I heard a funny story about John Wyndham (later Lord Egremont) that when he was Macmillan's private secretary in Downing Street (or possibly Admiralty House) he would sometimes, late at night, decide to play a little prank. He would telephone the Director of Security Services (in fact Hollis) at his home in Campden Hill Square and as soon as he got through he would shout down the telephone in an assumed accent: 'Aha! Villain! I know your secret!' – and ring off. After he had played this joke a few times, the Security Service put a tab on the calls and traced them to the Private Office of the Prime Minister. Red faces all round and a tremendous wigging from the PM.

This excellent story came to me from a source which left me in no doubt whatever as to its truth, but which was too private for me to use. But five years or so later I wheeled it out to illustrate an article I was writing for a French – or possibly a German – newspaper on the English sense of humour, or some such rubbish. Rather to my surprise, it was picked up by a hack on the *Sunday Times* who telephoned a few weeks later to say he had checked the story with Lord Egremont – something I would never have dared to do – and Egremont had denied it with the most extraordinary vehemence. At the time, I attributed this to the discernible assumption of the upper class that they have an absolute right to tell point-blank lies to the press (the same trait, I imagine, which explains Lord Home's denial that he was told about Blunt in 1964, which he has had to stick to ever since and which continues to cause general confusion. Hollis certainly told him and if Home were half a man he would admit it). The latest revelation – that Hollis was indeed suspected of having a guilty secret – not only explains Egremont's vehemence but may throw an unexpected light on his sense of humour.

To understand Roger Hollis's downfall and the continuing vendetta against him – we must go back to the atmosphere of the Sixties. At the time it was not so much fashionable as obligatory to believe that the country's salvation lay in the hands of the new 'classless' generation of upwardly mobile working-class folk who were just about coming into their own, many if not all of them with vicious chips on their shoulders. It may seem incredible now, but in those far-off days comparatively sensible people convinced themselves that Harold Wilson was a great statesman, Alan Brien was a witty writer, Don Ryder was a brilliant businessman, Lord Crowther-Hunt was an able administrator, David Frost had a sense of humour.

In the aftermath of Burgess, Maclean and then Philby, the duffle-coat brigade within MI5 saw its main chance. All the old-timers were suspect, most particularly those from a public school background. As Director-General, Hollis was constantly irritated by requests to investigate his friends and trusted colleagues. He refused them permission to tap his deputy's telephone (Graham Mitchell – Winchester and Magdalen, Oxford) and discouraged them from blackening the name of my poor cousin Guy Liddell, another deputy director who died as long ago as 1958. In both these instances he was unquestionably right. How many other colleagues he protected from harassment by these ambitious young creeps we shall never know, but by the time Blunt's turn came round his reaction must have been more or less automatic, and this time he was wrong. The lean and hungry new boys smelled blood, and this time they were right. The leader of the pack made himself so objectionable that Hollis, in exasperation, sacked him; he was re-hired by the rival firm MI6, put back on the interservice counter-espionage committee which is apparently known in Fleet Street as the Fluency Committee and, from the moment of Blunt's final exposure in 1964, Hollis was doomed. His greatest error was to have mistaken a soft-faced Cambridge homosexual for one of us. It is not hard to see where Chapman Pincher's information came from, or that the renewed hounding of Sir Roger is a simple continuation of the class war within MI5.

At least it all proved a useful diversion from the launch of the Social Democrat Party. For the future, we are told in *The Times* (which, in its own words, has itself 'given wider ventilation to the raw material') of the *Search for a new kind of Classless Spycatcher*: 'A wider social mix in its intake is being sought . . . A suspicion of left-wing activities, arising from a *Daily Telegraph* style view of the world, is not judged an especially bad trait as at present MI5 regards the far left as a greater threat to the nation's stability than the far right.'

Those who are groping their way towards an understanding of Times New English will deduce that MI5 is particularly anxious to recruit lower-class lefties. Which just shows how times have changed. Few, if any, intelligent children of the middle class are remotely drawn to the Soviet Union nowadays. But there is something oddly comforting in the knowledge that MI5 is once again trawling in precisely those waters where the future traitors will be found.

4 April 1981

Lady Spencer
Alexander Chancellor

The Spectator's 'Low life' columnist, Jeffrey Bernard, may not have the antecedents of the 8th Earl Spencer, a house of the magnificence of Althorp, or a wife with as many rocks as Raine. But he, too, has been ill – if not quite as ill as Lord Spencer, quite ill enough to cause alarm and induce reflection upon mortality. And now, I am glad to say, he is better, something which calls for celebration. Lady Spencer has set us an example which we might feel tempted to follow. We could, like her, invite the Bishop of Southwark to conduct a thanksgiving service. We could ask Mr Norman St John-Stevas to deliver an address and Sir John Mills to read the lessons. We could send out printed invitations to the grandest people we know. We could give a champagne lunch for two hundred and fifty people. And then we could pay for a notice in the *Daily Telegraph* listing all those who had been there. We could, but should we? What of Mr Bernard? Might not such a social event place some strain on his still fragile state of health? Might it not seem more like a wake than a thanksgiving? Might he not, poor man, be much embarrassed by such ostentation? We think he might.

19 May 1979

Winchester
Simon Courtauld

Winchester College has its sexcentenary this year. I was sorry to miss the celebrations held at my old school last month, particularly as I was interested to find out what had happened to my contemporaries, few of whom I see nowadays. To the vast majority of people – who did not benefit from a Winchester education – a Wykehamist is not a very endearing person. He is self-effacing, but complacent about his probably modest achievements; perhaps he has a job as a civil servant or in one of the professions; almost certainly he is considered to be unemotional and rather dull. Sir John Betjeman has made the Wykehamist seem even less attractive: 'Broad of church and broad of mind, Broad before and broad behind; A keen ecclesiologist, A rather dirty Wykehamist.' The cleaner sort of Wykehamist is a chap like Lord Bognor who, in Harold Nicolson's *Some People*, appears as someone who has benefited from the discipline of Winchester. It has taught him 'the value of mental and moral balance'. George Lyttleton, in his published correspondence with Rupert Hart-Davis, asks: 'Why are most of them such *prigs*? Cripps, Crossman, Douglas Jay all share an indefinable smugness. It [Winchester] is, I fancy, and always has been too close a community, with little fresh air from outside.' It all adds up to a rather unflattering picture, but I suppose one would admit that it has the ring of truth – recognisable in many Wykehamists of one's acquaintance though not, of course, in oneself. I wonder whether the impression is still valid today.

14 August 1982

Eton
Harold Acton

An English Education: A Perspective of Eton Richard Ollard (Collins)

Athletics combined with a classical education have produced the ideal Englishman since time out of mind, and Eton has continued to produce him – since when? Mr Richard Ollard has answered this question as completely as possible in his literary panorama of Eton's history and development. You need not be an Etonian to enjoy this vivid perspective. Most Etonian reminiscences tend to be obfuscated by sentiment or resentment, but Mr Ollard's vision is crystalline and he avoids the pitfalls into which his nostalgic predecessors have stumbled.

All of us will agree with him that Eton's animating principle and distinguishing flavour are aesthetic: 'the beauty of its setting, the nobility and individuality of the buildings that embody the original foundation'. As a King's Scholar he was perhaps better qualified to appreciate its aesthetic values than an Oppidan, for some of the housemasters' red brick dwellings are far from beautiful and in recent years the embosoming elms have gone the way of the slim Tuscan cypress, felled by incurable disease. Even the astigmatic tyro must have been impressed by the chapel and Lupton's Tower, the school yard with its central statue of Henry VI, and the echoing cloisters where we slaked our thirst with cool water in hot weather. Those who, like me, were bored by compulsory games, were less charmed by the sight of the fabled playing fields. Two elderly spinsters, Nora Davison and Mabel Spurrier, never wearied of depicting these scenes in watercolour, and I wish some had been included in the volume, which should have been bound in Eton blue.

Especially delightful are Mr Ollard's vignettes of the Provosts and Headmasters who left a permanent imprint on the college. Among the earlier Provosts Sir Henry Savile and Sir Henry Wotton were pre-eminent. After Wotton's long and arduous services abroad it was at Eton, Izaak Walton tells us, 'that his happiness then seemed to have its beginning; the College being to his mind as a quiet harbour to a seafaring man after a tempestuous voyage'. His celebrated pupil Robert Boyle wrote, that he was 'not only a fine gentleman himself, but very well skilled in the art of making others so'. Mr Ollard compares the influence of Henry Hales, the Greek scholar nick-named *Bibliotheca Ambulans* by Wotton, with that of William Johnson Cory two centuries later.

To Cory – a controversial figure since he was ignominiously dismissed by Headmaster Hornby in 1872 after nearly thirty years of teaching – Mr Ollard devotes his most eloquent chapter, explaining how he became 'an incomparable teacher, certainly the greatest in the history of Eton'. The Grecian spirit of Cory pervades the perspective. One of his memorable maxims was: 'every school should make the most of that which is its characteristic. Eton should continue to cultivate taste.' And the cultivation of taste should be combined with that of the reasoning faculties. The Eton Boating Song and a few poems in anthologies have kept Cory's memory green, but I suspect Mr Ollard is the first of many a year to emphasise his inspiring influence on colleagues and pupils who have handed on the torch.

Henry Green (Yorke) considered the masters 'a poor lot' and Cyril Connolly more or less concurred with him. Both were my contemporaries, yet I feel bound to support Mr Ollard's defence of the despised pedagogues. His list of them is too long to quote. Besides Cyril Alington, our ebullient and versatile Headmaster, and M. R. James, 'the greatest Provost for three centuries' and a unique scholar of mediaeval manuscripts and iconography (also famous for his ghost stories), we had an enviable variety of tutors with arcane talents and mild eccentricities. John Christie, the future founder of Glyndebourne Opera, would appear late in a dressing-gown for early school (which in those days was at 7.30 a.m.) A. S. F. Gow was the supreme authority on the primitive Greek plough. Aldous Huxley, who shared my classical tutor's lodgings for a while, was a linguistic stimulant with an aura of High Bohemia. W. Hope-Jones was an ardent nudist. C. M. Wells, we are told, 'played both cricket and football for Cambridge and for England: his knowledge of wine inspired awe in circles where such matters are not taken lightly: his skill as a fly-fisherman earned him an obituary in *Salmon and Trout*.'

My personal preference was for the oldest: H. E. Luxmoore of the exquisite garden, a Greco-Roman cameo of Cory's heritage, and the venerable E. L. Vaughan whose gift of Keats's poems now lies on my desk. That gigantic Headmaster Dr Warre, portrayed by Sargent in his prime on the chapel steps, was reduced to a pitiful wreck in a wheel chair. His successor Edward Lyttelton had been forced to resign owing to a sermon he preached in 1916, urging the advisability of a negotiated peace. 'The essential idea was not ignoble', is Mr Ollard's comment. At that period of bellicose blindness I should call it courageously Christian. With historical hindsight we must lament that his and Lord Lansdowne's more rational proposals fell on outraged ears.

Inevitably the topic of sex rears its dishevelled head in a chapter on

Love and Friendship. As Evelyn Waugh wrote in *A Little Learning*, 'Most good schoolmasters – and, I suppose, schoolmistresses also – are homosexual by inclination – how else could they endure their work? – but their interest is diffused and unacknowledged.' Cory fell in love with his pupils; so did A. C. Benson and Oscar Browning, but they flinched from 'the grossness of carnal relations'. Probably repression inflamed their sublimated passions. As Cory wrote:

> Show me what angels feel. Till then
> I cling, a mere weak man, to men.

Drugs were only connected with the Opium War in my time and the few boys labelled 'sods' were only guilty of furtive masturbations. A quotation from Brian Howard's diary evokes that precociously sophisticated friend who astonished Edith Sitwell with his Dadaistic verse in 1921. We tried, like Rimbaud, to be absolutely modern. There was nothing decadent about our enthusiasms: we painted and poetised in pristine innocence, and if we posed occasionally, it was to shock the philistines.

Most of my lasting friendships were formed at Eton and the old boy who wrote of it as 'five years in a lukewarm bath of snobbery' was disingenuous, for it was no more snobbish than other schools, possibly less. When I met George Orwell (Eric Blair) in Paris during the war our reminiscences of Eton were exchanged with humourous detachment in a predominantly American mess. I think we talked of Dame Clara Butt singing *Land of Hope and Glory* at a school concert, and of how glorious we felt at the time, as if we were living 'Amongst the bright and brave.' The bath grew warmer during our conversation, as in Mr Ollard's narrative, and we concluded that only 'Pop' was snobbish by popular standards.

27 November 1982

7 Sex

Contraceptive advertisements

Sir: I have been a regular reader of the *Spectator* for some years, and have noticed over this period that an advertisement entitled 'Durex Protectives' is regularly inserted by a Mr H. Fiertag of Dept S, Wardour Street.

For many years Mr Fiertag and his 'Protectives' have stood alone. Recently, however, he has been joined in this field by Safeguard of Newgate Street. The competition thus provided has no doubt led to a war of savage price cutting, to the grateful delight of those of your readers who are accustomed to apply to Mr Fiertag for marital aid.

But now the floodgates are truly opened: a recent issue contains advertisements for 'Adult Tapes'; 'Educational Video for the Children' (Adult Education, I wonder?); 'Lesbians and Bi-Sexual Women over thirty-five'; a 'Mature Widower'; 'Erotic Art' and 'Genuine Introductions'. It cannot be long before all those sad-sounding 'Company Directors' slip away from *Time Out* and surface in the pages of your magazine.

To revert to the man who started the rot – Mr Fiertag – why did he decide to advertise in the *Spectator* in the first place? Can it be that he thought (and thinks) your readers incapable of buying their own 'Durex Protectives' over the counter? I would like to think not, but the regular appearance of Mr Fiertag's advertisement suggests that he may be right. Therefore to demonstrate that there is no service which Mr Fiertag offers your readers that they cannot perform for themselves, I have bought a contraceptive device and sent it to you through the post. Had I done this at your request I would have packaged it more professionally in a plain unmarked envelope. But this being the age of letter bombs (Irish letter bombs, I should say) I thought it best to advise the contents on the back of the envelope.

H. E. Taylor, 15 Spring Street, London w2

24 January 1981

'That's not what I meant when I said, "Are you good in bed?"'

Good girls
Jeffrey Bernard

I was quite fascinated to read about the man who got a divorce because his wife wouldn't make love with him more than twice a week mainly because the court put so much emphasis on the fact that she'd had a convent upbringing. This emphasis was made in an attempt to vindicate the lady's reluctance and it showed, for the umpteenth time, just how little those who administer justice know about the facts of life beyond and outside the courts. When I was a lad everyone knew the form about convent girls and in, say, a dance hall, you always made a bee-line for a girl wearing a crucifix. Any girl decorated with such a charm was considered to be a 'racing certainty' in the bedding stakes. A crucifix may well work at repelling vampires but I've never known one to keep a wolf at bay. I've also been told by numerous East End correspondents of mine that Salvation and Church Army girls aren't the hardest nuts in the world to crack and I can only assume that those people closer to God than the rest of us simply have a kinder and more friendly disposition.

You don't have to be a professional writer or literary cocktail party habituée to know that Catholic lady writers dispense their favours in the most warm-hearted fashion, but I'm not, of course, knocking

Catholics or women when I say this. In fact, I thank their God for them. If Ireland went on the pill then I think the place would be packed with sex exiles not tax exiles. The thing is, women have so little to interest them. What really revolts me is the way men behave in so far as it just isn't possible to be a womaniser without being a shit. It's in the very nature of the beast. A man who's easy to get to bed is a silly, foolish fellow. A man who has to pay for it is also a little daft although I can't help envying the fact that he can afford to, and that brings me to the amazing business – and I mean business – of the brothel at 32 Ambleside Avenue, Streatham. You'll recall that the police kept the place under surveillance for twelve days and saw thirty men a day going in at £15 a shot which the girls split 50-50 with Madame Payne, and those transactions came to £7,200 by my reckoning. Doubtless you'll agree with me when I say I now *know* I'm in the wrong business having suspected it for years. What I did love about the case was Mr Donald Farquarson QC saying that some of the women the police found in the house when they raided it were 'amateurs' and that they were 'raising money for household purchases or for Christmas'. Bless them. And who should want to stop them?

Again we have the bit about the law not being in touch with life – Madame got eighteen months – although her clients included barristers and solicitors. The genius defending Madame said, in mitigation I assume, that the house at Ambleside Avenue was 'not an opulent New Orleans brothel', something I should have thought that anyone who knew how to spot the difference between Streatham and Louisiana could have told the judge. Incidentally, I suppose New Orleans was settled by Catholics, but I suppose some wag will write to tell me that it was Huguenots.

Anyway, the laws concerning brothels were, as it was pointed out in court, made to protect women presumably because they can't protect themselves. Well, you could have fooled me or anyone else who has seen the creatures sitting in places like Annabel's festooned in diamonds. If the law wasn't an ass then surely it would legislate to protect men from the rapacious little beasts with, of course, double indemnity clauses where crucifix-wearing girls were to be concern-ed. There must be exceptions, I know, and I'm sure that hysterical girl Joan of Arc was one. Perhaps if she had been a little more outgoing she might have saved her skin. If she'd been tried this week in the Old Bailey she'd have been acquitted on the grounds of her convent upbringing.

26 April 1980

Divorce
Jeffrey Bernard

All is not yet lost. Last Sunday I moved to a delightful flat in London, got divorced the very next day and then opened the *Daily Telegraph* on Tuesday to read the most moving story I have come across since *The Wind in the Willows*. The gist of it is this. Mr Bill Saunders, director of the Alcohol Study Centre based at Paisley College of Technology, has come out with the opinion that children should be taught the skills of drinking from the age of twelve, starting perhaps with two glasses of wine with a meal, or half a pint of shandy.

It's terrific stuff. Just think what else they could be gently led and talked into. Forget the drinking for a minute. What about preparing the twelve-year-olds for marriage? The centre – how dare they preside without asking me to sit at the table? – could arrange for twelve-year-olds to be whacked, ever so gently, over the head, say, two or three times a day with rolling pins. The force of the whack would, of course, increase gradually until they were old enough to be able to sustain quite serious injury. Twelve-year-old girls could be subjected to the sight of twelve-year-old boys reeling through the front door with empty pockets at about 9 p.m., extending the treatment until 2 a.m. at the age of fourteen or thereabouts. At the same time we must ensure that children should be brought up to cope with sex correctly. Perhaps two-minute spells of sexual intercourse at twelve for a start and then allowing them the good old British Coventry Climax after three or four years.

If any reader of this journal would like to back me financially I think we could have a really, great, profit-making Dotheboys Hall. Suggested curriculum: Rise at 10.30 a.m. Drink glass of Alka Seltzer. Climb into jeans and dirty jersey, go to kitchen, read *Sporting Life* over tea and toast, ignore girl for twenty minutes and then have row. 11 a.m. opening time. Leave house in huff and proceed to local. Half of shandy, write out betting slip – 5p yankee increasing to 50p yankee at age of sixteen – insult guvnor, threatened with expulsion and totter home to train set or snakes and ladders at closing time.

At 4 p.m, wake up with mild headache, stagger to kitchen for peanut butter sandwich and then two-minute burst of sexual intercourse on sitting room carpet in front of *Blue Peter*. 5 p.m., another row with girl, after listening to racing results on Radio 2. Walk to pub in manufactured huff dead on opening time. 6 p.m., learn to chat with local colonel, poacher, first world war veteran, doctor, do-gooder, village idiot, President of Women's Association. 9 a.m., punch-up with local tearaway. Practise left jabs to the head aiming half an inch higher for every whisky consumed. 9.30 p.m., sick in gents, back to bar and practise chatting up local scrubbers. 10 p.m., lunatic drunken bet on last race at Slough Greyhound Stadium. 10.30 p.m. game of conkers in public bar with another schoolboy. 10.45 p.m., warned by publican of bad behaviour. Order another glass of wine plus Mars Bar and sick again in gents. 11 p.m., throwing out time.

Fall in ditch on way home, take twenty minutes to find keyhole, hit on head with saucepan, eat cold dinner from oven. 11.15 p.m., up the forty steps to Bedfordshire – impotent. Tears, recriminations. Slumber. 3 a.m., wake up, stare at black ceiling and worry about shortage of pocket money and school blazer in hock. 6 a.m., wake up to hear twelve-year-old girl friend scream, 'You make me sick.'

Honestly, with that sort of grounding you could grow up to survive anything. The wretched school I went to, Pangbourne, was so ghastly I considered National Service to be akin to a holiday. If only we'd all been thrown in at the deep end what winners we'd all be! Actually, Bill Saunders is quite right. I only started drinking, gambling and fornicating because I was told it was all wrong.

Thank God it still is.

22 November 1980

Rape 1
Auberon Waugh

The Chief Inspector of Prisons seems to approve of an experiment in Maidstone Prison whereby victims of rape and sexual assault are encouraged to visit rapists and sexual assaulters in prison. This idea of confronting offenders with their victims has, apparently, been widely accepted in the United States, where I would have thought that it might qualify as a cruel or unnatural punishment such as is forbidden by constitutional law. In the apparent willingness of rape victims to attend these sessions, there need be no comfort to those who argue that women secretly enjoy being raped. Two uniformed policemen are present throughout. A stronger case might be made on the cruel and unnatural point by suggesting that even if the purpose of the women's visit is not to berate their tormentors, as I am sure it is not, the punishment of Tantalus has never yet been enshrined in our penal system.

But I do not suppose that these ladies consciously intend to tantalise the wretched prisoners. Such a thought may lie deep among their unconscious reasons for behaving in this way, but if so it is known only to God. Ostensibly, their purpose is to discourage rapists from pursuing their vocation and make them see the error of their ways by convincing them that rape victims are not just sex objects but also human beings, and probably quite boring ones, too. There is nothing so destructive of the sex urge as reasonable conversation.

Possibly this is why Women Against Rape, the extreme feminist organisation, takes such a dim view of the Maidstone experiment. The indignation of such women's groups can only be sustained within an atmosphere of conflict between the sexes. Describing the experiment as a device 'to get everybody off the hook', WAR's spokesperson, Ms Judith Kertesz, was quoted as saying: 'Rapists are ordinary, normal men who have the opportunity and think they can get away with it.'

This seems to reflect a somewhat jaundiced view of ordinary, normal men. No doubt Ms Kertesz has had some terrible experiences. Or not, as the case may be. But the real reason that some women are prepared to spend their time talking to rapists in prison is not, as Ms Kertesz fears, that they hope to make peace between the sexes – only the Kerteszes of this world are really aware of any conflict – any more than it is to entice, tantalise or punish men. Their real reason, I suspect, is simply that like many women they enjoy talking, and in Maidstone Prison they have found a literally captive audience.

I wonder which of these explanations can apply to the apparent passion of so many politicians for talking to trade unionists. The great difference here, of course, is that the trade unionists are not behind bars. In fact it is during the actual business of being raped that politicians feel it most important to hold conversations. Discussion has become part of the ritual. The accepted wisdom of the age is that any politician not prepared to hold discussions with trade unionists while being raped has only himself to blame if he is hurt.

Rape may be a tiresomely overdiscussed subject in its sexual sense – the number of cases involved simply does not justify the general hysteria; this is something I attribute to feminists' repudiation of their sexual role and the growth of lesbianism. It may have lost its meaning also in the sense that environmentalists use it to describe the building of a motorway over Romney Marsh or wherever. But I can honestly think of no better word to describe the capture and plundering of the nation's economy, the destruction of its industry, the theft of its savings and debauching of its currency by the trade unions, shortly to be followed, we are told, by control of its press and effective take-over of its political institutions.

13 February 1982 (extract)

*'Thank you Mr Smith — without my
glasses you're tolerably attractive too.'*

Rape 2
Alexander Chancellor

On Monday I discovered what the terrorists must have felt like when the SAS erupted into the Iranian Embassy. I was sitting alone in my office, trying to do some work, when quite suddenly I was surrounded by nine women. One of them pointed a camera at me and started firing away with a flashbulb. The others confined themselves to verbal abuse. My protests at this rather frightening invasion of my privacy were all painstakingly written down in a notebook by one particularly angry-looking woman. They explained that they represented Women Against Rape (WAR) and that they wished to be given space in the *Spectator* to present their case against what they claimed had been an incitement to rape in a recent column by Auberon Waugh. I said that such an interpretation of Mr Waugh's article, however distasteful they might have found it, was clearly absurd. Then one of them kept pointing at different sentences in the article, saying 'What do you mean by that?' When I explained that I hadn't written the piece, and that therefore I didn't mean anything by any of it, and that they had better go to Somerset to consult Mr Waugh, they cackled contemptuously, pointing out that I, as editor, was responsible for everything that appeared in the paper. To this I agreed, though I explained that I was merely responsible for publishing Mr Waugh's reflections, not for explaining or necessarily even for understanding them. In desperation, I had the police called, but by the time an officer arrived we had reached agreement about the basis on which they would depart. I signed an undertaking that I would read a pamphlet they gave me, *The Rapist Who Pays The Rent*, and write to them with my comments. They had been in my office for, I think, about twenty minutes when the policeman came in and asked me to repeat in his presence my request for them to leave. 'Buzz off', I said – a remark interpreted as the ultimate in male 'violence' against womanhood and gleefully recorded in their notebook.

27 February 1982

Judges and Sex
Jeffrey Bernard

If you ever doubted that the law is an ass then last Thurday's decision by three Appeal Court judges must surely have confirmed the fact. They ruled that a certain Brenda Mason was not being unreasonable when she rationed sex with her husband David to Saturday nights only. I have been pondering the dreadful Masons at leisure, but what struck me first about the case was the fact that the sum total of the judges' ages tots up to 198. That does, of course, make such a judgment fairly easy to make and, in the event of the said judges practising what they preach, then by my reckoning Lord Justice Ormrod who has been married for thirty-two years has had his leg over a mere 1,564 times. Lord Justice Dunn pips him on the post with a tally of 1,928 while Sir John Arnold with twenty-three years of marriage under his belt is almost a beginner. And there I was feeling guilty these past fifteen years, having once rationed a vicar's daughter I knew to sex fourteen times a week.

But the Masons themselves must be an odd couple. She claims to still love him and wants him back – what is this thing called love? – but why he didn't leave her when he first realised he was being put on short rations beats me. I mean, if it isn't reciprocal then get out. If someone doesn't want to go to bed with you – I suppose I mean me – then they're quite simply the wrong person by definition. Life's too short to play Dante to anyone's Beatrice, although I played the role a few times as a callow youth. In fact, I can remember standing all day in the rain, soaked through, by the corner of Canonbury Square once in the hope of seeing a certain girl walk by. Pathetic, isn't it?

Anyway, the paper I read about it all in added a rider headed 'Fading Passion'. That said, 'Newly-weds make love five times a week on average in the first year of marriage. But the passion soon wears off, and the average is only twice a week after the first year, a doctor of the Institute of Psychiatry in London said.' Who is this wretched doctor and how the hell does he know? I'm not in the habit of asking my married friends how frequently they have sex but a glance at their faces would seem to negate the doctor's calculations. They look simply dreadful. But he's a really bright spark is this quack and, as if we didn't know, he goes on to say, 'It is quite common for one partner to want sex more often than the other.' Apart from the fact that he forgets 'the other' is cockney for sex, I'm only too painfully aware of the fact. I can still clearly remember a case in point when I interviewed Raquel Welch over tea and biscuits in the Dorchester. Then there was the time when I shared a studio restaurant table with Ava Gardner, and I could have sworn I wanted it more than she did.

There's no stopping this quack though. He goes on to say that if a person makes love when they don't feel like it then they will be put off sex for ever. I think 'ever' could be a slight exaggeration in most cases but his notion of couples attempting to come to some sort of compromise is a stroke of genius. Why didn't I ever think of that?

'Tell you what, my dear. You have a headache tonight and I'll get legless tomorrow night.' 'All right, but what about Thursday?' 'Oh, I'll probably be too depressed.' 'Good, because Friday I'll be cooking all day and I'll be too tired.' 'Okay. See you Saturday then. Usual time. Usual place.' 'Right. Goodnight, darling.' 'Night.'

But these Appeal Court judges remind me of a sad joke. A sex therapist was delivering a lecture and asked some of the people in the audience to volunteer how often they had sex. One man stuck up his hand and said he had it once a day. Another said he had it twice a week and so it went on. Finally, he saw one cheerful looking chap who owned to the fact that he had it only once a year. 'Why are you looking so happy then?' he asked him. The man replied, 'Because tonight's the night.'

13 December 1980

J. Thorpe
Alexander Chancellor

It is no longer interesting to speculate whether or not Mr Jeremy
Thorpe is or ever has been a homosexual. Anyway, it is none of my
business. But if he ever did have tendencies of this sort, he has not
exactly proclaimed them from the rooftops. He is not, in other words,
a standard-bearer of the Gay Liberation Movement. And there is no
reason that I can think of why his acquittal at the Old Bailey, pleasing
though it may have been for other reasons, should be seen as any kind
of victory for British 'gays'. If anything, I would have thought, the
opposite, as Mr Norman Scott's performance in the witness box is
unlikely to have raised homosexualism in public esteem. So it was
therefore not just unlikely, but inconceivable, that a party of 'gays'
would wish to crown the celebrations of 'Gay Pride Week' by hiring a
coach and roaring down to North Devon to attend the appalling
thanks-giving for Mr Thorpe's acquittal. And yet when this little
titbit of unsubstantiated information was cast casually into Fleet
Street, it was seized and devoured by every newspaper in sight. It was,
of course, an obvious hoax, of which I will not name the perpetrators,
for fear that heads might roll and the gutters foam with blood. Suffice
it to say that the 'Mr Simpson' who last week telephoned the vicar of
Bratton Fleming, the Reverend John Hornby, to announce the
planned 'gay' visitation was nothing more than a cruel and malevolent
impostor, and not even a 'gay'. The extraordinary thing is that Mr
Hornby believed him and sought only to mitigate the embarrassment
by declaring that the church would be full (not true, as it turned out)
and that the 'gays' would have to make do with accommodation in the
village hall, to which the service would be relayed by loudspeaker.
Perhaps Mr Hornby's reaction should not surprise us, for on
television he appeared to possess in abundance those characteristics
which we have come to associate with many of those publicly
identified as 'friends' of Mr Thorpe – a disagreeable and slightly
sinister appearance and a capacity to say, do or believe almost

anything, provided it is in some way inappropriate. If the thanksgiving service was in itself a masterpiece of bad taste, Mr Hornby's sermon was even more so. 'God is so fantastic', said Mr Hornby, thanking God both for the jury's verdict ('With God, nothing shall be impossible!') and for 'that fantastic resilience' He had granted to Jeremy and Marion. 'My dears, don't you think if it had been you or I in Jeremy's or Marion's shoes, that we'd be either round the bend or in the madhouse or had a couple of coronaries . . ?' But enough of Mr Hornby. The really surprising thing was the gullibility of those hard-bitten Fleet Street journalists. Even Mr John Junor, the man who has edited the *Sunday Express* for countless generations, did not doubt that 'a coachload of poofs' was on its way to Bratton Fleming and practically gave himself a coronary when he thought about it. 'After you with the sick-bag please, Alice' were the closing words of his comment on the subject. But the fantasy world of Jeremy Thorpe has by now enveloped us all.

7 July 1979

Bums in Brideshead 1
Auberon Waugh

Hot on Richard Ingrams's sniffy review of Granada Television's *Brideshead Revisited* of a a few weeks ago came the news – to which the new proletarian *Times* exultantly devoted seven column inches on its front page – that *Brideshead* has not made the ITV top ten ratings, even for its first instalment on 12 October. So it would seem that bare bottoms are not the answer to the *Spectator's* problems, as may have been suggested from time to time. Quite apart from anything else, if we had too many bare bottoms we might lose the services of our distinguished television critic; on the understanding that Mr Ingrams almost certainly won't get this far in the article, I even dare to suggest that he missed the point of the bare bottoms in *Brideshead* when he wrote: 'I was sorry to see that the "gay" element in the story had been gratuitously pointed up . . . there was a quite unnecessary shot of naked bums on the Castle Howard roof.'

It seems to me that in his anxiety over the spread of homosexuality, Mr Ingrams has lost sight of the fact that long before bare bottoms were thought disturbing, or 'gay', or even pretty, they were universally recognised as funny. I am almost sure that the *Brideshead* bottoms were meant to be funny. Anyway, I laughed, and if I were editor of the *Spectator* I would make Ingrams write out fifty times: 'Bare bottoms need not be disturbing. They can be very funny indeed.' But perhaps Chancellor lacks the Power just yet.

Private Eye demonstrates the *Spectator's* problem in reverse. Pretty well the same people write for both publications, so there can be no question of jealousy. But it is inescapable that as *Private Eye* gets worse – its gossip and news pages less plausible, less funny, and more obsessed with homosexuality – its circulation goes from strength to strength until it now sells ten copies to *Spectator's* every one. My own conclusion is that there is only a very limited number of people worth addressing in Britain. In order to arrive at some estimate, we might examine the recent circulation figures for *Spectator*.

When Chancellor became editor in 1975, the magazine had had a very bad spell and its circulation was sinking fast. It continued to sink for the first two years of his editorship so that from its most recent peak of 48,000 in 1961 it had sunk to 12,000 average sales in 1977. Since then he has put on about half as many again. Whether the fact of the circulation's continued decline for those two years means that Chancellor, in his own small way, was Shrimsleying – in this case, of course, driving oafish readers away by his unashamed excellence – or whether the demoralised readership he inherited simply did not notice that there had been any change, I choose to disregard that residue of 12,000 readers at the bottom of the barrel. If they were prepared to read the *Spectator* from the middle of 1973 to 1975 they would be prepared to read anything.

Let us examine the 6000 buyers who have arrived since: intelligent, educated, humane, humorous people – are they really all that is left? My own guess is that we have caught only three quarters of them, and there are still 2000 left to be caught. When Mr Chancellor has that mystical figure of 8000 new buyers under his belt in addition to having published his 8000th number he will have the world at his feet. He will also be in possession of a power more unassailable than anything claimed by Mr Heath, Mr Benn or Sir James Goldsmith, of addressing the only people in England whose agreement or good opinion is worth seeking in the language and accents which only they understand.

7 November 1981 (extract)

Bums in Brideshead 2
Richard Ingrams

Some readers have complained to me that the last historic issue of the *Spectator* consisted entirely of one contributor attacking another and vice versa. So it is with some trepidation that I return to the great Brideshead Bum Debate, the main protagonists of which are myself (Anti-Gratuitous Gay Bums) and Auberon Waugh (Pro-Witty Life-Enhancing Bums). I was away in the North-East last week so I saw very little television and when I tried to watch Angela Rippon at Lindisfarne in a hotel bedroom the set unaccountably blacked out. On Tuesday night (*Brideshead* night) I was, as it happened, in Durham and my wife and I were enjoying a drink with Ms Sophie Waugh, daughter of the distinguished *Spectator* columnist. As nine o'clock drew near she became increasingly impatient to return to her college to watch *Brideshead* and it fell to me to drive her back. Thus it was that I missed the first few minutes of last week's instalment. I am informed on very good authority, however, that the opening scene included yet another bum – that of Lord Sebastian Flyte taking a shower – and that on this occasion it was a bum of the type that could in no way be described by Mr Waugh and his *Brideshead* supporters as a witty and amusing bum. Rather was it a heavily serious bum and of no relevance whatever to the story. This week's episode, as it happens, was bum-free, though we did see Lord Sebastian sitting in the bath with his friend Mr Ryder squatting by his side. This seemed rather an improbable scene to me, so I referred to Evelyn Waugh's text only to find that in the original version the scene takes place in Sebastian's bedroom while he is getting dressed. Why change it to the bathroom – except to introduce nudity?

I do not labour the point out of some anti-homosexualist obsession, but because what has been done to *Brideshead* is typical of the way television debases almost everything it touches. All the critics have said how faithful a transcription Granada and Mr John Mortimer have made of the book, overlooking the way in which the producers could not resist the Bum Factor, thus 'spicing up' the relationship between Ryder and Flyte to suggest a homosexual liaison where there is nothing of the kind in Waugh's story, and thereby reducing the serial, in my jaundiced eyes at least, to the same level as *The Borgias* or any other old soap opera.

14 November 1981

Bums in Brideshead 3
Auberon Waugh

Before returning for the last time to *Brideshead* and the great Bottoms Debate I suppose I had better agree with its instigator, Mr Richard 'Bottomy Bill' Ingrams, that I have an *exceedingly small* financial interest in the production. By the time income tax has been paid on it at the highest rate, plus unearned surcharge, the sum involved is so small as to be laughable. It would be a travesty of the truth to claim that every time Jeremy Irons or Anthony Andrews showed a cheek we opened a bottle of the Croft 1914 at Combe Florey. Only the slightly warped mind of a professional debunker could imagine that this trifling sum would influence my attitude to the vital question of bottoms. The suggestion is unworthy of him, and unworthy of the high office he holds as the *Spectator*'s television critic. It would certainly never occur to me to suggest that his own attitude is in any way shaped by the fact that he plainly has no financial interest in the film at all. Well, there we are then.

To recapitulate. Ingrams argues that the incidence and frequency of bare bottoms in Derek Grainger's production of *Brideshead Revisited* could only have been intended to inflame our passions and excite unnatural sexual desires. He finds no homosexual content in the novel, and bases a whole philosophy of bottoms on the supposition that Mr Grainger, the producer, and Mr Sturridge, the director, in consciously pandering to the corrupt appetites of the mass market, were contributing to its depravity. I would argue that there is a definite homosexual element in the novel, although it is artfully written so that it can be read in the drawing room as well as the smoking room and mean something slightly different in each place. I thought the handling of this element in the film was inoffensive, and only slightly less ambiguous than in the novel. Certainly my family laughed and cheered at every bare bottom, while Ingrams was deeply disturbed, supposing bitterly that it all looked very pretty in colour.

However, I would agree that there were rather a lot of them – there is some disagreement on the final bum-count, but I think it was eight – and the funny-joke brigade probably had a better time of it than the moral-outrage squad since the drawing-room bum, like the drawing-room fart, is a joke which improves with every repetition.

I now come to one of the few scenes where no bare bottom was in evidence. Perhaps in part because of this lack, the love scene between Ryder and Julia Mottram on board ship seemed to me the only serious artistic flaw in what was otherwise as close to being a masterpiece as the limitations of the original novel and of the television medium allowed. On this point I am particularly anxious not to be misunderstood, deliberately or otherwise. I was not yearning for another glimpse of the Ryder bum in any lustful or lubricious way. By the end of the film I found Ryder odious as well as unattractive. The only remotely amusing or likeable thing about him was the way he kept showing us his bum. If he had shown it us again on this occasion it would have allowed an audience of mixed sexes and ages to suppose that (on their level, at least) he was playing the scene for laughs and, on the principle of Pavlov's dogs, we would all have laughed heartily through what, in the absence of such a joke-signal, became an intensely embarrassing and distasteful moment.

Perhaps I had better explain myself further. It is a common place defence of sex on the screen to say that the act of lovemaking is a normal, natural and sometimes beautiful thing. Above all, it actually happens. It was there in the book. We all know about it. Most of us – God, how embarrassing – actually . . . is it not obvious hypocrisy to pretend otherwise? Why shouldn't the television show an activity which is familiar to most of us in our personal experience and which is certainly an organic element in the development of most love stories, or stories of human relationships?

The answer to all these questions is that whereas the act of sex is normal and natural, it is neither remotely normal nor remotely natural to watch two other people on the job. That is the central, unbridgeable difference between reading about it in a book and seeing it on the screen. Unlike many others, I have no objection to frankly pornographic films while not being, in any sense, an amateur of them, but their interest is confined to the single area of sexual curiosity. The great absurdity in the whole argument for 'acceptable' sex in drama is to suppose that you can drop a great chunk of sexual voyeurism into the middle of conventional social behaviour without destroying the whole balance and tension of the narrative.

The act of sex, as I say, is an intensely private thing between two people which happens out of sight of everyone else. The screen *must* leave its lovers at the bedroom door unless the film's purpose is sexual arousal, which is itself so intense and concentrated an emotion as to exclude, at any rate on celluloid, any other feeling or sentiment. In other words, it kills all personal involvement beyond the cold curiosity of the voyeur.

Which brings me to the matter of Diana Quick's nipple. Once again, I do not wish to be misunderstood. It struck me as a perfectly good nipple. She is right to be proud of it. Every year, as regular readers will know, I retire to the Mediterranean watering hole of Leucate, in the Aude, to complain about the bare breasts on display there. My point is always that whether the breasts are wonky and odd or whether they are perfectly formed, like Miss Quick's, what makes the female breast an object of veneration and erotic curiosity to the male is the intimate circumstances in which it is normally revealed. Publicly flaunted, it is of no more erotic curiosity than a well-turned shoulder blade.

But my reaction to the sight of Miss Quick's nipple being fondled by the expressionless oaf whom Charles Ryder had become was more complicated. Already I can hear the snake's whisper of Richard Ingrams accusing me of sexual jealousy, and for once I feel that old Bottomy Bill may nearly have got it right. But I do not suppose my reaction was peculiar, or even particularly odd. Let me explain.

In real life, I have been told, Jeremy Irons was wearing his underpants and nothing reprehensible occurred. In real life, I have read in my Hickey or Dempster, Miss Quick is already paired with an actor called not so much Mickey Finn as Albert Finney. If I had not once seen him as a reasonably credible Hamlet I would suppose that this choice might indicate Miss Quick's preference for the rough trade, which would rule most of us out in any case. But that is not my point. At the age of forty-two I have seen too many beautiful women throw themselves away on men who did not somehow seem quite up to their standards – the lovely Anna Ford on Mark Boxer, Lady Diana Fairytale on Prince Bat Ears – to have any illusions. One can't have them all. Life must go on. Jealousy will get one nowhere.

But it would be a peculiarly unsusceptible man who was not at any rate slightly in love with the fictional Lady Julia Flyte by the time we reached the shipboard scene. At very least, we were looking on her as an old friend. It was not only distasteful but also highly distressing to have to watch her being mauled by the oafish pooftah Ryder. I think that if ever the Granada contract comes up for renewal I will insist on that scene being cut.

19 December 1981

8 Books

Evelyn Waugh
William Deedes

Evelyn Waugh went to Abyssinia in the summer of 1935 as war correspondent for the *Daily Mail* with two books in mind. One, striking his rich seam as a travel writer, would be mainly serious and about the war. A novel might follow. As it turned out, the first book, *Waugh in Abyssinia*, possibly disappointed his own and his admirers' expectations. His novel, *Scoop*, hit the roof. Among our own fraternity in Fleet Street, where we are prone to narcissism, it is readily seen as his greatest work.

Abyssinia had good vibes for Waugh. In 1930 he had prevailed on *The Times* to send him to Addis Ababa to cover the coronation of Haile Selassie, Lion of Judah. The story goes that he *posted* his account of this event. BADLY LEFT ALL PAPERS ALL STORIES. But the journey inspired his novel *Black Mischief*, which was a success. It was unfortunate, incidentally, that the British Minister in Addis, whose daughter featured as Prudence in *Black Mischief*, should still be in residence when Waugh returned in 1935. I witnessed the reunion of Waugh and 'Prudence' in one of the capital's two dreadful cinema clubs, and it is the only time I have seen a woman dash a glass of champagne in a man's face.

Nature is pretty fair in her distribution of the talents. She will endow a politician of outstanding intellect with bad judgement; a poetic genius with a touch of dipsomania. She determined that Waugh should be a superb novelist and a very bad reporter. How else could the rest of us scratch a living? How otherwise would we have got *Scoop*? Living alongside him in the Deutsches Haus, which in *Scoop* became Pension Dressler, one got wind of the telegrams he received from an anguished *Daily Mail*. His comic telegrams in *Scoop* are emasculated versions of what arrived at frequent intervals from

Northcliffe House. He used them as spills when indulging his frightful habit of smoking a short cigar at the breakfast table. If Waugh had disappointed *The Times*, he dismayed the *Daily Mail*.

It must be borne in mind that this Abyssinian affair was the last of its kind. The later Sino-Japanese war was of a different genre. So was the Spanish Civil War. That for some of our craft was not a story but a crusade. Later they wrote books on how they had borne arms against Franco. Abyssinia was the last war to attract the circus. Fox Movietone sent Lawrence Stallings, famed and flamboyant author of those First World War hits *What Price Glory?* and *The Big Parade*, to head their outfit. The Westerns were unlucky to miss him. He and his gang got off rather lightly, I thought, in *Scoop* as Excelsior Movie-Sound Expeditionary unit to the Ishmaelite Ideological Front. Indeed, looking back on that galère, nearly all ghosts now, I feel moved to say that Waugh was charitable. One of our circle, a Texan, who does not feature in the novel, appeared in London some months after we all got back. He wore boots laced to the knee, a canary-coloured waistcoat, two cameras and a gigantic Stetson hat. As we parted in my office he wondered if I could put him in touch with Waugh. I directed him to Waugh's club and this must have come off, for a day or two later I received a card which read simply: 'That was not kind. E. W.'

It would not be fair, even at this distance from the forty-year rule, too closely to identify; but among the characters in *Scoop* can be traced Knickerbocker of Hearst's International News Service, Jim Mills of Associated Press, Sir Percival Phillips, veteran correspondent of the *Daily Telegraph*, Tovey, a *Daily Express* photographer, Drees of *Exchange Telegraph*, some wild Frenchmen whose names I forget, George Steer of *The Times*. I contributed, marginally, to William Boot's extraordinary baggage. The *Morning Post* thought it right that their correspondent should travel as a gentleman. Breeches, tropical suits and a variety of equatorial hats came with me, some of it in two uniform cases (stamped with my name) and a vast cedar-wood trunk lined with zinc to defy white ants. In Paris I paid for 294 lbs excess baggage. When this lot arrived in the Deutsches Haus, Waugh was enchanted. The cleft sticks were his own idea.

Holed up in Addis Ababa, first awaiting the war and then denied access to its main front, the spirit of the circus infected us all, including Waugh. There was, for example, one evening when after friendly poker Knickerbocker opined that Waugh and Aldous Huxley were the best contemporary writers. Waugh took this qualified acknowledgement of his pre-eminence as fighting words. He invited Knickerbocker to step outside the hotel where as if it were the most natural thing in the world, I found myself holding Knickerbocker's spectacles while they sparred in pitch darkness. No – and this is the odd thing – all of us were sober.

Though apparently impervious to the *Daily Mail*'s despairing telegrams, Waugh was not idle. He enjoyed more than one long interview with the Abuna, whose news value was negligible, and paid this pillar of the church the compliment of naming his pet monkey 'B'Abuna'. He discovered rich and ancient corners, such as the walled city of Harar, with joy and thoroughness.

Many characters he drew for *Scoop* are, as I say, even at this distance recognisable. (I never met Lord Copper or his foreign editor, Salter, but with recollections of Fleet Street in the early 1930 I have no difficulty at all in placing them.) More surprisingly, the plot he drew, though bizarre, had a strong substratum of reality.

As they travelled by Messageries Maritimes to Africa (mercifully, a boat ahead of me) Waugh and his warwarding companions were joined at Port Said by a mysterious individual named F. W. Rickett. They took note of his mysteriousness but failed to discover until it was too late the reason for it. Rickett was to sign an agreement with the Emperor on behalf of a subsidiary of Standard Vacuum Oil, giving oil and mineral rights over half the kingdom. The *quid pro quo* was to be a £10 million modernisation programme.

The night the agreement was signed in Addis Ababa Waugh was many miles away, exploring the ancient glories of Harar. Rickett's story was scooped up by two correspondents, Jim Mills of AP and Sir Percival Phillips of the *Daily Telegraph*. Mills cabled the entire agreement to America. Washington, thus suddenly drawn into an oncoming war, was aghast. The world was staggered. Eden, Laval of France, Cordell Hull, America's Secretary of State, consulted furiously and contrived to bust the deal. By any standards, Mills and Phillips had pulled off an astonishing scoop. Angry cables descended on all the other correspondents, but none more heavily than the *Daily Mail*'s on Waugh, still in Harar and out of touch. In *Scoop* this plot is, so to speak, inverted, with the mysterious Mr Baldwin playing the role of Rickett.

'Lightly as I took my duties and the pretensions of my colleagues . . .' Waugh was to write later. So he did. Yet it is not in the nature of man to work alongside professionals in any field, however oddly they behave, without feeling at times a certain wistfulness. Often I have wondered since how much such feelings may have stirred in Waugh. For in the end William Boot, his hero, came good. Lord Copper was right. Boot, from hopeless beginnings, scooped the world.

The general editor looked . . . 'It's news,' he said. 'Stop the machines at Manchester and Glasgow. Clear the line to Belfast and Paris. Scrap the whole front page. Kill the ex-Beauty Queen's pauper funeral. Get in a photograph of Boot.'

A touch of yearning there? Inside many reporters a novelist struggles to get out. Inside Waugh, with all his scorn for us, there could have been, who knows, a reporter wriggling about. Seeing what we got from Waugh instead, how very lucky we are that it didn't work out that way.

5 May 1979

Up the creek
Eric Christiansen

Estuary: Land and Water in the lower Thames basin A. K. Astbury (Carnforth Press)

By taking the long view, and tracing the great arteries of human life outwards from London, you can epitomise the whole of English civilisation in the main railway-stations. In that case, the offices of the

Spectator stand on a sort of cultural watershed. To the west, there is a moral slope that leads by leafy squares and airy terraces to Paddington, and Paddington still embodies the sort of world that goes with canons of Hereford guzzling tea on the Cathedrals Express, and boarding school charmers conning *The Pony*. The connexion with WC1 may appear tenuous at times, but on a clear day you can almost see Blenheim Palace from the upper windows of Doughty Street.

To the east there is another slope, both moral and physical, and it leads by way of Holborn Viaduct to Liverpool Street, Fenchurch Street, and London Bridge. From there, the lines fan out on either side of the Thames estuary, and the effect on the novice of this Antipaddingtonian experience can be painful. Half-wrecked, half-disinfected carriages, scrawled with skin-head slogans, hump the toilers *en masse* into a twilight of broken machinery, ruined factories, and flawed bungalows. It is a world so badly put together, so shored up with corrugated iron, asbestos and hardboard that simple explanations of its condition, like poverty, bombing, or local government, hardly cover the facts. When the streets end, the bungalows and huts carry on down the river, the theme is continued in dead car-bodies, unsorted junk, and caravan sites served by cut-price boating harbours.

Once the traveller reaches the saltings, he can pause by the tide-mark of aerosol cans (this is where they all come to die) and note that he has moved from the job racket, to the housing racket, to the retirement racket and the leisure racket almost without a break. A cruel joke has been played on the inhabitants. The great city has given them the freedom of the great river-mouth as Harold of Harold's Wood once gave Harold of Norway six feet of English soil. There's weakness in numbers down here. Out on the water, the rasping of the water-skiers drowns the unmistakable phut of Pitsea sportsmen wounding gulls with air-gun pellets. Along the outer face of the sea wall the broken glass twinkles cheerfully in the sun, and the boys from Vange race mopeds through the samphire. The former company director from Erith looks for places to hide the dismembered fragments of his mistress which he carries in his ruck-sack. This is the sort of place where Pip met Magwitch. They would miss each other in the crowd, nowadays.

Disturbing, very, for those who like to keep their Turner water-colours and their Giles cartoons on separate pieces of paper. However, this is what the whole coast will be like before the end of the century, and the marshes of North Kent and the Essex hundreds are merely undergoing a rather intense and sticky farewell kiss. It won't be long now, before they sink under the sea for ever, and Billericay Dicky will be able to hydrofoil to Holborn direct. In Roman times the marshlands were five feet higher; and no amount of conservation is going to keep them afloat. So the fastidious Paddingtonian may not find this an interesting subject. It's sad, but so is *Traviata*, and with *Traviata* you get the music, too.

But wait. Among the debris of the shore, a lonely figure moves, stops and looks. It is the figure of Mr A. K. Astbury, and he is looking at the past. In his waistcoat pocket he has a clipped day return to Benfleet, and in his mackintosh a pocket edition of Belloc's *The River of London* and a piece of Roman tile he has picked up from a lay-by. He is no longer young, but he stands in a bitter wind without flinching. Before his gaze, the marshes expand, islands emerge from the mudflats, and the roads, ships, houses and forts of a lost Britain take shape. Mark this man. On his shoulders he carries the weight of civilisation.

He has spent many years thinking about the estuary, and many years trying to persuade someone to publish his thoughts. He has finally had *Estuary* printed at his own expense. One of the officious half-wits who turned down his MS suggested he augment it with two chapters on the coming of the Saxons and the Vikings, and it is the only regret of this reviewer that he followed the advice. Otherwise, the book is a gem. It is not a history, nor a geography, but a series of reflections and notes on antiquities connected with the mouth of the Thames. What makes it remarkable is the author. He is wholly and unashamedly amateur, with no academic pretensions of any kind, no claim to technical expertise, no diploma in socio-archaeology, no Latin, no talent for playing the local studies market. He belongs to the old school; a pounds-shillings-and-pence yards-feet-and-inches man, who goes by Kipling, Buchan, Belloc, Rider Haggard and the 'Polish sailor' who lived at Stanford-le-Hope. Among the many proofs of his soundness, the lack of the author's photograph on the jacket is one some readers may regret; but there is no need for it. The book is the man.

Local history tends to breed lunacy, showmanship, or statistics. None of these appears in *Estuary*. Nevertheless, Mr Astbury is eccentric because he tackles historical problems with the assumption that they can be solved entirely by his own reason and experience, with only polite and rather distant acknowledgements to History Incorporated. He doesn't want to mug professors; he just wants to do things his own way. By explaining this way in detail, he acquits himself of any charges of fraud that might be levelled, and revels that even nowadays The Pursuit of Knowledge under Difficulties can be rewarded.

He got a job in the Thames Board at Purfleet in 1933, by 'the signal kindness' of one Timon Lockyer, and adds in a characteristic aside that it was 'a kindness for which I was never able to thank him adequately, or even at all'. For two years, he ate his lunch by the north bank sea-wall, and for much longer he travelled up and down the estuary, taking time off to visit Collins's Music Hall, where the physique of the North Country chorus girls convinced him that Lancashire was colonised by Norwegians. He investigated the brick, stone and timber relics of the river banks by asking workmen what they thought about them, and reading up the parish histories for further information; his equipment was a pair of wellingtons, a tide-table, and a railway ticket. This is not the approved way of doing historical research, and when it leads him to re-write the Anglo-Saxon Chronicle the results are poor. But when he deals with ferries, bridges, churches, chalkmines, old roads and landing-places, it pays off.

These things are discussed in a slow and digressive fashion, with the same assumptions about life and learning that were shared by the contributors and subscribers of the *Gentleman's Magazine*. It might seem questionable whether others really want to know whether East Tilbury Church was bombarded by the Dutch in 1667, or whether the plaque set up by No 2 Company of the London Electrical Engineers in 1917 was or was not destroyed on the orders of the War Office, but under the Astbury treatment the answer is definitely yes.

And his failures are sometimes as interesting as his successes.

There is the case of the vanishing Roman mosaic, which was said to have been built into the floor of Gray's church vestry. Mr Astbury persuaded the churchwarden 'to lift the edge of the carpet which covered the tiled floor. It was not possible to see the whole of it, for a heavy table covered the centre at which church officials were sorting out the collection . . .' Nevertheless, what he did see wasn't Roman. While searching for other Roman fragments on the eastern bank of Otterham Creek, he found a whole shore covered by the tide, but he was 'compensated for his lack of foresight' by the beauty of the apple blossom in the overhanging orchards, and the smoothness of the pasture. At Shoregate Creek he was marooned by another un-foreseen tide; not only did he fail to make any archaeological discoveries, but when he got back to Rainham at 2 a.m. he found 'the station shut, the recreation ground with its shelter locked, and the rain falling steadily, as it had been doing since I was cut off by the tide hours before. While standing in a shop doorway, wondering what to do . . .' Well, the story has a happy ending, which I won't give away.

Perhaps it was this sort of thing that put off the publishers. They must have found it disturbingly lacking in affectation. A non-fictional book without pretensions to superior wisdom or fine writing has become a rare and somewhat unwelcome event. This one proves that such graces are unnecessary. Despite a fair crop of blunders, it gives a careful and convincing picture of life on our most important river in times so remote that scarcely one of its modern features would then have been recognisable. They would not have to be remote for that, of course, as he shows by a last chapter on the nineteenth-century literary associations of the estuary. If all solvent Thames-dwellers buy this book, as I hope they will, both up and downstream from London, they will do themselves a favour and beat the system by backing an outsider. One day, they will be spraying CLIOMETRICS OUT all the way from Liverpool Street to Southend.

7 March 1981

Muggeridge
Mark Amory

Like it Was Malcolm Muggeridge Ed. John Bright-Holmes (Collins)

Malcolm Muggeridge has been revered and reviled as, among other things, a satirical gadfly, a political analyst, a lascivious hypocrite, an old ham and a saint. No one has suggested that he is a bore and for all of their 560 pages his diaries are not boring. His skills as a reporter are focussed on an excellent subject – himself – and if his interest fails in 1962, thus severely curtailing his days as a television sage, ours is still triumphantly engaged.

If he does not end at the end, nor does he begin at the beginning. We skip boyhood and a large chunk of youth to discover our hero in Russia at the age of twenty-nine. This is the crucial moment in his political life, when he has arrived with his wife to make a home in the New Civilisation (his phrase). He leaves eight months later a disillusioned man and life-long anti-communist. Most of us have heard about it before in his autobiography (third volume promised this year), in *Winter in Moscow*, the novel he wrote about it, or in a biography by Ian Hunter which appeared last year. It is as well, for the editor explains in a brief preface that he is against explanatory interpolation and expository footnotes and decided to let the diaries speak for themselves. This is a point of view, not often mine. Tolerably in control at home, I never really grasped who people were or what jobs they did, let alone what became of them, when Muggeridge was abroad. So I used Professor Hunter's book as a companion volume.

The effect of the bare text is a great increase in immediacy. Muggeridge is held in sharp focus, while all else is a blur, even his wife Kitty. As he worries about indigestion and money, sleeps on the floor when she has typhus, makes notes to himself to get on with his novel and considers suicide again, he is always vivid and alive. His self-pity crackles with energy, his mood shifts abruptly and exhilaratingly. There is no point in pinning him down; he and his opinions will be transformed in a moment. How he does his job as Moscow correspondent of the *Guardian* on the other hand can be pieced together if you have the will, a good memory and are a close reader. Similarly it is noticeable that his first entry is less than fully committed: 'Today I arrived in Moscow. Already I have made up my mind to call this the *Diary of a Journalist* and not the *Diary of a Communist*'. But you must go to Professor Hunter to be told that *before* he arrived he had said to A. J. P. Taylor, 'I am going to Utopia and I am sure I shall hate it', among other remarks that showed him already dubious.

We find him next working on *The Calcutta Statesman*. He is again taking language lessons, again urging himself to write a novel. Where Russia was depressing, India is melancholy and the twilight of Empire is almost as displeasing as the emergence of Communism. He seems like an earlier V. S. Naipaul, roaming the world, never at home, casting a cold eye that understands much and despises it. Then he is rather surprisingly on a horse, galloping about, though still with a bad stomach. On his way to a morning ride he shouted, ' "The morning is golden." It was. Sunlight hovering over everything like a golden mist. For years I have not felt so happy, been so aware of the sensuality of living . . .' Kitty, never described, comes out for a visit. They quarrel but make up. He has seen 'a woman at Sipi Fair, half Hungarian and half Indian, beautiful in a way, wearing an exquisite sari . . . I smelt emotional entanglement'. His nose was not deceived. The affair is detailed and touching when it is destroyed by his departure; his marriage, which we know is to end, or rather continue, happily, is a mystery.

The war is dismissed in twenty pages. For those searching to establish facts there is an important omission. In his autobiography Muggeridge spends four pages describing a suicide attempt. He swims out from Lourenço Marques at night and, before swimming back again, has a religious experience: 'there followed an overwhelming joy such as I had never experienced before; and ecstasy. In some mysterious way it became clear to me that there was no darkness, only the possibility of losing sight of a light which shone eternally . . .' Professor Hunter is too polite to call him a liar but he does consider the passage uncharacteristically understated, points out that Muggeridge never mentioned this experience to anyone, and that he had described a strikingly similar incident some years before in an unpublished novel. He decides Muggeridge is 'enmeshed in a web of fantasy'. I mention it because although there is nothing at the time, there is a reference on 30 March 1946, by which time the fantasy, if fantasy it was, has certainly taken hold.

With peace we come to the main section of the book, 200 pages of successful literary life and marriage in England. The ingredients are familiar and there is not much narrative thrust but the cast is star-studded and it is all highly enjoyable. Dull care has been left behind and even his digestive system seems in good shape.

Orwell appears, but already ill, with Muggeridge at his bedside subduing his natural contrariness: 'George said . . . he was quite convinced that judges like Lord Goddard wanted to keep hanging because they derive erotic satisfaction from it. Tried politely to indicate that I thought this utter rubbish.' Professor Hunter tells us that Muggeridge suggested that at the end of *Animal Farm* when the beasts take to two legs, 'A drove of fellow-travellers, such as the Dean of Canterbury, assorted *New Statesman* writers, and others, might put in an appearance going about on all fours'. Orwell was amused but thought it 'too unkind'. Tom Driberg appears with 'a face quite full of darkness and spreading darkness before it'. Graham Greene is met and discussed, Hugh Kingsmill is held in affection, Evelyn Waugh is not, even little David Pryce-Jones appears looking 'exactly like a successful banker'.

The account of editing *Punch* is a little thin. He begins with energy, declares himself 'impenitently a champion of bad taste' and aims to 'ridicule the age in which we live and particularly those set in authority over us'. There is a great row over a cartoon depicting Churchill as senile. The downward slide of the circulation is reversed. But soon he grows weary and by 1957 is glad to cease being The Fool at Lear's Court.

Muggeridge turned to television and snaps as its tentacles embrace him: 'Decided never to do it again. Something inferior, cheap, horrible about television as such; it's a prism through which words pass, energies distorted, false'. Perhaps there is a slight falling off in the book as sanctity approaches but in 1961, a few pages before the end, the old journalist gets another scoop. In Hamburg he 'dropped into a teenage rock-and-roll joint. Ageless children, sexes indistinguishable, tight-trousered, stamping about, only the smell of sweat intimating animality. The band were English, from Liverpool and recognised me. Long-haired; weird feminine faces; bashing their instruments, and emitting nerveless sounds into microphones. In conversation rather touching in a way, their faces like Renaissance carvings of saints or Blessed Virgins. One of them asked me: "Is it true that you're a Communist?" No, I said just in opposition. He nodded understandingly; in opposition himself in a way. "You make money out of it?" he went on. I admitted that this was so. He, too, made money. He hoped to take back £200 to Liverpool.' I like to think the Beatle he spoke to was John Lennon, before he could claim to be more famous than Christ.

There is a pedantic note to add. Editors are usually in a strong position because they have seen the manuscript and their critics have not. In this case John Bright-Holmes mentions that he worked from a typed copy transcribed from the originals and had 'the benefit and the pleasure of Mr Muggeridge's help and advice.' The selection is his and I have no complaints though I would be interested to know if there were earlier or war diaries not thought fit to be included. But for once we have also the passages quoted by Professor Hunter. A comparison is disquieting. In eighteen lines under 4-6 January, 1936, there are numerous discrepancies. Forty words are left out of the first paragraph, a sentence from the second, Hugh is turned into 'Hugh Kingsmill who lives in Hastings', a sentence is introduced. 'The waves pounded in' is changed to 'The waves poured in', but that is presumably a slip in transcription. An 'and' is substituted for a full stop. Another sentence is omitted at the end. No indication is made of any of this.

Now none of this seems sinister. Other spot checks found many fewer differences. I have no way of knowing which version is accurate, though presumably editors cut rather than add something of their own. What is omitted is very like what is included. The motive would seem to be brevity rather than censorship with the possible exception of Kay Dick being described as grotesque in Professor Hunter's version but not in this one. To mark alterations every few lines is tedious and distracting; but if there are few they should be so marked, if many, we should, in the popular phrase, be told.

18 April 1981

The Webbs
J. Enoch Powell

The Diary of Beatrice Webb: Volume 1: Glitter Around and Darkness Within Edited and introduced by Norman and Jeanne MacKenzie (Virago)

From girlhood until the eve of her death at eighty-five Beatrice Webb, *née* Potter, confided to her diary a revelation of her thoughts and feelings, unsparing to the point of cruelty and unblushing to the point of humiliation. Rousseau is fuddy-duddy by comparison. Introspective and intensely personal though the diaries were, the diarist could not bring herself to procure their destruction. At twenty-six, anticipating death, she recorded the 'wish that all these diary-books, after being read (if he shall care to) by Father, should be sent to Carrie Darling' (a schoolteacher friend who was at that time in Australia). She herself, in later life, typed them up and the typescript and the original are available in microfiche as well as at the L. S. E. So she can hardly be surprised or dismayed that they are now being published in four volumes, edited, indexed, with secondary matter excised but without expurgation.

The first volume of the four, which now appears and which runs to her marriage to Sidney Webb in 1892, will, I suspect, be the most revelatory. What it reveals is an extremely introverted woman, by instinct religious, by prejudice Tory, by nature passionate, neurotically inclined to self-doubt and self-examination, and obsessed with the fear of spinsterhood. ('Oh woman, you are passing strange. God preserve me from a lover between thirty-five and forty-five. No woman can resist a man's importunity during the last years of an unrealised womanhood'; or again, 'it is almost necessary to the health of a woman, physical and mental, to have definite home duties to fulfil: details of practical management and, above all things, someone dependent on her love and tender care.') It was an obsession which sometimes verged on nymphomania.

But this warm and womanly person had to bear an intellectual cross. Hers was neither a powerful nor an original mind; but she was imbued with the conviction that somewhere, if only one could acquire and analyse it, there existed the information which could resolve the social and human ills that she perceived. This it was that made her a reluctant socialist. Yet all the time, until Sidney Webb took it and buried it for her, there was the nagging conflict with an instinct and emotion which told her different. The following entry not only illustrates that conflict, but is a good specimen of the diarist's style:

I have in my mind some more dramatic representation of facts that can be given in statistical tables and in the letterpress that explains these – illustrations of social laws in the terms of personal suffering, personal development, personal sin. But this must be delayed until I have discovered my laws, and as yet I am only on the threshold of my inquiry, far enough off, alas, from any general and definite conclusions.

More compromising still (age twenty-six): 'Social questions are the great questions of today. They take the place of religion. I do not pretend to solve them. Their solution seems largely a matter of temperament.'

Best of all, and most Tory of all, take this (age twenty-seven):

That false metaphysical idea of rights as some unalterable result, determined in quantity and quality, due to all men alike, is working its wicked way in our political life. The right of a man, that is to say the natural right of a man, apart from what other men contract to give him as their fellow, is surely only the sum of external forces which react on the internal force.

This is not some sexless Fabian or female Beveridge, such as we thought we had heard of. The deviation of the reality from the common assumption is so great that the several items call for verification.

Would Disraeli himself have quarrelled with this brilliant self-confession of a Tory (age twenty-five)?

In practical politics, if we are forced to interfere through government with the sequence of events and to introduce new factors which will interfere with the natural order of things, is it not safer on the whole to be governed by the instinctive cravings of society than by theories based on 'little knowledge'? Why should we not regard society as an individual, and acknowledge that it is natural and right that it should gratify the sensations and desires through the agency of self-government? Is it not possible that government is not a thing external and foreign to the community but merely the external organ by which the society adjusts its actions to the conditions of the surrounding medium?

The religion is to match. On the way to the East End Beatrice Potter cannot resist, and cannot explain why she cannot resist, Holy Communion at St Paul's: 'Prayer is a constant source of strength. I like to sit in that grand St Paul's with its silent spaces; there is a wonderful restfulness in the great "House of God".' 'Beautiful communion service at St Paul's. While I knelt before the altar I felt that I had at length made my peace with my own past, that the struggle with bitter resentfulness which began as I knelt at the same altar the Sunday after his marriage had at last ended.' A year later, 'this Sunday last year I took the communion at St Paul's and prayed earnestly against bitterness and evil feelings. This day I take it again.'

Which last entry brings us to Beatrice and Joseph Chamberlain. Somebody ought to put these diaries and the other sources together and write the story of that passionate infatuation which dominated this woman from twenty-five to thirty-two, which she herself knew to be 'eccentricity bordering on madness', and which passed through phase after phase of exaltation, mortification and humiliation. It would be a subject worthy in its own right of high literary and dramatic talent. In a review no more than the slightest impression of it can be given.

Beatrice Potter met Chamberlain in 1883 when he was the rising radical hope and Gladstone's President of the Board of Trade, and she fell for him hopelessly. It was not her first love. She had had, at the New Inn, Gloucester, in 1877 'one (!) of my first and most romantic flirtations', and in 1882 she had an affair in Switzerland with a professor of mechanics by the name of Main, which after the event she was to describe thus: 'Two young human beings on the threshold of life and on the verge of an ever-uniting love, parted for ever – one to die, the other to live a life of . . .?' It is not at all clear to what extent Chamberlain at any point reciprocated Beatrice's passion; but for most of the time until he married the American Mary Endicott in 1888 he played a cruel cat-and-mouse game with her, in which his sister and other relatives aided and abetted him.

To her credit, she was never under any misapprehension about his character, which she accurately assessed: 'I felt his curious, scrutinising eyes noting each movement as if he were anxious to ascertain whether I yielded to his absolute supremacy.' 'He is neither a reasoner nor an observer in the scientific sense. He does not deduce his opinions by the aid of certain well-thought-out principles . . . He is an organ of great individual force, the extent of his influence will depend on the relative power of the class he is adopted to represent.' 'His diplomatic talent is unquestioned and is manipulated in his administration of public and local affairs and in his parliamentary work.' 'I could not have idealised that man, though I loved him so passionately.' 'His aims are denoted by enthusiasm and ambition – in his means he is not scrupulously honourable or loyal, and he is indifferent to the morality of his associates so long as they serve his purpose. In his relationship to me there has been a strange lack of chivalry and honour; in mine to him, of womanly dignity.' Finally, after Chamberlain's marriage, 'he must become a Tory. The tendencies of his life are already set in that direction: hatred of former colleagues, sympathy with the pleasure-loving attractive class of "English gentlemen", with which he now associates.'

Despite this penetrating insight, Beatrice remain enslaved from the beginning to the end, repeatedly reviving forlorn hopes, devoured by daydreams, consumedly jealous when Chamberlain married, and even after that remembering with a pathetic compulsion every anniversary of events in their association. It was from all this that Sidney Webb at last rescued her, giving her – for she was acutely class-conscious – 'a new surrounding to my life, a new scene laid in the lower middle-class . . . Past are the surroundings of wealth, past the association with the upper middle-class, past also the silent reserve and the hidden secret . . . My step downwards in the social scale is probable, but if it is his gain it will not be my loss.' From then on, it was second-rate hotels, conferences and reports, correspondence and business, 'with a few brief intervals of "human nature" ', which 'I do not think that the inhabitants of the hotel suspect.'

The book closes with the actual marriage (registry office) and a brilliantly cinematographic fade-out:

Travelled from Darlington to Durham in the same train as Chamberlain and his wife. Watched them set out to walk to the Sunderland train and standing by the side until we speeded out of the station. He was looking self-complacent and somewhat self-conscious, quick to perceive whether he was recognised by the casual travellers. He has lost that old intent look – the keen striving expression of the enthusiast stimulated by ambition. His wife was a plain little thing, but sweet and good and simply dressed. He was on his way to make a big speech at Sunderland. I was on one of my innumerable journeys 'in search of knowledge'. I shuddered as I imagined the life I had missed.

23 October 1982

George Borrow
Michael Wharton

George Borrow died on 26 July, 1881. How many people read his books today? Very few, I imagine, though his name is no doubt remembered for its Gypsy connections. Yet he was once a very celebrated writer; a cult-figure during his lifetime and for long afterwards; subject of several biographies (one by Edward Thomas); and in the 1920s appeared an imposing Collected Edition of his works in fourteen volumes. But the centenary of his death has been little noticed in the literary world. He is decidedly out of fashion. Will he pass out of memory altogether? I hope not. For the strange books of this strange man, once read – certainly when read at the right time of life – can never be forgotten.

He was born at East Dereham in Norfolk in 1803, his father being a Militia Captain of Cornish descent, his mother the daughter of a Norfolk tenant farmer of Huguenot origin. As a boy, travelling with his father's regiment about the British Isles, Borrow acquired a taste for outlandish places and outlandish people – notably gypsies – and a distaste for the ordinary, and for what he called 'gentility'. He had a precocious aptitude for languages. By the age of twenty he claimed – and in Borrow's case the word 'claimed' must be emphasised – knowledge of French, German, Italian, Spanish, Portuguese, Danish, Irish, Welsh, Latin, Greek and Hebrew, as well as Romany, the language, at that time still a philological mystery, of the Gypsies. That his claims were not altogether unfounded was shown when, after an unusually long period of the youthful latency often found among remarkable men, in which he worked as a hack writer and lived (in his own phrase) 'a life of roving adventure', he came to the notice of the Bible Society, which was impressed by his linguistic abilities and gave him the truly quixotic task of distributing Bibles in Spain, where the Spanish version of the Bible was then forbidden.

Out of the letters he sent from Spain to his employers, describing his exciting and picaresque adventures (not all of them connected with the circulation of Bibles) he fashioned a book, *The Bible in Spain* which, published in 1842, made him instantly famous. His problem now was how to continue and expand this fame which he had always felt to be his due. *The Bible in Spain* is full of hints of secret knowledge and mysterious, exotic characters. Urged by his publisher to write his autobiography, he produced, after ten years of toil and anguish the extraordinary book *Lavengro* which, with its sequel, *The Romany Rye* (or 'Gypsy Gentleman') gives him, far more than *The Bible in Spain*, his claim to immortality. Yet the reviewers who had praised his previous book gave this one a hostile reception. Borrow was furiously angry; and however much he may have despised the 'lackeys and lickspittles', the 'canting hypocrites' and the 'foaming radicals' who attacked him, he never really recovered from the blow. He had found material security by marriage to a comfortably-off widow and returned to live in his native Norfolk, spending the long, sad decline which was to be the rest of his life in planning books which never got finished, in far-fetched philological studies and bad translations, varied, until age made him immobile, with restless journeying about Europe. An added cause of bitterness was that his own romantic and haphazard studies of Gypsy lore and language had been overtaken by other men's more systematic and academic research.

Such are 'the facts' of Borrow's life. To us they are only interesting because, transmuted in his writings, they are the groundwork of something unique in English literature, as Borrow himself was unique among English men of letters. He would probably have scorned the term. A fine horseman, boxer, prodigious walker (summoned to London for his first interview with the Bible Society, he is said to have covered the one hundred and twelve miles from Norwich in twenty-seven hours), he must have been the most physically robust of all English writers. Six foot three in height, he was a man of imposing, even awesome presence. An admiring Gypsy said of him: 'he was almost a giant, a most noble-looking gentleman, as it might be the Mayor of England.'

Borrow would have liked that. For he was his own hero. Everything he wrote, whatever it may appear to be about, is about himself. That is what made it so difficult to write his autobiography. If the 'facts' of his life did not fit his heroic image then they must be made to do so. One of his characteristics, so unconscious as to be inoffensive, even endearing, is that in all arguments and encounters he always comes off best. He is a supreme egoist. Aware of this autobiographical difficulty, and by nature secretive and evasive, he changed the title of his book from the original 'An Autobiography' to 'Life: a Drama', then to 'Lavengro: A Dream' and finally to the form in which it eventually appeared. No wonder critics and readers were puzzled. Yet this ambiguity, this doubt about what is fact and what is fiction, is part of the curious fascination of the book. Perhaps without knowing how, Borrow had hit on a kind of writing, half autobiography, half novel, which exactly suited his purpose.

Even the earlier parts of *Lavengro*, where he sticks, at least to some extent, to the true facts – his discovery of the Gypsies, that ancient, outlandish people still living their own hidden life in nineteenth-century England, his experiences as a hack writer in London, where he meets a whole collection of characters from an Armenian merchant to a pea-and-thimble man who have nothing in common but their extreme oddity – have a highly idiosyncratic quality. But it is when he quits London for the country that the book begins to acquire the peculiar enchantment which belongs to Borrow alone.

It is the summer of 1825, that time between the last days of the stage-coaches and the coming of the railways when England must have been more beautiful than it has ever been before or since. Tramping the roads, Borrow has a long series of adventures and chance encounters (as well as some highly contrived ones). One day he meets and is entertained in a fine house by a gentleman who (like Dr Johnson) has a compulsion to touch objects to 'avoid the evil chance'; next he buys a tinker's pony and cart; he is poisoned by Gypsies and saved from death by a Welsh preacher who believes he has committed the Sin against the Holy Ghost; he sets up camp in a lonely dingle; he meets and fights the ferocious Flaming Tinman, the terror of the roads; he lives for a time, in total chastity (the real Borrow seems to have been completely sexless), with a tall, beautiful, flaxen-haired workhouse girl, the incomparable Isobel Berners, who falls in love with him but is finally driven away by his cruel attempts to teach her Armenian; he is visited by a sinister but learned priest, conspiring for Catholic emancipation, whom he continually bests (needless to say) in scholarly arguments (Borrow's hatred of 'Popery' was as fierce as any Orangeman's); he meets an old man who has spent his life learning Chinese but has never learned to tell the time; and so on and so forth.

What saves the book from mere sentimental open-roadism and romantic gypsyism is the sense of a unique personality which pervades the whole. Borrow is a mass of contradictions. He was a writer who, when he stopped writing in the good plain style which he inherited from Defoe and Smollett, often wrote so badly, with his Victorian apostrophes and set purple patches, as to make the reader groan aloud; yet even the very badness and crabbedness of his style, particularly in the mannered, stilted dialogues he has with trampers on the roads, can have a certain charm because it is so unmistakably his own.

He was a man who, though scornful of gentility and fond of poor and wandering people, even criminals, the stranger and more eccentric the better, became angry in his later years because he was not made a Justice of the Peace and could not get on in polite, particularly literary-polite or 'intellectual' society. He upheld the virtues of old ale and pugilism but at the same time wanted to be taken for a Victorian country gentleman. He was a man of vast physical health, strength and courage, yet suffered all his life from what would now be called 'depressive anxiety' and it is perhaps not generally realised that the phrase 'there's a wind on the heath', which must have appeared on thousands of cosy 'English countryside' calendars, comes from a dialogue in which Borrow speaks of his longing for death. He praised openness and plain speaking but was himself a man of habitual self-concealment (and there is evidence that he may indeed have had a great secret to conceal: that he was not the son of Captain Borrow of the Norfolk Militia but of a Gypsy, one of that race, despised and distrusted by the 'respectable', for whom he felt so strong an attraction and who, it is said, often took him for one of themselves).

As an English writer he is a completely isolated figure. His opinions on all subjects were scornfully reactionary. Of the other writers of his century he knew little and cared nothing (he once said of Keats, 'have they not been trying to resuscitate him?'). He is a literary monolith, a survival of old England to be prized all the more in times when England herself seems to be foundering altogether. I first read *Lavengro* in adolescence fifty years ago; going back to it now with some trepidation I find that in spite of everything the old spell still works. A hundred years after Borrow's death others may perhaps discover and take delight in this extraordinary man.

25 July 1981

PLR
Auberon Waugh

One never thought one would applaud any decision of the Arts Council on its policy towards literature, and closer investigation reveals that it is too early to start cheering yet, but if Sir Roy Shaw and his merry arts persons find, as I sincerely hope they will find, that their funds are frozen (if not reduced) this year, and if they adopt the 'unthinkable' option of closing down the Literature Department and ending its patronage of the literary arts (thereby saving slightly less than one per cent of the Council's revenue) they will have earned the undying gratitutde of all who care for the health of English letters.

All, that is to say, apart from four hundred-odd 'writers' and would-be writers who have received awards or bursaries in the past years, and those still hoping for them. It is one of the advantages of having a government which chooses to use the rhetoric of monetarism in place of an economic policy that just occasionally it can be persuaded to make small cuts in public expenditure in those areas which are actually harmful to the recipients. If, as I half suspect, the motive of the Arts Council in suggesting that it will put an end to literary subsidies is to provoke as noisy an opposition as possible to the whole idea of cuts in government expenditure on the arts, then this should suit the government's purpose very well. The sum involved is, as I say, tiny – about £611,000. The publicity excited is commensurate with the closing down of five major teaching hospitals, two steelworks and a shipyard. The real money spenders (and money wasters) are the four great national companies – National Opera, National Theatre, Covent Garden and Royal Shakespeare Company – but economies demanded there, and vindictively applied, would undoubtedly result in the cultural impoverishment of the nation.

Nor, I am convinced, is it the government's real purpose to save money. Spending other people's money is too much fun for that, and in fact this government, for all its monetarist avowals, is overspending at a greater rate than any previous government in the history of the nation. But it has to convince itself, and us, and the rest of the world, that it is serious in its intentions to cut public expenditure. To this end the howls of anger excited by a cut of £611,000 – a sum so tiny as to be completely invisible in the budget deficit of £10,500 million – represent a triumph for government policy, or at any rate for the presentation of it.

But it is not my purpose to argue that the Arts Council's ending of subsidies to literature would be helpful to the government, so much as that it would be a good thing for literature and a good thing in itself – a positive contribution to the intellectual vitality of the country such as the Arts Council has not yet made, to the best of my knowledge, in its thirty-six years of existence.

In urging this course of action I am fully aware that there are contrary arguments to be put. Mr Channon, the Minister for the Arts and Sir Roy Shaw can accept my pleading or they can choose to listen to the Writers' Guild of Great Britain whose chairman, Ms Eva Figes, has received no fewer than three grants from the Arts Council for work which Robert Nye (no doubt himself a beneficiary) has described as 'creating the *moment from inside*, vividly, patiently, admitting every ounce of its current ambiguity, so that [her] sentences read like heart beats'.

I do not propose to enter into a discussion of the Figes heart-beat technique at this stage; the Writers' Guild argument is well put in ordinary English by Mr Ian Rowland Hill, its general secretary, in a letter to *The Times*: 'with libraries and education authorities spending less money on purchasing books and with prices being forced up, now is the time for increased funding, not a total abdication.'

To this Sir Roy Shaw replied a few days later that 'whereas dance, drama and music must rely mainly on the Arts Council for support, literature is very heavily supported by libraries, which are separately funded.'

Although on this occasion Sir Roy appears to be on the side of the angels, I feel he misses the point. The libraries, far from helping writers, have destroyed any hope of earning a livelihood from writing books for all but a handful of authors. No first novelist today can hope to earn a living from the practice of his craft. Librarians talk as if they are doing a favour to the author when they buy his novel and lend it to forty or fifty readers for nothing, pointing out that few of the borrowers would ever think of buying a novel for themselves, but the sad truth is that free libraries have nearly destroyed the market, as they were bound to do. The Government has at last acknowledged this by its proposal to pay ½p per borrowing up to a limit of £500 (or 100,000 borrowings) on each title but this should not be seen as 'support for literature' so much as a belated and inadequate recompense for an act of piracy. It is the posture of a highwayman who kindly offers his victim a few pence back in the hope that he will continue to cross Haywards Heath every night to be robbed.

I write these words with some pain, as a man who has published eleven books in the last twenty years, five of them novels, but who gave up novel writing ten years ago when it became apparent that no literary novel was ever again going to earn more than £2000 (or its equivalent) for any but a tiny handful of old favourites. For myself, I will not be tempted to write another novel by the offer of ½p a borrowing on a maximum borrowing, I should judge in my case, of 20,000 – that is to say £100 on top of a library royalty of some £600 for the purchase of 1000 copies. Nor, when would-be novelists look into the economics of the matter, will many of them be tempted to start, even if publishers are still prepared to look at the work of unknown fiction writers. I should judge that a payment of 5p a borrowing, with an upper limit of £5000 a title (or 100,000 borrowings) would be the least needed to get things started again. Even this would cost only £20 million, or less than a fifth of one per cent of our budget deficit, for a service which, in times of mass unemployment, may prove only slightly less important or useful than the National Health.

But direct government patronage is not the answer. It is as a reviewer, rather than as a writer of books – and general student of the literary scene – that I would urge Sir Roy to consider that the influence of Arts Council patronage in literature has been detrimental, and that it should be stopped for this reason if no other. My qualifications for this are that for the last eleven years I have reviewed at least one, sometimes many more books every week. In that time I have been searching publishers' lists in the endless quest for any books worth noticing. The Arts Council's Annual Reports for the last ten years trace not only its support of such disastrous ventures as the *New Review* and *New Fiction Society* but also list authors who have received awards. Many names are repeated, but ninety per cent of them are still completely unknown to me – if they ever published anything, it sank without trace.

The remaining ten per cent include five or six respectable writers, but the bias apparent in the choice – towards anyone prepared to keep blowing on the dead embers of the Modern Movement which could be seen to have lost all heat forty years ago – has been a disastrous one for the vitality of English letters. One could blame the Literary Director for this, a mysterious and uncouth Australian called 'Osborne' but I suspect that any other Director would have been as bad. The very fact of discretionary awards creates it own aura of 'expertise' or pseudism which must prove at best obfuscatory, at worst cliquish and corrupt.

My last argument is addressed through Mr Channon to the Chancellor. Writers both represent and create a large part of the intellectual climate of the nation. If they are encouraged to look upon the nanny-state as their proper source of sustenance, so eventually will everyone else. It is my observation that those ineligible for government *largesse* are as a result more, not less, critical in their attitudes, towards those whom the authorities judge eligible.

1 August 1981

'We gave up using animals because we thought it was too cruel.'

Joan Crawford
Peter Ackroyd

Late one night, I turned on my telephone answering machine, only to hear a demented voice screaming, 'Wire coat-hangers? *Wire* coat-hangers!' The significance of this escaped me – was it a cry from the heart, or was it an irate customer mistaking me for a department of Peter Jones? It was only when I read, several days later, the reviews of *Mommie Dearest* that I understood. This is a film about Joan Crawford's relationship with her adopted children. As a result of it, a strange fever has gripped America: audiences turn up with wire coat-hangers gripped in their hands. In one scene Joan Crawford, in a fit of terrible rage, beats her daughter with just such a hanger. At the same moment, members of the audience hit each other with theirs.

I shall return to this particular scene in a moment, since it must count as one of the most extraordinary in recent film history, but it is the 'cult' status of *Mommie Dearest* which is most remarkable. In America most of its dialogue has been memorised and the audience shout it out as the narrative unfolds. 'Goodnight, good luck and goodbye' is the tearful exit-line of one of Miss Crawford's boy-friends, and the audience roar out the 'goodbye' with him. When Miss Crawford tries to strangle her daughter, in full view of an appalled woman journalist, the audience scream out 'Kill! Kill!'

Let us not mince words: I'm sure Miss Crawford would not want us to. This is a film patronised primarily, though not exclusively, by homosexuals – Joan Crawford being a *monstre sacrée*, a Hollywood Salome to whom large numbers of homosexuals are indebted for their gestures and their conversation and, occasionally, even their clothes. I once wrote a book about the psychology of such matters and it would be otiose to repeat it here: let's just say that the tradition of the masculine goddess is an ancient one. We have simply moved from

The Golden Bough to the silver screen. Of course many audiences might have preferred to see Stanley Baxter rather than Fay Dunaway in the central role, but they are grateful for what they have. The notion of the 'star' is entrancing, in any guise, because it represents the concept of personality untouched by ordinary human feeling. The camera peers into Joan Crawford's face as if it were moving towards a bright, blank wall.

Miss Dunaway looks approximately right; she wanders through a house which resembles the ground floor of Swan and Edgar's, her shoulders as square as a theodolite, the arched eyebrows and the V-shaped mouth forming a perfect circle across her face. And then the onslaught begins; when Miss Dunaway stares, her eyes are like basilisks. Anything human melts within a thirty-yard range. In this film, her children bear the brunt of it – the beatings, the stranglings, the attempts to lock them away in convents. It is a Twentieth Century Fox's Book of Martyrs.

But back to the wire hangers. Joan Crawford, her face caked in white moisturing cream so that she resembles a pantomine clown, is wandering around her young daughter's bedroom; she is smiling, in a rather pained way, at nothing in particular. We have already seen her drinking tumblers of gin, so we suspect the worst. The daughter hides under the covers of her bed. Miss Crawford starts riffling through the infant's wardrobe, perhaps wondering if the clothes might still fit her, when a spasm of rage distorts her already strangely moulded features. 'No wire hangers! No wire hangers!' She brandishes one above her head like an axe. 'What are wire hangers doing in this closet? Answer me!' Pandemonium now breaks out in the cinema, and those with wire hangers tighten their grip upon them: a great tragic scene is being created out of thin air. She is Lady Macbeth who cannot find a missing button, Clytemnestra who has mislaid her bus pass.

Then, oh no!, she finds another wire hanger. 'Why? Why?' she screams, raising her eyes to heaven as if to scorch God. 'Tina! Get out of that bed!' This is the moment. As she beats Tina with the hanger, the audience give wild cries and hit each other with theirs. And then she is forcing Tina on to her kness and making her scrub the floor; suddenly she throws cleaning powder all over her daughter (at this point, in America, some members of the audience use talcum powder instead) and makes a sudden, tottering exit. Her adopted son now creeps tearfully out of a nearby bed and says to Christina Crawford, 'I'll help you clear it up.' 'No,' says Christina in terror, 'No. Go back. Strap yourself in.' It seems that Joan Crawford tied her little son to his bed. It is the culminating moment.

Now here is the paradox: this is a serious film, in no way designed to be deliberately funny; and yet it reduces audiences to hysteria. How could the director, and Fay Dunaway herself, have so miscalculated the mood that, instead of a psychological study of a haunted and bitter woman, we have high comedy of a rare kind? Chekhov was dismayed when his comedies were treated as solemn dramas; how much more disappointing to have created a comic masterpiece by accident.

Certain doubts have been raised about the authenticity of Christina Crawford's biography of her mother, from which this film was made; it has been said that, out of malice or anger, her adopted daughter has embellished the record. But this is, of course, beside the point. If you live the myth of the 'movie star', as Joan Crawford so relentlessly did, then you must expect that same myth to continue and even to grow after your death. There are hints within the film of a real person beneath the make-up – Joan Crawford was clearly terrified of failure, and it was this fear which drove her to the kind of absurd perfectionism and competitiveness which marked her life. An interesting film might well be made out of such an extraordinary personality – apparently devoid of self-doubt and yet filled with fear. But it would have to be of someone working in a different medium – in the cinema such matters are of little account; the legend has to triumph over the reality. And so *Mommie Dearest* becomes a kind of homage to the monster herself – the emotions are so splendid, the scenes so dramatic, the experiences so incandescent. At the end, we see Joan Crawford in death, perfectly made up, the shoulders as square as ever. She is bathed in a faint blue glow, as though the arc lights had been only momentarily dimmed.

5 December 1981

Dali and Picasso
John McEwen

The retrospective of Salvador Dali's work is the best attended exhibition, with the exception of the great Constable memorial in 1976, that the Tate has ever mounted. So far, over 180,000 *paid* visits have been recorded, and no doubt the climactic days now upon us will push this figure beyond the quarter-million. By any standards it is an astonishing response.

Popularity is not, however, necessarily an indication of artistic merit. On the contrary, it usually means nothing more than that a great deal of effort has gone into the publicity, and no artist has been a more extravagant or, as the Tate attendance proclaims, successful self-publicist than Dali. In mitigation it must also be said that self-publicity, like popularity, need not discount artistic worth. One has only to remember Cellini or Courbet or Whistler to know that and to know also, as in the case of Courbet, that it does not necessitate popularity either. So with Dali, however much his own exploits have served to confuse the issue, the work is all – and at the Tate there is more than enough of first-rate quality to prove that he is one of the great artists of his time.

Ever since he became overtly right wing in his political sympathies and rich enough to make it a rule that he should earn 20,000 dollars every day before breakfast, Dali has not been popular with the intelligentsia. Thus the critical consensus has slowly ossified into the pronouncement that he is a minor artist, who painted some acceptable but derivative pictures on his first contact with Surrealism in the late Twenties, but who soon vulgarised the ideas of Freud and subsequently of everyone else to his own flagrantly commercial advantage. This ruling is the legacy of his banishment from membership of the surrealists for 'glorifying' Fascism, and it hardly tallies with the Group's adulation of Dali in the years of Surrealism's fullest international flowering, of Freud's high regard and the continued friendship and admiration for the artist of those two stars of twentieth-century art, Picasso and Duchamp. Nevertheless it is to the Tate's credit that it has staged this exhibition – already a hit at the Paris Beaubourg – and refreshing to read Simon Wilson's whole-heartedly supportive catalogue introduction.

The dust of the Spanish Civil War has finally settled with the establishment of democratic government in Spain, and a more favourable view of Dali is a symptom of the same. It must confirm him in his low opinion of politics and high opinion of himself; a high opinion justified at the Tate by an abundance of masterpieces and the intelligence and sustained energy of his visual enquiry from the mid-Twenties to the present. His jewellery might have been included and a few more objects, but otherwise the selection is exemplary, protecting him as it does from some of the kitsch excesses of his later work while nevertheless having the courage to promote the best of it.

It is another complacently held art-historical assumption that Dali's significance as an artist is as an illustrator of Freud. This is justifiable as far as it goes, but in diminishing the originality of Dali's imagery it draws attention from the real significance of his artistic contribution. Dali, of all twentieth-century painters, has most concerned himself with the preservation of traditional painting's values. Even as a student he repudiated the trendily impressionistic efforts of his teachers in favour of the technical virtuosity of conservatives like Meissonier, whom the professors affected to despise. 'I was expecting to find limits, rigour, science,' he has said of his art-school days, 'I was offered liberty, laziness, approximations.' Cézanne he still sees as the artist who opened the door to this fashion for newness at whatever cost; modern art in its self-destructive decadence and Russian communism in its tyrannical mechanisation he considers the scourges of our age.

Modern art did not confront the visual threat of photography. In the form of Picasso's distortion and fragmentation of the image it resorted to self-annihilation. Dali in optimistic contrast has com-batted photography by mastering a painterly technique that out-dazzles any photographic image and applies this super-realism to imagery that can be conjured only by the human eye. The camera, even the cine-camera of *Le Chien Andalou*, the brilliantly inventive film he made with his friend Bunuel, is confounded. As for the creeping and deadly influence of the machine, that Dali finds most hatefully expressed in the regimentation of totalitarianism, this too he has opposed from the outset of his career as bitterly as any D. H. Lawrence. The sexual softness of his forms, his love of putrefaction in nature (the sort of feeling that makes a person less guilty of throwing an apple core rather than a plastic cup out of the window) is the essence of his anti-mechanical vision. The soft watch, his most surprising discovery, is a perfect symbol of unmechanised time – time, that is, governed by emotion and not the clock. And all this expressed in a technique that enables him to convey the visual effects of heat and to incorporate the ethereal colours of putrefying flesh – atmospherics eerily appropriate to an age of atomic bombs and piece-meal slaughter – in a way quite new to painting.

The immense Picasso exhibition in New York represents the counterpart – if not in scale, certainly in ideology – of the Dali show. Dali considers the equally Catalonian Picasso as his only contemporary artistic peer. He also sees him as a polar opposite: hell-bent on the destruction of art, while Dali by contrast is the guardian of its authenticity and tradition. Picasso consumed succeeding artistic fashions till the day he died, giving the overall impression of someone with the monstrous ambition of wanting to bring art to a close. Dali, for all his self-publicity, is much less egocentric in his earnest endeavours to find a way forward for painting. The course of these enquiries was altered for him by Freud's observation at their single, momentous meeting that in classic paintings one looked for the sub-conscious – in a surrealist painting for the conscious. Dali's later works accordingly address themselves to the pictorial science of the Renaissance and even to its religious subject matter, while the most recent pictures of all seek to incorporate the discoveries of holography and nuclear physics with the aid of stereoscopic viewers and double-imagery. They are more suggestive of the possibilities for painting rather than outright answers in themselves, but do not falter in technique or purpose. The selection admirably isolates these exploratory intentions.

It is the spirit, the heroic scale and supreme attention to the detail of Dali's pictorial defence that is cowing. The fact that he has also found time to create a vast audience for painting (other peoples' as well as his own, no doubt) through his own remorseless exhibitionism – rather in the way Muhammad Ali has done for boxing, once also an activity in need of an audience – only increases one's sense of awe at his fanatical energy and dedication. In the end it does make him a phenomenon almost the equal of Picasso; while considered purely as a painter – and surrealist comparisons are obviously the most apposite – what he lacks in imagistic complexity beside Ernst or Magritte he compensates for in his greater visionary power and refinement of technique. Nor, as is also commonly assumed, has he lacked influence. He is revealed as a father of such latterday movements as Pop and Photo-Realism, Oldenburg and Warhol his most grotesque parodists, though he must feel disappointed in his heirs. Nevertheless he leaves a legacy of affirmation and hope in the continued relevance of painting as a means of communication in the modern world, and will surely one day be vindicated.

PS: The best way to avoid the crowds for the exhibition is to enroll, for an annual subscription of £8, as a Friend of the Tate, thus obtaining the privilege of the two hours viewing time set aside for the Friends and their friends from 11 a.m. on Sunday mornings. Otherwise the only solution is to go at the 10 a.m. opening time.

5 July 1980

The singer's voice
Alfred Alexander

It is surprising how little we know about the physiological aspects of voice production. The only facts we know for certain are that the voice is produced by the vibration of the vocal cords and that the resulting sound (a so-called 'mixed' sound) is amplified by the resonators of the pharynx, mouth, nose and chest. We have no idea in what manner anatomical structures correlate to a big voice, nor do we know what gives the voice its carrying power and beauty. Our ignorance in so important a field may well be deplorable. But if one is scientifically honest, one can only say that the singer's sound qualities are due to some lucky shape of one resonance area or another: all the claims to the contrary made by many singing teachers are sheer humbug.

One sad fact which we *do* know is that beauty and power of the singing voice are transient, and that for reasons beyond our understanding they can fade without any sign of illness or disease.

The 'singer' can be defined for our purposes as a person of adequate musicality, who is gifted with a voice of such power and beauty that competent judges confidently recommend singing as a career. Approximately one person in 50,000 possesses such gifts. As we rely for population statistics on the figures of the Registrar General whose returns put England and Wales together, one in 50,000 means that in England and Wales, where there are yearly circa 800,000 births, about sixteen first-class voices are born every year. If the lifetime of a voice is thirty years, which is probably an over-estimation but a convenient measure as the thirty-year span is the unit of the generation, then five hundred or so great English and Welsh singers are active at any one time.

Vocal performance itself is perfected by neuromuscular control which can be improved by persevering training, similar to the case of the athlete whose reflex activities are improved by diligent and assiduous effort. We know that vocal beauty depends on the five points of:

1. Precision of sound, i.e. accurate intonation
2. Purity of sound
3. Vocal range
4. Openness and evenness of timbre throughout the reach
5. A vocal adaptability which permits technical and expressive qualities to emerge freely.

The method leading to the attainment of these aims is called vocal technique.

Where do the best voices come from? Contrary to widely held beliefs, there is evidence that their incidence rate is the same all over the world. However, a voice must not only be there, it must also be *known* to be there, and be discovered for its musical function. This discovery rate varies enormously in different parts of the globe. Italy and Wales, for example, do not produce proportionately more good singers than other lands: but the high musical awareness, particularly of Italy, has made it rather unlikely for a really good voice to remain undetected.

The current wealth of fine Australian singers has been attributed erroneously to Australia's phonation, sunshine, dryness of climate, Italian immigration etc. The true reason is that, in line with musical awareness, Australia's discovery rate has risen rapidly. Similarly, the fact that Britain now produces so many good singers is due to the country's greatly increased, as well as socially extended, musical activity.

The moment of consciousness of his voice ('sonognosy') is a true turning point, influencing all future activities and emotions of the singer's life. Its timing varies. Some singers were already aware in their childhood of the ability to make a noise which was better than that of their school-fellows. Other fine voices (e.g. Kathleen Ferrier's) were accidentally discovered in adult students of music who had opted for singing as a second subject. Once sonognosy has occurred, singers have to learn to live with their voice. Realising that the voice behaves as if it were a Siamese twin, or a semi-independent living organism of its own, they develop the most intense commitment towards their twin. This devotion to the voice is for the non-singer very difficult to understand and forms a notorious peril in the relationship of singers with non-singers – even musicians!

The demands a voice makes on the singer are incessant and incisive. The voice claims precedence over all personal relationships. Every link of a singer with a person of the opposite sex is, from the outset, a *ménage à trois*, with the voice being number two. Fortunately, most voices make it clear that smoking is undesirable and, in fact, very few singers smoke. Dietetic fads are common among them, but these are generally harmless and often helpful as they may express instinctively felt needs. Not surprisingly, though, any one item a singer's voice craves, may be anathema to another.

In contrast to instrumentalists or conductors, singers conform neither in their educational nor in their social background to a standard pattern. Some well-known singers were hardly able to scrape together a couple of passes at 'O' level, whereas others hold university degrees in highly complex subjects. Their physique, as well as their physical fitness, differs enormously: some singers have represented their countries at Olympic Games while others may be unable to walk more than a few steps without pain.

Whether singing is a desirable career is open to doubt. Whichever way the career goes, the strain is enormous. The exposure in singing, unparalleled in the performing arts, is so taxing that it can cause the breakdown of the requisite moral fibre – and of a career with the voice in perfect order. The waiting for opportunities, the endless chain of forgotten promises and disappointed hopes, the paraphernalia of the auditions and the attendant periods of suspense can be heart-breaking. Singers are now even forced to audition for agents who may know little about music or voices – an iniquity no other profession has to bear. If the career is successful, a potentially critical audience has to be faced afresh on every occasion. To mitigate the tension *before* a performance by the use of alcohol or other drugs is an expedient which has never helped in the long run and caused many a disaster. Afterwards, the beginner and established performer alike have to brave the critics, well aware that the untutored public only too readily accords the personal opinions of music journalists the weight of judicial verdicts.

The voice always presents problems, and the fear of losing it is never far from a singer's mind. Every morning the singer steps into the bathroom to test the 'twin'. If the voice feels well, all is well, but if the twin is out of sorts, the singer is at once upset and worried. Singers are generally reputed to react hypochondriacally to minor physical troubles, but this accusation is unjustified. The attitude of non-singers to coughs and colds is governed by the fact that such indispositions do not place their capacity to earn their living in jeopardy.

The purely technical aspects of singing are comparatively readily acquired, and it has been claimed that singing's basic technical requirements contain nothing that a competent instructor could not teach, and a gifted pupil could not learn in one afternoon's session. However, a singer can hear his or her own voice only in a somewhat distorted way, and needs critical assessment of the sound produced, with constructive suggestions for the mechanics of its improvement.

He has therefore, more often than not, to embark on the choice of the right teacher. This is complicated by the fact that even very experienced teachers are able to help only in certain cases and not in others, which explains why the very same teacher can be rightly referred to as 'brilliant' by one pupil and 'hopeless' by another.

A great number of textbooks on singing exist but most of them contain a good deal of nonsense. Many are written by teachers with charlatan ideas, who paint gloomy pictures of the danger of having one's voice 'ruined' by rival methods. This danger is, fortunately, non-existent: no one can ruin someone else's voice, though persistent attempts to force a pupil to measures which do not suit him could have a bad effect and cause prolonged difficulties. Nor, for that matter, can one ruin one's own voice by singing music that, in the opinion of whoever it may be, is not suitable for a certain voice. The only thing which could damage a vocal cord is the strenuous and violent forcing of a voice which does not respond willingly.

The person trained to inspect the mechanism of singing is the laryngologist; though his crucial gadget, the laryngeal mirror, was invented by a singing teacher and not by a doctor. His main asset is that by seeing with his own eyes that all is well, he can convincingly reassure a singer who is tormented by doubts about the state of his cords. An understanding laryngologist can be helpful with minor problems; he can become a trusted friend, and the link thus established is for some singers more necessary than for others. For serious voice problems, though, he can be found pretty useless.

Supplementary to his technical needs are the singer's artistic needs, which must be met by a person with the training and capability of a conductor, though he may be called *répétiteur* or coach. There is also the intelligibility problem: critic and public blame singers for not being able to understand, and accuse them of bad enunciation or pronunciation. They fail to realise that for physical reasons a listener unfamiliar with the libretto cannot possibly understand more than a small proportion of the text; good pronunciation of foreign languages does not necessarily help, particularly when an orchestra complicates the issue. On the other hand, people who know the text intimately are not reliable either, because they are convinced that they understand every word. In this dilemma the singer has to follow his own instinct and, realising that one cannot achieve the impossible, try to impart to his sound the correct colour of the overtones of the respective language.

The professional outlook for singers is not good, although no other profession is taken more seriously by those engaged in it. The individual effort made is often enormous, and even passionate over-ambition is not at all uncommon: but the present abundance of gifted and competent singers has greatly worsened their career prospects, and it is becoming increasingly evident that apart from all the art and musicianship a stroke of good fortune as well is needed for a decisive success. Only one among 2000-3000 singers achieves international recognition. The second most favourable outcome, a national reputation, is gained by one in 300 or 400. For many young singers, chorus-work is a good experience, but the would-be soloist often finds this eventually unsatisfactory and frustrating. Ancillary activities, e.g. the teaching of singing or music, can give satisfaction, but there can be no doubt that many singing careers, begun with high hopes, come to a disappointing end.

However, against these risks must be set the wonderful feeling of giving, by means of one's voice, such intense delight to others. And even more important than that, perhaps, is the singer's own 'transcendental ecstasy': an incomparably glorious sensation (when all goes well!) of physically sensing one's own beautiful sound, and experiencing in this a fulfilment and a happiness which amply compensates for all the anguish and humiliations which had to be endured.

9 January 1982

The late Alfred Alexander was an ear, nose and throat surgeon and the author of several books on opera.

10   The television critic's television set

Muck and brass
Richard Ingrams

Staying with friends in London during last week's train stoppage I had reason once more not to regret my decision to watch television in black and white. Like almost everyone else nowadays my friends have colour and it always comes as a nasty shock when you see someone like Sandy Gall in all his purple glory with strange, unnatural-looking hair. Apart from that there are the commercials, many of which feature loving close-ups of food. The sight of a fried egg or fruit pie in full living colour is not a reassuring one late at night, though in black and white it is not quite so distasteful. My host, a man of traditional left-wing views, was very keen to watch a serial called *Muck and Brass* put out by the new Midlands company, Central TV. This features Mr Mel Smith, the fat man in *Not the Nine O'Clock News*, as an unpleasant business tycoon in Birmingham getting the better of other unpleasant business tycoons. In last week's story he was busy buying up a local football club in order to develop the site. The story was so complicated that despite my host's assurances that the series represented a brilliantly accurate picture of the capitalist system at work I remained unimpressed, not to say baffled. But it was when one of the many unpleasant businessmen was sick in the Gents after a heavy lunch, producing what Barry Humphries has graphically described as 'a technicolour yawn', that I thanked 'whatever gods there may be' for my flickering black and white set waiting for me at home.

30 January 1982

Altitude of the set
Richard Ingrams

Sometimes, I must say, I regret my complete lack of scientific knowledge. I have discovered a fatal flaw in my new television set which I'm sure that someone like Dr Jonathan would easily provide an explanation for. Despite its irritating habit of cutting off people's legs my old set had one great advantage, namely that you could get LWT programmes as well as Southern on it. I always assumed that this was in some way due to the fact that I live at a high altitude. But the new set does not respond in the same way. I get the legs all right but no LWT.

13 January 1979

TV in the room next door
Richard Ingrams

I was away in Wales for most of last week walking along Offa's Dyke and therefore saw no television at all. I find I slightly miss not seeing the *Daily Telegraph* if I am on holiday – but only slightly. What is certain is that I do not miss the telly one little bit and I doubt if anyone does. Not that one can altogether avoid it. Most hotels now feel obliged to provide colour tellies in every room along with the make-your-own-tea kit and you are likely to be kept awake at night by the sound of nonsense coming from next door. In one hotel in Monmouth I was obliged to bang on the wall with my walking stick to silence a programme about a racing trainer. Two nights later in Hay-on-Wye I was kept awake by *Question Time*, about which I wrote last week. I could hear enough to get a rough idea of what was going on. Lord Devlin was one of the speakers and an opinionated token woman with a very loud voice. She might have been an MP or possibly a left-wing journalist. The other two speakers were indeterminate but I imagine they included a right-winger to balance the strident woman. In other circumstances it might have been rather tantalising to hear only the muffled noise of the programme through a flimsy wall – Day's ponderous voice putting the questions, the views for and against, the woman speaker banging away, Lord Devlin's more moderate tones, the occasional bursts of laughter and applause from the audience – but in this case it didn't seem to matter at all. I felt, when my fellow guest finally switched off his telly and a beautiful silence ensued, that I had watched it all.

14 June 1980

Ingrams and the Bhagwan

Sir: In common with a growing number of other people (see, e.g., your forthcoming payment of libel damages to Mr Ronald Harwood) I am sick of being lied about by Richard Ingrams who, himself corrupt, is unable to recognise honesty in a man like Ram Dass, about my television interview with whom he was writing in your issue of 21 June. 'I understand', Ingrams writes of the Indian guru who taught and influenced Ram Dass, 'that the Guru is the same Bhagwan Shree Rajneesh about whom Levin wrote three glowing articles recently in *The Times*'; he adds that Ram Dass 'apparently runs the Mexican branch of Rajneesh's outfit', and claims that I suppressed these facts for sinister reasons. But they are not facts; they are Ingrams's inventions. Ram Dass's guru was not Rajneesh, nor does Ram Dass have anything to do with Rajneesh or 'Rajneesh's outfit', in Mexico or elsewhere.

Ingrams then goes on to retail the usual dirty little bits of gossip about Rajneesh – usual both in that these particular ones are endlessly repeated and also in that dealing in dirty little bits of gossip now constitutes practically the whole of Ingrams's life. He repeats them in the characteristic poltroon's manner ('. . . there have been the usual allegations ... so they claim ... there have also been reports ...') that he adopts when he does not believe a word of what he is peddling. The allegations about drugs he picked up from the *Daily Star* (no less characteristically knocking that newspaper with one hand while stealing from it with the other) and embellished. The fact is that one of the girls in the case Ingrams alludes to has since admitted that the claims made in court about drug-running 'on behalf of the Guru's organisation' were lies.

Ingrams goes on to refer to the fact that Ram Dass, when he was a professor at Harvard, took LSD, and attacks me for not 'querying' his comment on these experiences, though 'Levin ... must be aware that terrible tragedies have befallen LSD takers in their search for enlightenment'; the sight of Richard Ingrams thus asserting the claims of conscience is rather like hearing a ponce extol the virtues of romantic love.

I have just been dictating replies to the scores of people who have written to me in calm, matter-of-fact tones about my television conversation with Ram Dass; all these correspondents saw and understood his openness, serenity, love and wisdom. (No doubt Ingrams would dismiss them all as homosexualists, or indeed downright Jewists.) I prefer their capacity for understanding to Ingrams's terrified refusal to admit the possibility that there might be something in the universe larger than his own pimples.

A final word to you, Sir. Week after week in your columns, Ingrams deploys some gaudy lie to 'explain' why he has not bothered to watch any television at all; in other weeks he makes it clear that he has watched for only a few *minutes*; at other times he writes about programmes he has not seen; constantly, he uses his space, as he uses the pages of his own magazine, to pursue private vendettas and spites. I have known nine editors of the *Spectator*, and you are the only one sufficiently lacking in professional self-respect to accept such standards from one of its contributors.

Bernard Levin, London W1

28 June 1980

The budgie on the set
Richard Ingrams

In recent days the neighbours' budgerigar, temporarily entrusted to our care, has been perched on top of the television and a small dog called Buffy sits in front of the set mesmerised by the bird. The arrangement has its advantages for me as the eye can easily stray from the boring images on the screen to the happy creature hopping up and down on its perch, gazing at itself in the mirror and from time to time ringing a little bell with its beak. I am thinking of installing a bird or possibly a fish tank as a permanent fixture.

A budgie on top of the telly is the last sort of thing you expect to see in the home of Richard Foster, the main character of *A Family Affair* (BBC1), yet another series about the home life of a box-wallah – an Indian Civil Service expression meaning merchant or businessman. In the Fosters' suburban home everything is neat and tidy. The scene at the breakfast table is immaculate, the telephone is one of those slimline ones which Anthony Wedgwood Benn helped to popularise when he was Minister of Technology, and the dog is a placid-looking labrador rather than a mongrel terrier with a budgie-fixation. The scenario is a sort of Reggie Perrin one without the jokes: harassed box-wallah having affair with secretary, droopy son at university, pompous boss with moustache and bags under eyes. The BBC has mounted quite a run of these sorts of shows recently, apparently in the belief that there is a demand for good-looking bank managers having an identity crisis or sales executives cracking up under menopausal strains. Perhaps the next one could feature a manic television critic running amok. I found myself showing the most advanced symptoms of frustration during the second episode of *A Family Affair* – itching, compulsive foot-stamping, the desire to let out high-pitched shrieks. The soothing sight of the budgie hopping up and down did nothing to avert the crisis.

26 May 1979

11 Death

Ways of dying
Taki

According to Ernest Hemingway there are two ways to murder a lion. One is to shoot him from a motor car, the other to shoot him at night from a platform or the shelter of a thorn boma, as he comes to feed on a bait placed by the 'sport' and his guide. Hemingway wrote this in 1934, and called the people who murder lions 'Shootists'. He also wrote that these two methods of killing lions rank, as sport, with dynamiting trout or harpooning swordfish. Although Papa is my hero I cannot get round the fact that he did, after all, shoot animals – although not from automobiles – and considered himself a sport for doing so.

My current hero, John Aspinall, is much braver than Hemingway. He faces wild animals without a gun. To me that's real sport and I warmly recommend the Princess of Wales to visit Howletts and Port Lympne as soon as her honeymoon is over. If the same principle applies to red deer as, say, to wounding a beater instead of a bird, Princess Diana should never shoot anything again. Anyway, I don't think women should be allowed to slay animals, or indeed anything except militant feminists.

Killing cleanly was an obsession with Hemingway and is becoming one with me. Where people are concerned, not animals. For example, I would hate to kill Gaddafi or Khalkali cleanly; they both deserve slow and humiliating deaths; and so does Arafat. For myself I would love to die as Sadat did. Death, after all, can raise one's status, and the smartness of certain deaths is indisputable. Death on the battlefield enhances one's reputation posthumously, as does death through drunkenness. My ancestor, Alexander the Great, died of drink but his detractors, who were desperately trying to cut him down to size, spread vicious rumours that he died of malaria. (Typically, those Turko-Cypriots who now pass for modern Greeks were furious last year when the truth finally came out.)

If Hannibal had died in Zama, his reputation would have been even greater than it is. Instead, he lingered on, hounded by the Romans and finally died of poison. Death by disease, poison or drugs is plebeian and vulgar. The most notable death of all was that of the great Mithridates. He asked his slaves to kill him, in fact ordered them to do so. Mithridates, who incidentally is Aspinall's idol, was probably the greatest man ever. He claimed descent from Darius and Sileucus. He thought very little of the Romans, describing them as nothing but regimented farm labourers. When he was sixty-five years of age he was planning to cross the Carpathian mountains from the Crimea and teach the Romans a sharp lesson when he learned that his son had gone over to them. That was too much for an honourable man. One can withstand desertion by allies, women, friends but not one's son. When the venal Phanasis went Roman, Mithridates got his slaves to do a Mishima on their master.

Napoleon failed miserably where his own death was concerned. Imagine how much greater he would have been if he had been killed by the charge of the Hessian Guard, instead of the cancer that got him in St Helena six miserable years later.

Modern tycoons are notorious for the humiliation of their deaths. Charlie Engelhard, the platinum king, ruined an otherwise good record by asking for a Coca-Cola while he lay dying from a stroke. Onassis ruined his opportunistic streak by not choosing to fall on his sword once he realied what a mess he had made of his personal life. Thus he lingered on pathetically and full of tubes while Jackie KO commuted from New York to the American Hospital in Neuilly.

Of the French, whom I consider to be way below par in matters of honour, only three, to my knowledge, died well; all three were presidents of the Republic. They died in the saddle, which might not be a very noble way of dying, but they did, after all, die in bed with their mistresses – something, which, I am sad to say, will never happen to the future king of England.

24 October 1981

Lord Mountbatten
John Hackett

The people whom Mountbatten knew must number millions – quite apart from the many millions more who knew Mountbatten. He will be very easily remembered. He moved through his acquaintance with the brilliance of the king-fisher, darting along the stream in a blinding, breath-taking flash of electric blue. Some of those who worked with him found him rather irritating: others even went so far as to describe him as a little obtuse. What few would deny is that he shed a light on whatever company he was in that was not easily equalled. The life that was so brutally snuffed out by the work of squalid trolls was one of radiance beyond their ken. It was not, it must be admitted, entirely beyond his own. To be wholly unaware of the shape and texture of his own aura a man must be either very stupid or a saint. This man was neither.

I first met him when I was eleven years old. He was then Flag-Lieutenant to the Prince of Wales on his Australian tour and stayed, with the other three closest members of the Prince's staff, in my mother's house in Adelaide. Not long ago I came across the bread-and-butter letter he wrote. It was as charming as it was discursive. Many years after that, when he was Chief of the Defence Staff and I was Deputy Chief of the General Staff and we had over the years come to know each other quite well, I brought one day to the office a picture of all those beautiful young men with their signatures on it, the most beautiful of all being the god-like figure in naval uniform under which was written 'Louis Mountbatten'. Dickie looked at it with something approaching awe. 'You must be very careful with that', he said. 'That's a historic document.'

It was impossible not to love this man, even if – and perhaps in part because – you also had to laugh at him a little. Once there was a great party in the house of Admiral Sir Frank Hopkins, C-in-C Portsmouth, to dine in Nelson's cabin in HMS Victory, newly done up the way it had been in the great days. We all met in the C-in-C's house to change. Dickie arrived in a rig that was clearly maritime but equally clearly not RN. As an ignorant but not wholly unobservant soldier, I had a careful look at this. Several possibilities went through my mind, of which one, as at least a decent outside bet, was Trinity House. He came over to me. 'Now you're one of our more intelligent soldiers', he said. 'Tell me what I'm wearing.' Wild horses could not have dragged Trinity House from me. 'I don't know,' I said, 'Peruvian navy?' 'Good heavens', said he. 'Peruvian navy, indeed! Trinity House!' He said it in a way that positively invited genuflection. Later, in Victory after dinner, I could hear him saying to one duchess after another (it was always useful to have a duchess or two for occasions like this): 'You see that chap over there? He's one of our more intelligent soldiers, but when I was wearing Trinity House rig before dinner he thought I was in the Peruvian navy!'

Everyone who knew him has his own store of Dickie stories. I have several of my own. Some of those you hear are very funny but I have never heard one that was malicious. He may have attracted an explosive blast from those already damned beyond redemption, who in the words of the song I used to know in County Donegal about poteen, 'be they Christian, pagan or Jew', will carry a bitter load of guilt to the grave and far beyond. He has never attracted malice.

Everyone who knew anything about him was aware that he wanted to be First Sea Lord, to set an entry in the book against the earlier intolerable and ignoble slight to his father. Contemporaries who knew his active, energetic ways would gloomily reflect over the Plymouth gin that he would get there all right, and it would take the Navy years to recover. But he was a very high-class professional, a 'communicator' – as they call those who know about 'making signals' and all that sort of thing in the senior service – who played in the top division of the league. He was brave. Of course he was brave: bravery – whatever 'bravery' means, and not even Aristotle in the Nichomachean Ethics could clear that up entirely – is in fighting men no more than another professional skill. He was brave, but he was also very capable. He could take a long cool view and if in the political arena he sometimes went a bit wrong on the detail, he knew where he was going and never lost sight of the objective, even if it was one that not everybody could see – and not all of those who could found welcome.

Above all he had style, a richness and a splendour which the pathetic little men who blew him and his boat apart can never hope to match this side of doomsday.

There can never be another, for the mould into which fate poured the rare metal of which Mountbatten was made is broken now. The *Immortal Hour*, known so well to so many of my generation, is virtually unknown in this. 'How beautiful they are, the lordly ones . . .' Rutland Boughton's phrases come back to me over the half century since I heard them first.

Mountbatten was one of the lordly ones. However you look at Dickie Mountbatten that is the company in which he belongs, not least because of the true humility without which there is no entry to it. We shall not see his like again, and there will be very many who will find the world he has left a poorer and a sadder place without him.

1 September 1979

General Sir John Hackett ended his army career as Commander-in-Chief, British Army of the Rhine.

Lord Butler
William Rees-Mogg

Rab Butler was the most lovable politician of his generation. Of those who did not become Prime Minister his work was the most substantial and is already proving the longest lasting. Indeed, there are few Prime Ministers who have left behind so important a legacy. It will always be asked why he did not become Prime Minister, which at least is better for a man than for it always to be asked why he did.

I first met Rab Butler during the period after 1945 when he was reconstructing the Conservative Party. The post-war form of the Conservative Party owes more to his creative ideas than to the work of anyone else. I first got to know him well in the period after he had lost his first wife and ceased to be Chancellor of the Exchequer in 1955 and 1956. That was a low point in his fortunes, from which he made a remarkable but never a complete political recovery. He never had quite the same power in the Conservative Party as he had enjoyed under Churchill's leadership and he had an uneasy relationship with Harold Macmillan during his time as Prime Minister.

Apart from his work in education and the Conservative Party, Lord Butler was one of the two best post-war Chancellors and indeed rather better and rather more important than Roy Jenkins, who ranks next to him. It is interesting to contrast these two admirable and civilised English statesmen. Rab was not much of a European. For better or worse, he cared more about the English farmers and became reconciled to Europe as the Community turned out to be good for them. He had Roy Jenkins's determination, but perhaps not his bravado. In similar circumstances, I believe he would have been capable of standing in Warrington, but I doubt very much whether he could have been persuaded to stand in Hillhead.

I always remember Rab as one might always have remembered Samuel Johnson: not by his specific works, but by his conversation. In the first place, one could never discuss any political subject with him without learning of aspects of it which one had not considered. A political conversation with him was symphonic in character. It would move through the whole range from the most serious analysis of policy to the most lighthearted discussion of personalities. But he understood the whole range of politics, both in terms of ideals and of the limitations of reality, in a way that very few men I have known have ever understood anything.

His conversation was not malicious, but it was ironic and ridiculous and his sense of their absurdity sometimes disturbed his more pompous colleagues. He had more humour than wit and the delight of his conversation was that strange fantasies would half-emerge in an ironic form when discussing serious subjects. This could happen in the House, where he would use his gift for oblique expression in order simultaneously to reveal and to conceal parts of his mind. It could happen on public occasions. I can remember at some great Rhodesian dinner, when he was in fact engaged in winding up the Federation, that he offered reassurance to the white settlers by saying: 'Those of you who have made your homes in Africa

– and when I say homes, I mean homes ...', and received tumultuous applause from an audience plainly unaware that no meaning could be attached to so gnomic a reassurance.

But it was in private conversation that he was at his most enjoyable. There is a story which I think he tells in his memoirs of his conversation with Churchill shortly before Churchill resigned: Churchill said to him about Eden's succession, 'I think I have made a terrible mistake'; and what Rab most enjoyed was Churchill's following words which were, 'It's all right, old cock, it isn't going to be you.' Many of Rab's stories had an ironic element about himself and all of them had some double element, just as the Churchill story reveals doubts about Eden (which Rab fully shared) as well as putting Rab himself in a slightly ridiculous light.

It was not always clear where the elements of his fantasies came from. I remember shortly after I had got to know him, that someone at a dinner attempted to introduce us. Rab replied: 'I know William Rees-Mogg well. We served together in the Afghan wars.' The Afghan wars were then a much more suitable subject for humour than they are now.

About the same time, I came back from a meeting in the North with him and stopped overnight at Halstead. Rab, for some reason, became concerned that he had inconvenienced my sister, with whom I then shared a house, and walked round the borders of his garden scooping up great quantities of tulips and daffodils. He commented: 'It is more important to be generous than to be efficient – that is what I learned at the Treasury.' Again, the remark has the feel of a succession of receding ironies and if Eden was intended to be put in a slightly unfavourable light by the Churchill story, the Treasury was equally intended to be put in a slightly unfavourable light by his comment.

It cannot be said that Rab was happy with Harold Macmillan. They were in many ways complementary. Rab, much the more creative man with a deeper insight into the processes of politics. Macmillan, with a harder, more Scottish view, perhaps less wise in counsel, perhaps more effective in action. It was, of course, Macmillan who stopped Rab Butler becoming Prime Minister and who wrecked the Conservative Party in doing so. He stopped him in 1956 because he wanted the job for himself. In 1963, he stopped him again for motives which are perhaps less clear. I have always though it was a matter of conscience: Macmillan found it difficult to behave well to a man to whom he had once behaved badly.

What is certain is that in 1963 Rab could have had the leadership had he stood out for it. It would not have been possible for Lord Home to form a Government unless Rab had agreed to serve under him. I was at the time one of those who urged Rab to stand out and I still regret that he did not. He later took a philosophical view of his own decision, though it was inevitably a wound that never quite healed. But for the great happiness of his second marriage it would, I think, have been unbearable. Hardly any other statesman in English history has narrowly missed becoming Prime Minister twice.

He came to think that it made less difference than I have argued. He thought he would have won the 1964 election which Lord Home came quite close to winning, but that a year or two later people would have become bored with him and the pressures which ended Macmillan's own leadership would have ended his. Yet, in fact, 1963 was a critical year for the Conservative Party and therefore for British politics. Between 1945 and 1963 under three different leaders, Rab held together the Conservative Party's heart and its head. Since 1963, the heart and the head of the Conservative Party have never been on the best of terms with each other. There was wisdom about Rab's politics which even the most gifted of subsequent statesmen have not found. His wisdom and humour will live for their lifetimes and perhaps beyond in the minds of his friends.

13 March 1982

Uncle Alec
Auberon Waugh

A few years ago I came across a slim volume of poems by Alec Waugh published in 1918, when he was in a prisoner of war camp. Some of these lines written in the trenches struck me as really very good indeed, and as part of a conscious and sustained policy of cheering him up about his writing I told him so. He received my congratulations with his usual urbanity, although I never really knew how successful my policy was proving – on another occasion I was able to tell him that a young nanny we employed preferred his books to those of Evelyn Waugh, on yet another that his book about Bangkok was still remembered there by some of the older residents. But I suppose it was some sixty years since he had written the war poems, and he might have preferred to be reminded of some more recent achievement.

Among the poems (published by Grant Richard under the general title *Resentment* and dedicated to Barbara Jacobs, daughter of W, W, and later to become Alec's first wife) is a juvenile piece 'The Exile' written as a sixteen-year old at Sherborne:

'When they bring back the thing that once was me
And lay it in some quiet grave to rest,
Say that a weary river, long distrest
With aimless wanderings winds at length to sea.'

In the context of his death last week at the age of eighty-three, I suppose that this is what we should say: that a weary river has wound at length to sea. But his teenage poem also contains the injunction: 'Weep not that I am gone' – and I must admit that I find myself overwhelmed by a great, engulfing sadness. Alec Waugh may not have been a greater writer but he was a great survivor. From his survival as a professional writer, year after year for over sixty-five years, we could all take comfort – not just his family and friends, but every aspiring writer in the country.

Because of the last war, which he spent for the most part in the Middle East, he did not enter our lives until quite late on, and he was then introduced more than anything else as a biological curiosity. When my father, whose affection for his older brother never wavered, announced that we had a hairless uncle who would shortly be coming to stay, my younger sister Hattie asked in some alarm whether he also had the normal number of fingers and legs. We must have seen other bald men – Alec lost his hair gallantly in the service of this country during the Great War – but for some reason this remained his chief identifying characteristic until we were older, when we were let into the secret of his voracious sexual appetite.

This aspect of his personality got off to a bad start. Asked to leave Sherborne for what is nowadays called 'the usual thing', but was then unmentionable, he went to Sandhurst where he quickly acquired a reputation for sexual prowess. But when he came to marry Miss Jacobs, amid embarrassingly sentimental scenes from my grandfather who was an old friend of the bride's parents, he met a problem. As he delicately describes in one of his many autobiographies, he couldn't get into her, achieve penetration or whatever: 'I who was called Tank at Sandhurst could not make my wife a woman.'

Many would have been discouraged by this, but Alec applied himself with renewed vigour to the rest of the female sex achieving, by his own account, some considerable success. 'Venus has been kind to me', he observed in his old age. On meeting my wife for the first time, he introduced himself: 'I am Alec Waugh, sixty-five and still interested in women.' At the age of seventy he wrote his first pornography, or 'erotic comedy', called *Spy in the Family*, about a lesbian seduction. I thought it a very sporting effort. He stills grins at me from the back of its cover – bald, slightly simian and lecherous as ever, in an open striped blazer with a silk scarf tied nonchalantly around his wrinkled neck.

At the age of about eleven, I was sent to stay with him. By this time he had married the spirited Australian whose possession of a private fortune provided him with a home, during his visits to England, until her death in 1969. It would be nice to record my memories of him from this visit, but I had been programmed to watch only for his baldness and my chief impression of the occasion, I am sorry to say, was of the extraordinary wealth of my Waugh cousins. They lived in a beautiful eighteenth-century red-brick house in its own park at Silchester, near Reading. It was slightly smaller than our house and I noticed they did not have a butler, as we then did, but I had never before seen wall-to-wall carpeting, or an automatic radio-gramophone, never tasted Coca-Cola or peanut butter. His children – Andrew, who now commands the naval station in Hong Kong; Peter, who lives something of a hermit's life in Berkshire but has developed a technique with photographic plates which will make him famous; and Veronica, the toast of her generation, who married a business man and now decorates furniture – made more of a mark. But I remember Alec, who had recently seen *South Pacific* in New York, miming the song 'I'm Going to Wash that Man Right Out of my Hair'. This seemed to me very droll.

I saw more of him later when I was stuck in hospital for nine months after a machine gun accident in the army. My father who was not really at his best in the role of hospital visitor, seemed to resent his brother's getting in on the act, which is the background to the letter reproduced in Mark Amory's edition of *The Letters of Evelyn Waugh* (Weidenfeld 1980): 'The man who calls on you purporting to be my brother Alec is plainly an imposter. Your true uncle does not know your whereabouts . . . Did your visitor offer any identification apart from baldness – not an uncommon phenomenon? Had he a voice like your half great uncle George? Did he wear a silk scarf round his neck? Was he tipsy? These are the tests.'

The last question reflects my father's opinion that after the great success of *Island in the Sun* (1956) – everybody agreed that it could not have happened to a nicer person – Alec never drew another sober breath. Alas, like many of my father's decisions about the human race, it was based more on an artist's vision than on any first-hand perception of the world around him. One of my sisters, who visited Alec in some mid-Western university where he was Creative Writer in residence a few years later, described him as living in a sort of cubbyhole above the student's canteen, from where meals were sent up to him on a plastic tray which he warmed on a radiator.

But he always cut a dash on his visits to London, appearing in suits which grew nattier and nattier as the years rolled on, entertaining large parties of friends to lavish meals at his various clubs. I became a friend of his only after the publication of my first novel in 1960.

Despite his enormous generosity as a host and kindness as a friend, I don't believe he ever paid a school fee and certainly made no very conspicuous contribution towards the support of his widowed mother. Of course, he simply did not have the money, but above all, he was a free spirit. In old age, he resembled nothing so much as a tortoise – toothless, slow-moving, unaggressive, benign, with a little piping voice so soft as to be almost indistinguishable. Like a tortoise, his natural equipment was designed more for survival than for battle and conquest. But he was a Waugh, and I find myself inexpressibly bereaved.

My last glimpse of him was outside the Athenaeum, where I delivered him last December after a convivial evening at one or other of his curious, elderly dining clubs. He was too old for the outing and I was sickening for some illness; both of us were rather drunk. In the taxi he started singing hymns, and I left him weaving between the Corinthian columns, a tiny, upright, strangely dignified figure, singing his little bald head off: 'All people that on earth do dwell Sing to the Lord with cheerful voice.' I shall miss him terribly, but I suppose, as he put it himself, the weary river winds at length to sea, so there it is.

12 September 1981

'Okay, so you're an Englishman, he's a Scotsman, and I'm an Irishman. What's so funny about that?'

would rather be 'undertakers' and weep at what Mervyn and his like have done to the 'decomposing ecclesiastical corpse' in the last twenty years. He does not ask himself why the corpse twitches when the surgeons hack away at its ancient liturgies and ordinals. Only in horror movies do corpses cry out. In real life, protest from such a quarter would suggest that the patient is still alive. But, although one ought to be angry with the foolish old men who are responsible for the decay of religion in the last few decades, I found myself illogically disarmed by this book and fully warmed to his frank belief that the modern church is thunderingly boring.

18 September 1982

Christmas*

Christmas is based on a fact; not on the literal accuracy of every word in the Gospels, but on the fact of the Incarnation. If it is not true that the Word was made flesh in the person of Christ, then the story of Christmas may, like all good stories, offer moral and psychological truths, but that is all. It will be no more than a legend, and the edifice of doctrine and worship which the Church has built upon it will be as false as the original fact. But it is also true that the Incarnation cannot be proved by ordinary historical or scientific methods: its fact only becomes apparent through faith. If the Church is to make anything of its duty to preach the Gospel at Christmas, it has to explain the fact in strictly religious terms.

Today's Church does not readily supply such an explanation. Some of its bishops do not even believe it themselves. Many more regard the exposition of religious truth as an affront to the good nature and patience of the few that care to listen to them, and are content to conduct their carol services, and make a few remarks about the lack of love in the world and the humble circumstances of Christ's birth. If they are sentimental, they will go on about how Christmas is a time for the children; if they are austere, they will complain about the enjoyment of carnal pleasures at such a time; if they are political, they will point out that while we eat our turkey, a third of the world is making do with rice.

If this is the Church's handling of Christmas, the 'commercial Christmas' regularly railed against each year is the last thing that Christmas need worry about. The cribs on show in big stores may well be the nearest representation of Christian truth that many children ever see, the atmosphere of festivity and consumption the only ghost many adults know of a great feast of the Church. Indeed, in the semi-secular, commercial Christmas, two vital principles are observed – that the occasion is for a family, however broken, and that the purpose of all the spending and effort is mainly to give. These are Christian principles which are reinforced by their widespread annual observance.

All that the commercial Christmas suffers from is its vagueness. It acknowledges that the birth of Christ was a Big Moment for mankind, from which we should learn and which we should commemorate, but on why, what and how, it is confused. If there is no institution ready to remedy the vagueness, the strength of belief will inevitably degenerate. The hungry sheep look up and, receiving little attention from their pastors, settle for Christmas pudding.

What makes the failure of the Church in this respect so odd, is the quality of the truth bequeathed to it. It would take a man of remarkable eloquence and clarity to bring the doctrine of the Trinity home to an ignorant audience, but in Christmas the Christian religion finds its most accessible moment, the moment when God, that most inaccessible of concepts, became a man.

Becoming man means becoming something that every man may understand, and therefore something which any clergyman should be able to explain. Where a generalised concept might mean nothing, a specific fact is intelligible. It is possible (though not especially pleasant) to visit Bethlehem today and experience the bleakness of the Judean hills in winter, or simply to point to a map to show where the events took place. The story of a particular time, place and person can be told.

The more often, fully and beautifully the Church relates the events of Christmas, the more inevitably will their 'relevance' appear to those who listen; and the more the listeners learn, the more they will wish to know what else happened, where the story began, and whether it has ended. Souped up, watered down, over-generalised, Christmas is reduced to the ordinary things which, by its events, were made extraordinary. The precise story of how the Word was made flesh is the most truthful that words can tell, and becomes less so with each alteration.

Nor does the Church have to speak with condescension of these simple events, as if they were a show put on to convince the foolish. They contain more than any intellect can ever grasp. It is almost unbearably difficult, if delightful, to imagine the Redeemer of the world being born in a stable, He 'whose glorious, yet contracted light, wrapt in night's mantle, stole into this manger'. There could be nothing stranger than that God should have implanted his Word in a speechless baby (the Latin *infans* means, literally, wordless), or that he should have prepared his coming by so many signs, and then come by stealth.

Many who are exasperated by the weakness and secularism of trendy religion have driven themselves into a position where, in order to save their faith from dilution, they have made it antithetical to the world. To them, in particular, the Church can give a proper answer at Christmas. We are told that 'God so loved the world, that he gave his only-begotten son, to the end that all that believe in Him should not perish, but have everlasting life'. In these circumstances, it is presumptuous to hate the world. Christ's life on earth forbids anyone to regard his own life as pointless. The moment of his arrival is a moment of joy, which is what Christmas, however debased, has remained. It would be nice if the sermon on Christmas morning simply said, 'eat, drink and be merry, for today we live'.

18 December 1982

* Unsigned leader by Charles Moore

3   Power

Jeremy Thorpe's acquittal
Ferdinand Mount

Mr Jeremy Thorpe stands in the privacy of his own balcony, a free man. It is a riproaring finale – but a finale to what? Greek tragedy was never like this. Once again, you would have to riffle through Trollope to find such a mixture of high places and low life, such a meeting of the grand and the grubby. And this stunning reversal of fortune in the final chapter has more in common with the twists of a high Victorian novel than with the remorseless spinning of the Fates.

Even Trollope, though, for all his interest in ecclesiastical life, might have drawn the line at laying on a Thanksgiving Service in the North Devon village of Bratton Fleming for his hero. The rector describes this new *Te Deum* as 'a thanksgiving for the way God has answered our prayers for Jeremy and Marion in their ordeal.' Oh God, oh Bratton Fleming!

As to the conduct of the actual trial, only the most temperate and delicate comments are permissible; there is nothing much to be added to the points Alan Watkins made so well in the *Observer*. But it is worth harking back to the Minehead committal proceedings for a minute. Those who have criticised the reporting or indeed the existence of committal hearings usually argue that for the jury to hear the evidence twice may harm the interests of the defendant. But in both the cases where the dramatic nature of the evidence provoked this argument – the Thorpe case and the case of Dr Bodkin Adams – the jury *acquitted* the defendants. You could just as well argue that Mr George Deakin's decision to call for the magistrates' proceedings to be reported *helped* both himself and his co-defendants. The best argument against the existence of committal proceedings remains that they cost a lot of money and serve no good purpose; but if they are to stay, they should be reported, as Sir David Napley for one thinks.